The Philosophical Foundation of Alt-Right Politics and Ressentiment

The Philosophical Foundation of Alt-Right Politics and Ressentiment

William Remley

ROWMAN & LITTLEFIELD
INTERNATIONAL

London • New York

Published by Rowman & Littlefield International, Ltd.
6 Tinworth Street, London SE11 5AL
www.rowmaninternational.com

Rowman & Littlefield International, Ltd. is an affiliate of
Rowman & Littlefield
4501 Forbes Boulevard, Suite 200, Lanham, Maryland 20706, USA
With additional offices in Boulder, New York, Toronto (Canada), and London (UK)
www.rowman.com

Copyright © 2019 by William Remley

All rights reserved. No part of this book may be reproduced in any form or by any electronic or mechanical means, including information storage and retrieval systems, without written permission from the publisher, except by a reviewer who may quote passages in a review.

British Library Cataloguing in Publication Information
A catalogue record for this book is available from the British Library

ISBN: HB 978-1-78661-197-0
ISBN: PB 978-1-5381-4799-3

Library of Congress Control Number: 2019949094

Contents

Introduction	1
Part I: The Philosophical Foundation of Alt-Right Politics	**21**
1 *Philosophia Perennis*, or the Art of "Anamnesis"	23
2 René Guénon and Traditionalist Philosophy: "Those Were the Days"	37
3 Julius Evola's Traditionalism	59
Part II: Social Dominance Theory and Sartre	**93**
4 General Outline of Social Dominance Theory	95
5 Group Formation, Hierarchy, and Human Freedom in Sartre's *Critique of Dialectical Reason*	119
Part III: *Ressentiment*	**159**
6 Alt-Right, *Ressentiment*	161
Bibliography	179
Index	185
About the Author	195

Introduction

There is an increasing belief not only in America but in Europe as well that progress has at best stagnated, that the past and not the future holds the key to saving humankind from the decadence of the modern world, and that everyday normal citizens are increasingly set upon by "foreigners" who appropriate their wealth and invade their culture. In Europe, some leaders have already declared death to liberal democracy in favor of an "illiberal state" tethered to authoritarian leadership. The need for a strong warrior-type leader, it is argued, is necessary to fend off an otherwise hostile world by building walls instead of bridges, erecting barriers to head off the real and imagined foreign threats, and waging a ceaseless battle on those so-called liberal elites who embrace multiculturalism and a globalist creed.

In the United States, these sentiments are echoed in slogans such as "Make America Great Again" and in policies designed to put "America First," all of which underscore the domestic as well as worldview of those who share this political philosophy. Since its inception, America has laid claim to a liberal democratic style of government with various well-known philosophical tenets, yet the underlying beliefs or political philosophy of one of the movements that opposes liberal democracy, the alternative right ("alt-right"), are relatively unknown. Just as important and equally murky is the question of how people are attracted to this political philosophy and why they are so intrigued.

An exact description of the alt-right is, at best, somewhat nebulous. Like most political ideologies, alt-right politics is not monolithic but inclines toward an amalgamation of many threads of thought. However, the movement tends to be characterized by its intense use of social media to disseminate its message along with a provocative slant designed to catch the attention of the public. At a more fundamental level, the alt-right eschews anything connected to the "establishment" conservative movement, especially principled conservatism. Coined by Richard Spencer, founder of the National Policy Institute, the alternative right is a loose set of far-right ideals centered on ethno-nationalism, or "white identity"; isolation from foreign entanglements; and the preservation of "Western civilization" as fundamental tenets of faith. Spencer describes the alt-right as an all-inclusive ideology embracing the ideas of, among other groups, neoreactionaries (NRx-ers), or Dark Enlightenment, as well as adherents of Guillaume Faye's archeofuturists, who seek a return to the older traditional means of existence and a type of libertarian form of government that supports "traditional Western values and civilization" but without abandoning the technological advances of present-day society. Also included within Spencer's "big tent" are human biodiversity adherents as well as "race realists," who push scientific racism of the type prevalent in the nineteenth century. One common theme of the alt-right is, however, its strident rejection of universalism and egalitarianism associated with democratic forms of government.

From a more philosophical point of view, most alt-righters argue for a complete break with establishment conservative philosophy and are more aligned with the philosophy of the French New Right, which seeks the replacement of any organized state with one that champions open markets and individual sovereignty. Importantly, the movement also sees a return to Catholic traditionalism, prevalent before the Second Vatican Council (1962–1965), as the means to "rejuvenate" an otherwise profligate society.

While the ties between President Trump and the alt-right are difficult to define, he is generally considered a hero of the American alt-right for his independent, antiestablishment stands. However, it is Trump's attitude and, more importantly, his policies toward immigrants, Muslims, Mexicans, and Asians as well as others that have garnered him the most support from alt-right believers. In a speech to his followers shortly after the 2016 election, Richard Spencer said America belongs to white people, whom he called "children of the sun," a race of conquerors and creators who have been marginalized, but now, in the new era of then President-Elect Trump, were awakening "to their own identity."[1] Spencer went on to assert that, until the last generation, America was a white country designed for white prosperity and white posterity. To be white, at least according to Spencer, is to be a creator; an explorer; and, most of all, a conqueror—the choice it seems is either to "conqueror or die." Presumably, what it means to conquer is to subjugate anyone who is not white.

The underlying question surrounding alt-right politics is how it has achieved such prominence in American political life. The dominant narrative explaining the shift in American politics in the 2016 election, essential to the rise of the alt-right, has been that working-class voters feel themselves economically and politically left behind by those who rule the "swamp," better known as Washington. Those who lost their jobs to foreign outsourcing or have experienced stagnant or falling incomes, it is said, rose up to punish the establishment.[2] In contrast to this so-called dominant explanation, the theme I wish to put forward is that it is not the economically based "left behind" story, but the perceived threat to status within the social hierarchy that has propelled the alt-right movement to its place in American political prominence.

In support of my claim, I argue three main but interrelated points. While many view the alt-right movement in terms of fascism, this is generally a wrong or at the very least a misguided assumption. My first argument, then, is that alt-right politics has its own philosophical foundation in the traditionalist movement most recently associated with the thought of René Guénon (1886–1951) and Julius Evola (1896–1974) but which can be traced back to at least the fifteenth century through the closely interconnected notion of perennialism. Traditionalist philosophy generally promotes a hierarchical, antidemocratic, elitist, and overtly racist political structure. But the real issue is to understand, in far more depth, what it means to advocate a traditionalist political philosophy

In as much as traditionalism adheres to a strictly hierarchical social structure where some groups are favored over other groups, my second inquiry concerns not only *how* but *why* group formations based on hierarchies naturally occur within any given society. I rely on the concept of social dominance theory (SDT), which concerns itself with *intergroup* relations and whose analysis begins with the basic observation that all human societies tend to be structured as systems of group-based social hierarchies. In conjunction with SDT, I also point out that Jean-Paul Sartre makes a similar point in his *Critique of Dialectical Reason*, where he primarily analyzes *intragroup* dynamics. Moreover, Sartre's ultimate concern is with human freedom, which he believes diminishes as groups become more organized and ultimately institutionalized. Both SDT and Sartre observe that, when individuals form groups, they organize themselves though function—everyone has a role to play—which is hierarchical in nature. Within the hierarchical social structure, one or more groups deemed superior dominate and oppress inferior groups, but, when these hierarchical structures break down, as I argue they are in America and in Europe, the dominant group, fearing its imminent displacement at the top of the hierarchical social structure by groups thought to be inferior, will use its position of dominance to erode and curtail the individual freedoms of those perceived to be usurpers.

From the fundamental hypothesis of SDT, a "basic assumption" follows: most forms of group conflict and oppression can be regarded as different manifestations of the same human predisposition to form not individual but group-based social hierarchies. Consequently, a "trimorphic structure" emerges, which both produces and maintains the hierarchical society structure: the age system; the gender system; and the arbitrary-set system, where racism is but one example.

These hierarchical structures tend to play out in various ways, but in America whites have historically been in a position of power within the social hierarchy that depends on the domination and oppression of those at the bottom of the hierarchy. The lower part of that social hierarchy has historically been inhabited by African Americans, who initially came to this country as slaves but also suffered domination through the fantasy of "separate but equal" legislation of the Jim Crow era (1875–1954). With the rise of the civil rights movement beginning in the 1950s and the various legislation inspired by that movement, the white dominant social hierarchy began to break down. While blacks are citizens of the United States, the *ressentiment* of certain groups of whites has been directed at others, mostly noncitizen immigrants from Mexico and Central America, Muslims, and to some extent Asians. What these groups all have in common, however, is a lack of whiteness. Today, some whites consider their position within the social hierarchy as threatened. They fear the loss of status, either real or imagined, at the hands of groups they deem inferior. Consequently, we see whites striking back through either outright discrimination and violence or political movements, such as the alt-right, designed to maintain the social hierarchical status quo.

Associated with the concept of SDT is the question of why individuals, who perceive themselves to be at the top of the social hierarchy, react the way they do when they again perceive their position as threatened. Some may discount any psychological basis for racism because they see those who espouse racism but fail to alter their behavior when presented with compelling proof to the contrary as irrational and, therefore, not philosophically worthy of inquiry. In my third main objective, I take a different approach by relying on the philosophical and phenomenological arguments of Jean-Paul Sartre based on Nietzsche's concept of *ressentiment* to understand why this phenomenon occurs.

Much like Nietzsche's concept of *ressentiment*, Sartre believes that racism is an emotion, or a passion, aimed directly at a particular person or group that seeks to suppress their rights or to exterminate them. As such, racism cannot be an opinion. As an emotive behavior, the racists' consciousness first and foremost is unreflective consciousness of the world as being afraid of something or someone. In America, that fear manifests itself in a certain white paranoia of loss of domination in the social hierarchy, which gives rise to *ressentiment*. Consequently, action is spontaneous, unreflective consciousness that constitutes a certain existential level in the world.

Yet, as is generally the case, the path of life is littered with difficulties, which means that the racist's emotions are transformative mechanisms allowing him to cope with the difficulty. At times, life's difficulties may seem too difficult to overcome, and, even though one feels the need to act in the face of overwhelming obstacles, no obvious pathway may be apparent. It is in these circumstances that the racist endeavors to alter his world and live as if the connection between things and their potentialities are not governed by deterministic processes but by *magic*. By altering his behavior, the racist apprehends an old object in a different way such that it becomes a new object for him. The end his emotional behavior seeks is to act upon the object through the agency of a particular means so as to confer upon that object another quality, a lesser existence, or a diminished presence, all without altering the object's actual structure. *Ressentiment* is the manner in which those who feel disaffected manifest their emotional behavior toward groups they deem inferior. The alt-right political movement in America is a reflection of those pent-up emotions brought to bear against various social groups, especially nonwhite immigrants.

I begin the discussion in chapter 1 with perennialism, which generally has its origin in the Renaissance with the translation of the *Corpus Hermeticum* (ascribed to Hermes Trismegistus) by philosopher–priest Marsilio Ficino. Originally believed to date to the time of Moses, the *Hermeticum*'s provenance proved to be incorrect, and, in fact, it was ascertained that the text was written between the first and third centuries of the Common Era. As a result, perennial philosophy was discredited and seemed for a time to die out. However, it did survive in eighteenth- and nineteenth-century France among Freemasons and those interested in mysticism, who fundamentally believed that all tradition derived from one single tradition predating the ancients.

To a large extent, perennialism is about not forgetting the past, but it is certainly much more than that. In its attempt to unlock an inner knowledge that recognizes a divine reality, it places the end of human reality in the knowledge of an imminent and transcendent being as a spiritual Absolute. As such, it seeks a timeless wisdom thought to be passed from religion to religion, with existence itself designated as the primordial tradition. Thus, perennialism and traditionalism are essentially synonymous as universal, eternal, and immutable.

The combination of perennialism with Hinduism (Vedanta–Perennialism), which René Guénon later espoused, also took shape during this period by, among other organizations, the Asiatic Society of Bengal. Established in Calcutta in 1784, this society was the first one devoted to the study of the Orient. The society's publications argued for the Indian origin for the European sciences and favored Hinduism over Hermes. In the United States, perennial philosophy got its impetus through the Theosophical Society, established in New York City by Henry Olcott in 1875. The society was charged with conducting research into comparative religion as well as discovering ancient wisdom found in the books of Hermes and the Vedas, or perennial philosophy. Like Guénon, Olcott believed the perennial philosophy originated in the Vedas. As the English translations of the Hindu texts, especially the *Bhagavad Gita*, became available, others in America were also drawn to them. Notably, Ralph Waldo Emerson read the Hindu translations, and they form an important basis for transcendentalism. Emerson also subscribed to a form of perennialism when he wrote that the Bible must be considered as the ethical revelations generally, including the Vedas, and not just the Jewish religion. I should also mention that perennialism extended well into the twentieth century, most famously through Aldous Huxley's *The Perennial Philosophy* (1944).

The discussion of perennialism extends into that of traditionalism in chapter 2 with René Guénon, who is widely considered the originator of traditional philosophy. Early in his life, Guénon became interested in the study of initiation, fundamental to perennial philosophy. Initiation is generally composed of two aspects: exoteric and esoteric. Exoteric initiation marks entry into the religious community, with Christian baptism playing the role of exoteric initiation. Esoteric initiation, on the other hand, grants access to divine grace with its possibility of salvation. It is this latter aspect of initiation, especially in non-Christian Masonic form, that interested Guénon. Moreover, Guénon not only immersed himself in the study of Hinduism, but he was the first traditionalist to search for an unimpaired initiatic tradition.

As I have said, Guénon is considered the originator of traditional philosophy, but the story does not end with him because many of his followers further enhanced traditional philosophy, including such associates as Ananda Coomaraswamy, Frithjof Schuon, and Titus Burckhardt. In presenting the philosophical aspects of traditional philosophy, I chose to analyze Guénon and Julius Evola as the two who have the greatest influence on the movement—Guénon as the highly theoretical originator and Evola as the much more concrete builder of traditional philosophy.

There are several concepts that underlie alt-right politics. My argument is that, on a fundamental level, the philosophy of traditionalism is central to its understanding and is actually its starting point.

Traditionalism entails the strongly held acceptance that there are certain beliefs and practices that have existed since the beginning of time. Yet those beliefs and practices that should have passed from generation to generation have, since the beginning of the Middle Ages, been lost to the West. According to traditionalists, the modern West is in crisis as a result of the loss of this transmission.

While relatively unknown outside of a small intellectual circle, Guénon rose to public awareness during the interwar years. Perhaps his most famous work, *The Crisis of the Modern World*, underscores the belief in this fundamental traditionalist principle. I should emphasize, and as Mark Sedgewick shows in his book *Against the Modern World*, traditionalism is a very loose movement with no strict structure. Not unlike liberalism or almost any political theory, there is not just one liberalism but many "liberalisms"; so it is with traditionalism. As such, a traditionalist may prefer an established practice over a different kind of practice that has replaced the old one. For example, the replacement of Latin in the Catholic Mass gave rise to those who believed the deviance from Latin was an abomination of Catholic tradition.

In an early work, *A General Introduction to the Study of Hindu Doctrines*, Guénon adopts three central elements in the traditionalist philosophy: first, he adheres to a theological, rather than a sociological or anthropological, approach. For Guénon, Hinduism is the repository of spiritual truth; second, Guénon believes that Hinduism equates to Vedanta; and lastly, Guénon believes in "a primal truth," or what is better known as perennialism, as the understanding that all religions share a common ancestry in a single perennial religion that subsequently took several forms throughout the ages, including, Zoroastrian, Pharaonic, Platonic, and Christian.

While perennialism forms one of the major elements of traditionalist philosophy, in subsequent books, Guénon advanced two more central principles of his philosophy. First, he attacks the ideas of theosophy, spiritualism, and the occult and enunciates two key and interrelated positions: counterinitiation and inversion. By the term counterinitiation, Guénon means initiation into pseudo or false traditions, such as theosophy, which he sees as the inversion of true tradition. Counterinitiation, therefore, does not lead to perennial philosophy but away from it. While counterinitiation is the inversion of initiation, inversion is not restricted to questions of initiation. Rather, inversion is an all-pervasive characteristic of modernity that declares that, while everything that is held dear is actually in decline, people mistakenly believe they experience progress. Along the lines of Oswald Spengler, Guénon sees the West in the process of deterioration, a point that alt-right adherents ardently adopt. But for Guénon the villain is Western materialism replacing metaphysics (as spirituality or religion) by a superstitious cult of reason that values only those things that have no value. This type of reasoning can be seen, for example, in today's Christian conservative movement whose generally right-leaning politics believes that same-sex marriage—and indeed homosexuality in general—drugs, lawlessness, abortion, and a multitude of other sins have denigrated American culture and only a "return" to God and Christian "values" can save us now.

The concept of the decline of the West is, perhaps, one of the most powerful ideas of traditionalist philosophy. Manifested today in slogans such as "Make America Great Again," there is an overriding sense that an amorphous, idealized past holds the key to the future, that Western culture is infected with godless mores, and, on a less ethereal level, that immigration and its perceived associated lawlessness together with non-Christian religions have "watered down" Western, white culture almost to the point of extinction.

Not only did Guénon believe the West was in decline as a result of materialism, he also saw the white race under attack by the so-called yellow peril of his time. Historically, this was the period of the rather rapid and devastating loss of the Russian army at the hands of Japan in 1905. At the time, Guénon's defense of the white race involved two prongs: first was a Franco-German (white) entente, and second was the desire for the West to take control of Chinese philosophical resources.

These same themes resonate today among alt-right supporters, who fear the imminent demise of the white race at the hands of those races considered inferior. Labeled the "Great Replacement," alt-right advocates argue that the white race is being inundated by inferior races and will, in a very short time, become a minority. The Unite the Right rally in Charlottesville, Virginia, in the summer of 2017 witnessed white, mostly male, participants chanting "Jews will not replace us" or its counterpart "you will not replace us" in support of their Great Replacement ideology.[3] It should be clear that the idea of "us" is the white race and the "you" are all those who are not white. While these phrases are popular among the alt-right, they are commonly exemplified in another slogan known as the fourteen words: "we must secure the existence of our people and a future for white children."

Guénon's solution for the decline of the West forms another major tenet of traditionalist philosophy. He argues for an Eastern tradition to save the West from collapse. He sees the West as obsessed with the illusion of materialism coupled with a corresponding intellectual regression, which not only means the West is no longer able to understand what intellectuality (i.e., spirituality) is, but it also explains its lack of understanding for Eastern civilizations as well as the period before the Renaissance, that is, the European Middle Ages (Guénon sees the Middle Ages as marking the start of the decline of the West). What Guénon is really arguing for is a restoration of the West to an appropriate traditional civilization. But how best to accomplish this goal? A certain intellectual (again, spiritual or metaphysical) elite is necessary to receive traditional teaching "by an assimilation of Oriental doctrines" to shepherd the West in the direction of a traditional civilization.

Chapter 3 brings into focus the writings of Julius Evola, whose name is oftentimes linked to the founding of traditionalism. Having said this, he is probably the most important collaborator of Guénon, and, while other traditionalists provided shape and form to the movement, Evola gave it a new meaning. Evola became acquainted with traditionalism in the late 1920s, but it was not until the early 1930s that he recognized its true importance. In 1934, Evola published his most famous book, *Revolt against the Modern World*, in which he envisions the political domain as hierarchical, heroic, ideal, antihedonistic, and even anti-eudemonistic.

While Guénon was of utmost importance to Evola, so were two nineteenth-century thinkers, Friedrich Nietzsche and Johann Jakob Bachofen. From Nietzsche, Evola adopted the idea of the *Übermensche* while Bachofen articulated the binary typology of uranic (pertaining to the heavens) and telluric (pertaining to earth) civilizations and with the concept that human society progressed from an early matriarchal (sensuous) to a patriarchal (spiritually pure) society. Evola, however, reversed Bachofen's binary positing and argued instead that Western civilization's decline has "progressed" from uranic to telluric (male to female).

As with Nietzsche, Evola emphasized action as uranic, which he associated with the Hindu *kshatriya*, or warrior caste. While Guénon thought spiritual authority superior to temporal authority, in Hindu terms, the *brahmin* superior to the *kshatriya*, Evola thought quite differently. He was of the view that both castes were originally one and separated only in the decline from primordial tradition. This decline produced what Evola viewed as a "desacralization of existence": first, individualism and rationalism; then collectivism, materialism, and mechanism; and, lastly, an opening to the forces that are not ascendant to humans but rather below them. At the same time, Evola saw what he termed the law of regression of castes, a form of inversion, operating with power passing from the priestly and military castes (highest) to the merchant caste (bourgeois democracy), and finally to the serf caste (proletariat and lowest). In Evola's mind, the primordial sacral caste was uranic and also pre-Christian, while Christian Catholicism, with its allegedly nontraditional conception of a personal God, was telluric and characteristic of modernity.

Evola also differs from Guénon in the solution he offers. For Guénon, the transformation of the individual through initiation under the influence of an elite is the means to transform the West as a whole. Evola, on the other hand, called for self-realization through the reintegration of man into a state of centrality brought about by uranic action as the Absolute Individual. Transformation here was not so much the means but the consequences.

Regarding fascism, with which Evola's name is often associated, both the Italian fascists and the Nazis rejected Evola's traditionalism. For several years in the 1930s, Evola sought to influence both Italian and German fascism. In each instance, he was rejected probably because he espoused a far more radical position than either of the two fascist organizations. Eventually abandoning his idea of infiltrating a party, he instead determined to penetrate an issue—race. In 1941, he published *Synthesis of Racial Doctrine*, which radically attacked the racial policies of the fascists and the Nazis, arguing against a biological determination in favor of a spiritual definition of race. Even though Evola harbored a distaste for Jews, he argued the problem was spiritual. In other words, Aryan and Jew should not be understood in biological terms but rather as denoting typical attitudes that were not necessarily present in all individuals of Aryan or Jewish blood. The real enemy was not Jews, biologically defined, but global subversion and antitradition.

In his discussion of race, Evola adheres to a strict hierarchical system with the Nordic (white) race superior to all others. In comparison to the lower Mediterranean race, Evola sees the Nordic as the race of active men who perceive the world as presented to them as material for possession and attack. On the other hand, the Mediterranean soul, typified by its vanity, seeks to show off in a noisy, exaggerated manner. Much as Guénon did, Evola argues that the Aryan peoples of the world descended from a race that once inhabited the Arctic. In an era that predates history, this land was the home of a super civilization—super in the sense of its connection with the gods—known as Hyperborea. The Hyperborean were forced to migrate due to an unknown cataclysmic event that destroyed their homeland. Forced to migrate, they eventually settled in what is now Western Europe. This pure Aryan race ultimately became the proto-Nordic race of Europe, which founded, according to Evola, the greatest civilization.

In his writings, Evola asserts that "the one who says yes to racism is the one in which race still lives" and that the one who has race is intrinsically a foe of democratic ideals. In today's world former Counsel to the President Steve Bannon echoed Evola's words when he called on members of France's National Front Party to "let them call you racists . . . wear it as a badge of honor." True racism, then, resides in the "classical spirit," embedded in the Nordic race, which is rooted in the exaltation of everything that has form, face, and individuation, as opposed to what is formless, vague, and undifferentiated.

After laying out the philosophical foundation for alt-right politics with its absolute emphasis on social hierarchies embracing an elite dominant class with all others subject to its supremacy, I then move to a discussion of social dominance theory (SDT) to further understand not only how social hierarchies come about but the dynamics involved in their establishment.

Chapter 4 enters into a discussion of group-based social domination to support the argument that, within the American social structure, whites have been the dominant group, often oppressing those in the out-groups. In articulating intergroup relations, SDT has as its foundational thesis the basic observation that all human societies tend to be structured as systems of group-based social hierarchies. This system minimally entails a hierarchical structure consisting of one or more dominant and hegemonic groups at the top and one or more subordinated groups at the bottom. Those at the top usually possess a disproportionately large share of what is called positive social value, that being those material and symbolic things for which people ordinarily strive. An example would be the wealth dichotomy between the 99 percent and the 1 percent, which usually translates into authority and power; obviously, wealth; and social status, among other things, for the dominant group. On the other hand, subordinate groups possess a disproportionately large share of negative social value, which manifests itself in low power and social status. SDT attempts to identify the mechanisms (the "how") that are responsible for producing and maintaining this group-based social hierarchy.

SDT relies on the observation that human group-based social hierarchies consist of distinctly different trimorphic stratification systems: (a) an age system where adults have more power over children and young adults; (b) a gender system in which males have disproportionate social power compared to females (patriarchy); and (c) an arbitrary-set system, which comprises socially constructed groups based on certain characteristics, such as ethnicity, nation, race, social class, religious sect, or any other socially relevant group distinctions. In such systems one group is politically or materially dominant over the other.

After laying out the contours of the trimorphic nature of this social hierarchy, I then discuss the primary assumptions upon which SDT is based. These assumptions fall into three categories: (a) while age- and gender-based hierarchies tend to exist within all social systems, arbitrary-set hierarchies invariably emerge within social systems, producing economic surplus; (b) most forms of group conflict and oppression are different manifestations of the same human predisposition to form group-based social hierarchies; and (c) human social systems are subject to the counterbalancing influences of *hierarchy-enhancing* (HE) forces, producing and maintaining ever higher levels of group-based social inequality (police, legal systems, and economic or financial institutions), and *hierarchy-attenuating* (HA) forces, producing greater levels of group-based social equality (civil rights organizations, social welfare organizations, charities, and religious organizations).

Given these assumptions, SDT argues that group-based social hierarchies are driven by three proximal processes: (a) aggregated individual discrimination, such as everyday acts of discrimination by one individual against another; (b) aggregated institutional discrimination, which is produced by the rules, procedures, and actions of social institutions, resulting in a disproportionate allocation of positive and negative social value (Jim Crow laws); and (c) behavior asymmetry, which recognizes the differences in the behavioral repertoires of individuals belonging to groups at different levels of the social power continuum, all of which are partially regulated by legitimizing myths ("whites possess superior intellect").

The extent to which an individual accepts legitimizing myths depends on whether that individual endorses a system of group-based social hierarchy. This generalized orientation toward group-based social hierarchy is referred to as social dominance orientation (SDO), an important topic that I discuss at length.

The mechanisms SDT describes tend to make group-based social hierarchies ubiquitous and stable, but they also provide these social hierarchies with certain other characteristics; chief among them is ever increasing disproportionality (income inequality), hierarchical consensus (high degree of agreement within the social group as to which group is dominant and which is subordinate), and resiliency (while group-based hierarchies tend to be stable, there are times when the arbitrary-set systems are cataclysmically overthrown, such as in the French Revolution. However, one can argue that in no case has an egalitarian transformation actually succeeded. As Sartre has shown, the revolution will most likely return to what he calls the practico-inert in one form or another).

Having provided the broader outlines of SDT, I then discuss its more practical, specific mechanism designed to produce and maintain group-based social hierarchy. Much like Sartre posited, SDT accepts that the human mind both forms and is formed by human society. I am always thrown into a situation inhabited by others who will mold me and form me into what I am or what I am not. As a result, understanding the nature and dynamics of group-based social inequality requires an understanding of the psychology of group dominance. One of the ways in which the psychology of group dominance expresses itself is through the mechanisms of SDO.

SDO is defined as "a very general individual differences orientation expressing the value that people place on nonegalitarian and hierarchical structured relationships among social groups." Accordingly, SDO expresses support for the domination of certain socially constructed groups over other socially constructed groups. These various groups are usually defined on the basis of race, gender, nationality, skin color, religion, or any other distinction that can be brought to bear. While individuals will differ as to the degree to which they desire group-based inequality, understanding the intensity and distribution of SDO within the group allows insight into the dynamics and overall hierarchical structure of societies.

In Europe, social class has historically defined the primary continuum for social stratification and as a result has been the group distinction most likely to activate social dominance drives. In the United States, however, race (broadly defined) has and still is the most likely primary motivation of social stratification and therefore the most likely to trigger SDO.

SDT uses empirical research to establish a correlation between SDO and certain types of beliefs or ideologies, which generally shows that people with low group status or power are more likely to acquire low levels of SDO, whereas those with high group status or power are more likely to favor the domination of inferior groups by superior groups. In support, I point to recent studies that support this theory, which indicate a significant increase in SDO among Republican voters in the last election cycle. SDO has been shown to be a reliable predictor of those within society who utilize ideologies to enhance as opposed to attenuate hierarchy, those who seek out social roles that will perpetuate group-based social domination, and those who discriminate against groups in social segregation or resource allocation.

The next question is how people acquire different levels of SDO. Generally, there are three major influences on the level of SDO one may acquire: socialization and experience, situational contingencies, and temperament. It has been found that people from dominant groups adopt higher levels of SDO than those from subordinate groups, the reason being people's general desire for positive self-esteem is ordinarily compatible with hierarchy-legitimizing myths for those in dominant groups, thus making group superiority seem natural to them. Moreover, the status of the group itself is related to SDO. Those in high-status groups (men, whites, and heterosexuals) exhibit higher levels of SDO than those in lower-status groups (women, blacks, Hispanics, and homosexuals). Where there are several stratified groups, SDO is linked to the relative status of each group. In summary, increasing group status is linked to increasing SDO across all samples, population, culture, and group status designation. People generally have consistent orientations toward group dominance, and SDO levels are reliably related to one's own group status.

I have mentioned the importance of legitimizing myths to SDO, but at this point I delve into the subject in more detail. Social ideologies are an important instrument to guide people's actions, justify beliefs, and approve or condemn the behavior of others. Indeed, in periods of social change ideologies become increasingly important as people either welcome or oppose that change. However, it is the social implications for intergroup relations that ideologies have, rather than their specific content, that orient people toward those ideologies in ways compatible with their levels of SDO. In the Charlottesville demonstration by white supremacists, various ideologies were at play. The use of torches in a nighttime demonstration and the chanting of slogans such as "blood and soil" were reminiscent of Nazi parades along with their concomitant ideology. Alt-right leader Richard Spencer described the parade as "theatrical and mystical and magical and religious." But the video of the march shows mostly young, white males, united within the group by the fear of a loss of power conferring status within the social hierarchy protesting the perceived subordinate groups they seek to dominate.

After the discussion of group-based social hierarchies and their deleterious effect on so-called inferior groups, in chapter 5, I lay out Sartre's discussion of social group-based formations and their effect on human freedom. Sartre's primary concern is with intragroup dynamics, or why groups come to be organized in the manner in which they are; the question becomes, what is it that causes humans to curtail their freedom in an almost maniacal desire to organize the group and, then once organized, to institutionalize the group.

As he does in a great deal of his philosophical undertakings, Sartre is keenly interested in human freedom—its sources, effect, sustainability, and demise. I turn to Sartre's *Critique of Dialectical Reason* to not only support and complement the conclusions reached in the discussion of SDT but also to understand how Sartre sees group-based hierarchical social structures eroding the very idea of human freedom. I begin the process of laying out Sartre's scheme of group formation with what he describes as the most basic entity—collectives. Fundamentally, collective structures occupy the practico-inert field of impotency. If collective praxis is constituted as a kind of stasis, in contrast, groups are marked by their undertakings and their constant movement of integration, which tends to turn them into pure praxis by endeavoring to eliminate all forms of collective inertia.

I then analyze Sartre's concept of group formation starting with isolated individuals; next to the group-in-fusion; followed by the statutory group (the "pledge"), the organized group, and finally to Sartre's last group—the institutionalized group. Sartre's political notions can play out only within a social environment, but what that environment entails involves Sartre in a complex analysis of what he calls group formations, which he understands as fundamental to human development. Regarding human freedom, Sartre offers a sliding scale, arguing that the group-in-fusion offers the highest level of human freedom with the least amount of alienation. However, as the group organizes its activities by function, the scale is reversed—alienation takes over human freedom. Eventually, when the group institutionalizes itself, we not only see human freedom lost in a sea of sameness and obedience, but we also witness the rise of politics in a *milieu* of a "cult of personality."

The discussion of why individuals come together to form groups embroils Sartre in an analysis involving the quest for unity once a group is formed. But it is not necessarily individuals within the group that interests Sartre, but rather the effects of maintaining group unity. In the early stages of group formation, we see the individual locked within what Sartre calls the practico-inert—a position that sees individuals as impotent to effect change—through to the stage of the organized group. Once the organized group is formed, it could go in one of two directions: it could remain in the realm of organized functionality, or it could enter into a more structured environment where alienation overtakes freedom as the organization strives to unify itself by institutionalizing itself. Sartre sees the organized group becoming "degraded" in terms of human freedom as it seeks to solidify its pledged unity by institutionalizing its praxis.

Sartre begins with the quasi-sovereignty of the organized group, based on function, but he introduces the group to an element of fear: even though individuals within the group may adequately perform their function, they may still find themselves outside the group at any moment. This fear means that freedom becomes afraid of itself as it ultimately gives way to an increasing sense of alienation. The consequences are varied in Sartre's portrayal, but fundamental to his analysis is the development of a new group unity centered on the incarnation of a single sovereign whose policies are defined by his personality alone. While still within the group, this sovereign becomes the untranscendable third who provides a necessary, albeit illusory, unity while at the same time individual sovereignty gives way to the structure of obedience, representing a decline in individual freedom.

As the group refuses to dissolve, in fact there are now serious apparatuses (laws, the police, the judicial system, etc.) in place to assure that dissolution is unlikely including the pledge, which sanctions violence in the form of repression and terror. The members of the group submit to the will of the sovereign and his quasi-sovereignty as violence without reciprocity. Sartre's analysis points out the dangers not only faced by individuals within the group, but the freedom they once associated with the social bonds of solidarity. Indeed, the sovereign's demand for complete integration dissolves all individuality save for one individual—the sovereign.

Once we go beyond the mere organization of the group to its institutionalization, we witness the emergence of a "new individual" who has enjoyed the sovereignty and freedom of the group-in-fusion but who has come to accept the quasi-sovereignty of the organization, all for the sake of unity within the group. Now, Sartre points out the deleterious effects of the bureaucratic institutionalization of human praxis through the centralizing mode of the state and its oppressive apparatuses designed to curtail dissent and individual expressions of freedom. Sartre's analysis proves to be complex, but the message is quite clear. The institutionalization of human praxis with its centralized and "scientific" orientation can lead only to the effacement of human freedom that Sartre so fervently desires to maintain.

Sartre shows the inherent dangers in human relations that may commence as well intentioned but invariably lead to unintended consequences. The group, united through its pledged inertia, entrenches itself in a hierarchical structure. Its malaise assures the group that it will seek—at all costs—its elusive sense of unity. The common individual, now defined by her function or the very role she plays, experiences the fear of exclusion brought about through excess. To protect the group, but at the same time insulate and isolate it, a "container" is constructed, the effect of which is to remove the leadership from the masses and further instantiate the bureaucratic institutional structure of the expert. At this moment, Sartre asserts, freedom becomes afraid of itself.

Sartre brings us to an end point as he describes the rise of the leader that gives way to authority and sovereignty of one person. Much like what has been written recently concerning President Trump's takeover of the Republican Party, Sartre is describing a transformation of a political organization (a group) into a cult of personality. In fact, former Senator Bob Corker admonished his Republican colleagues for being "cultish" and "fearful" under President Trump. In Sartre's portrayal, sovereignty grounds authority, which means that everyone's quasi-sovereignty is immobilized. Authority becomes lodged in the relation of one individual to all the rest, which can come to full fruition only in the institutionalized group. Yet it is the common person's impotency that allows power to constitute itself, but this does not necessarily mean that freedom is lost forever.

Once the theory of social domination has been discussed, from both a sociological and philosophical point of view as well as from an intergroup and intragroup perspective, in chapter 6 I bring together the thought of Friedrich Nietzsche and Jean-Paul Sartre and their theory of racism based on *ressentiment*. In the previous chapters, I built the case that alt-right political philosophy is fundamentally based on traditionalism. Part of that philosophy is a racist-oriented outlook based on white nationalism and supremacy. The question I ask in this chapter is why people are attracted to this type of philosophy, or, in other words, what motivates them to adhere to an alt-right political philosophy. My argument dispels the notion that devotees of alt-right politics are economically disaffected, or "left behind." Rather, I argue they are driven by their fear of losing their hierarchical status within the social structure. That fear, in turn, results in *ressentiment* toward those they perceive inferior. I turn primarily to Sartre and his discussion of anti-Semitism, and while Sartre focuses on anti-Jewish racism, what he says applies equally to all forms of racism and not to just one particular type. However, to understand Sartre's ideas, the discussion must begin with Nietzsche's "man of *ressentiment*."

Nietzsche's discussion of *ressentiment* distinguishes between what he describes as the master and slave mentalities. In our present-day circumstances, the slave mentality or morality Nietzsche speaks of represents those attracted to alt-right politics. As one might expect, the slave morality is seen as a reaction, an inversion, a corruption; it is dominated by the negative. The overpowered slave, who revolts ideologically against his condition does so by *inventing* a series of distinctions by which to condemn his master as "evil" and to affirm himself, not directly and spontaneously, but indirectly and "reactively." It is clear that an ethics of *ressentiment* is not merely an expression of bad character, regardless of its principles and rationalizations.

Nietzsche's *ressentiment* entails the act of deception, the clandestine and the opaque. Moreover, *ressentiment* relies on a dyadic relationship; ordinarily, one cannot have *ressentiment* directed at oneself. Rather, the slave believes himself worse off than his master and takes revenge regardless of whether the master is imagined as a single, specific person or some vague group to which that person belongs. *Ressentiment* aims at other individuals, other groups, or other institutions; its very essence requires that one's view be directed outward instead of back to oneself. To exist, slave morality insists upon a hostile external world, which provides the necessary external stimuli to act at all, yet that action is fundamentally reaction. In language that foretells Sartre's later argument, Nietzsche explains that "man seeks a principle through which he can despise men—he invents a world so as to be able to slander and bespatter this world: in reality he reaches every time for nothingness." The reverse is true for the noble (Nietzsche's master) whose acts are spontaneous and who affirms life though passion. *Ressentiment* is, on the other hand, a nonreflecting, bitter emotional state oftentimes linked to a slight or injury that is either real or imagined. Just as often it is premised on fantasies and frustrations of revenge, which further exacerbates the *ressentiment*.

One should keep in mind and, in fact, Nietzsche tells us that a race of men of *ressentiment* is bound to become eventually cleverer than members of any noble race; it will also honor cleverness to a far greater degree, namely, as a condition of the existence of the first *ressentiment* as the evil enemy, or *"the Evil One."* And it is this description that, in turn, allows the man of *ressentiment* to view himself and his attitudes as righteous and himself as the "good one." This evil one arouses fear in the slave because it is the slave's belief that "power and dangerousness are assumed to reside in this evil, a certain dreadfulness, subtlety and strength, which do not admit of being despised." For Nietzsche, it is clear that the man of *ressentiment* must divide the world in two; to affirm his very existence, he must portray that existence in Manichean terms.

Even though there is no direct correlate in the German language, there is a purpose for Nietzsche's use of the French term *ressentiment*. Frustration is an emotional feeling and *ressentiment*, which derives from the Latin *resentire* and means to feel, denotes a strong and often harsh emotion balanced between vulnerability and imagined vengeance on the one hand, and an aristocratic sense of honor on the other. In short, the resentful person has ingrained feelings, while the noble self overcomes those feelings and acts. No matter what language one utilizes, *ressentiment* harbors a feeling of vulnerability and implies reaction to an offense that includes schemes of revenge. As has been pointed out, however, more often than not these slights are imagined and the schemes are nothing more than fantasies of the imagination.

But what is it that brings *ressentiment*, this emotional, psychological state of vengeance and vulnerability to fruition? For Nietzsche, *ressentiment* is primarily concerned with power, but not just as a feeling of self-pity for one's own plight in the world; rather, it is a personal vindictiveness or blame for a perceived and, perhaps, preconceived injustice. Moreover, *ressentiment* is typified by its obsessive nature, but it is not generally expressed as a specific desire other than as an amorphous yearning for revenge. This type of revenge seems to manifest itself in an abstract desire for the utter humiliation of its target followed by its total annihilation. One should not believe, however, that *ressentiment* is self-destructive. On the contrary, it is the ultimate emotion of self-preservation and self-affirmation at any cost.

Ressentiment is a psychological form of repressed vengeance arising out of several key factors. Initially, the man of *ressentiment* desires to lead a certain kind of life that he deems of importance and is generally thought of as a life of supremacy. Nevertheless, his weakness creates a feeling of inferiority or impotence. Next, this feeling of impotency assumes the essential role of a feature of one's own psyche. The result is the man of *ressentiment* sees himself as permanently and ineluctably weak. Of even greater concern is the fact that his loss of power is seen not as some aberration, but as evidence of his constitutional impotency. In the end, the man of *ressentiment* believes himself powerless, yet he retains his arrogance and his false sense of superiority. Thus, his will to power remains intact. Finally, the man of *ressentiment* refuses to resign himself to this ignominious impotency; his sickliness or impotence does not eliminate his desire for control; it only makes those feelings more acute. It is this third definitional characteristic that sets *ressentiment* apart from other attitudes. The man of *ressentiment* maintains his commitment to his original goals and aspirations and refuses to accept his inability to realize them. From a psychological point of view, the man of *ressentiment* is torn or alienated by the tremendous tension between the desire to live the life he values and the belief that he is powerless to attain it. To affirm his own existence, the man of *ressentiment* must negate the other who he sees as an absolute other. It is only through negation that the man of *ressentiment* is able to recognize himself within a community and become ensconced as a member of the "club."

In his short book, *Anti-Semite and Jew*, Sartre describes the psychological disposition of the racist. Whatever a racist may be, Sartre refuses to characterize their views as opinions because those views, aimed at particular people, seek to suppress their rights or exterminate them altogether. Consequently, Sartre sees racism as a psychological passion that cannot be based on experience. Here, Nietzsche and Sartre are in agreement: in Sartre's description of passion, he states that ordinary hate is associated with provocation—I hit you, you return the favor—but the racist experiences no such outward insult. Rather, the hate the racist harbors "precedes the facts that are supposed to call it forth." A predisposition toward hatred is not only fundamental to the very being of the racist, it is primordial. The racist's passion and psychic drives necessarily manifest themselves in a subjective position that preconceives an "idea" of the targeted group as to their nature as well as their societal role. Thus, because it is not the outcome of some external force, racism must be seen as a total free choice. Sartre makes another key point at this juncture: if the racist is controlled by his passions, those passions also control his world view. The racist, driven by psychologically generated drives, projects those passions onto the world and all those who inhabit it. The racist, reminiscent of Nietzsche's slave mentality, perceives a hostile external world and reacts with hate.

Sartre believes the racist adopts a "syncretic" outlook that is always already present in all circumstances. By syncretic, Sartre means behavior that is submerged in the content of behavior itself rather than behavior that imposes its own demands on the elements of the situation. In probing this type of behavior, Sartre finds the racist possess a basic fear not only of himself, but for the truth as well. This fear emanates from the form of truth itself with what he describes as its ever elastic character of indefinite approximation. The racist rules out reason and rationality in his search for impenetrability. Hate is freely chosen because hate is a faith. As Sartre argues, the racist feels no compulsion to look within himself; his being lies entirely outside of himself, and, as a result, the racist runs away—he flees himself—from the very awareness of himself as a person.

Sartre's view is parallel to Nietzsche's whose "man of *ressentiment*" also directs his view outward instead of reflecting on himself. For Nietzsche as well as Sartre, this is the essence of the slave morality, and it is the essence of the racist. In probing the origin of the man of *ressentiment*, Nietzsche finds them in the masses or the herd. Sartre sees the racist in similar terms. They move among the anonymous crowd, they are the middle class who inhabit mostly the towns and rural areas. In short, they are every bit of Nietzsche's herd. These people perceive themselves to lack power, or, as I argue they no longer feel at the top of the social hierarchy; rather, immigrants, foreigners, and people of nonacceptable religious faiths (non-Christian) have threatened that very social order. As a result, both Sartre and Nietzsche believe the other has a profound effect on human subjectivity in general, and for the man of *ressentiment* in particular who can affirm his own existence only through the negation of the other.

In American political and social life, the top of the hierarchy has been occupied by whites while historically the bottom has been the domain of blacks. But, as the black middle class began to form as a result of the civil rights movement of the 1960s, new classes of subordinate outgroups began to take shape, namely, new immigrants, non-Christians, women, gays, and other minority groups. These groups are seen by some whites within society as a threat to the existing group-based social hierarchy.

NOTES

1. Joseph Goldstein, "Alt-Right Gathering Exults in Trump Election with Nazi-Era Salute," *New York Times*, November 20, 2016, https://www.nytimes.com/2016/11/21/us/alt-right-salutes-donald-trump.html.

2. It is interesting to note that research into the voters in the 2016 primary elections found that the estimated median annual income of Trump supporters was approximately $72,000, compared to the national average of $56,000 and to Clinton and Sanders supporters of only around $61,000. This seems to negate the idea that Trump supporters are actually "left behind," at least economically. Nate Silver, "The Mythology of Trump's 'Working Class' Support," *FiveThirtyEight*, May 3, 2016, https://fivethirtyeight.com/features/the-mythology-of-trumps-working-class-support/.

3. For a discussion of the meaning of many alt-right symbols and slogans, see "Deconstructing the Symbols and Slogans Spotted in Charlottesville," *Washington Post*, August 18, 2017, https://www.washingtonpost.com/graphics/2017/local/charlottesville-videos/?noredirect=on&utm_term=.481daaca5353.

Part I

The Philosophical Foundation of Alt-Right Politics

ONE

Philosophia Perennis, or the Art of "Anamnesis"

To a considerable extent *philosophia perennis*, or what is commonly referred to as perennialism, is about not forgetting the past, a past that extends beyond acknowledged history to embrace the mysteries of both myth and legend. For in that past lived a so-called golden age—a period one might rightly think of as magical—where people did not perish, and the mysteries of the cosmos, so keen for perennialists to rediscover and keep alive, were known to all.

In its desire to resurrect an outward forgotten time, perennialism, attempts to unlock a particular type of inner knowledge that comes about through a discipline involving spiritual practices as a "metaphysic" recognizing a divine reality, and a human psychology similar to or even identical with that reality.[1] As an ethic, it places the final end of human reality squarely in the knowledge of an imminent and transcendent ground of all being as a spiritual Absolute, ineffable in terms of discursive thought, albeit susceptible to direct experience.[2]

While many believe that perennialism deals with an "original" religion, common to all religions, this is not necessarily the case. Rather, the concern is more with understanding the underlying, basic shared metaphysical human reality found in the West through the philosophy of Plato and the writings of Hermes Trismegistus, whose name means "thrice great"—king, philosopher, priest—and in the East through the Hindu Vedanta.[3] As we shall see, Guénon combines the Eastern practice with the Western style of perennial philosophy to form his specific concept of traditionalism, which brings us to the issue of how traditionalism and perennial philosophy intersect.

Philosophia perennis speaks of a timeless wisdom or truth passed down through many religious beliefs; it is both without form and beyond all conceptions. As Harry Oldmeadow explains, "this universal wisdom, in existence since the dawn of time and spiritual patrimony of all humankind, can also be designated as the primordial tradition."[4] Tradition is, therefore, synonymous with perennial philosophy as universal, eternal, and immutable, which is a sacrosanct principle of the traditionalist view and seminal to Guénon's work. As Lord Northbourne describes it, the *traditional mentality* is "characteristic of societies in which a revealed Religion together with the accompanying Tradition, exercises a predominant influence."[5] By contrast, what Northbourne terms the *progressive mentality* is "one in which a science founded on observation, together with humanistic philosophy based on that science, is the mainspring of thought and action."[6] Unfortunately, in the eyes of traditionalism over the last several centuries the latter mentality has overcome the former and entrenched itself as the dominant force.

Traditionalists point out that every great religion adheres to such a principle. For example, Plotinus formulates his principle of prior simplicity by saying there must be something prior to all things which is simple, and this must be different from all that comes after it.[7] Augustine argues that the Christian religion existed among the ancients, and, in fact, has never ceased to exist. Likewise, Lord Krishna in the *Bhagavad Gita* declares that his message has been proclaimed since the beginning of time.[8] Consequently, the primordial tradition as *philosophia perennis* is of suprahuman origin outside of any anthropological, evolutionary thought.

While traditionalism and perennialism are stitched together as timeless, universal, and immutable truths known since the beginning of time, it is essential to understand that their basic tenets or principles must, in turn, be passed down or transmitted as truth that finds its formal expression in myths, rituals, symbols, and, importantly, doctrines revealed through divine revelation. Under traditionalist notions, revelations are neither understood in any psychological sense nor can they occur as the result of purely human initiatives. Rather, revelation must be experienced, and certainly Guénon expresses it as "remembering anew" through a divine unveiling of the primordial tradition.

At its very core, however, perennial philosophy is, as Aldous Huxley explains, composed of "doctrines." By this Huxley means that its claims do not appeal to experience in any phenomenological construct nor are mystical experiences necessarily cross-culturally identical, rather doctrines are the intellectual component concerned with the grasping and formulating of truth and the eradication of falsehoods. Huxley points to four very general doctrines that guide perennialism's thought:

- First: the phenomenal world of matter and of individualized consciousness—the world of things and animals and men and even gods—is the manifestation of the Divine Ground within which all

partial realities have their being, and apart from which they would be nonexistent.
- Second: human beings are capable not merely of knowing about the Divine Ground by inference; they can also realize its existence by a direct intuition, superior to discursive reasoning. This immediate knowledge unites the knower with what is known.
- Third: man possesses a double nature, a phenomenal ego and an eternal self, which is the inner man, the spirit, the spark of divinity within the soul. It is possible for man, if he so desires, to identify himself with the spirit and therefore with the Divine Ground, which is the same or like nature with the spirit.
- Fourth: man's life on earth has only one end and purpose: to identify himself with his eternal Self and so to come to unitive knowledge of the Divine Ground.[9]

The legitimacy of metaphysical truths does not depend on "gifts of infused grace"; rather, for perennialists, they are self-evident to the intellect. As such, these doctrines derive their existence from metaphysical "intuitions" thus discounting the necessity to discern the truth of such axioms from "experience."[10] The use of the term intuition takes on special meaning for perennialism, especially for Guénon. In as much as metaphysics stands above rational thought, the truths that are metaphysically self-evident can only be conceived by the use of a faculty not belonging to the individual order whose operation can be characterized as "intuitive." However, and Guenon makes this distinction, perennialism's notion of intuition should not be regarded as having anything in common with contemporary philosophy's conception of intuition as merely an "instinctive and vital faculty that is really beneath reason and not above it."[11] What perennialism refers to here is more precisely termed "intellectual intuition," or what Aristotle in his *Posterior Analytics* referred to as the pure intellect, the faculty that possesses a direct knowledge of principles. Simply put, perennialism deals with supra-individuals in a supra-rational order. Accordingly, the theophany, or mystical intuitions perennialists speak of are essentially ineffable. Not subject to rationalization, they are revealed mystically through the symbolic.

Just as perennial philosophy does not assert the identical nature of cross-cultural mystical experiences, it also shuns any identity between Eastern and Western philosophical traditions; instead, it looks to the truth value asserted by each as indicative of their shared character. Perhaps, the fundamental insight of perennialism is the fact that truth, perceived through human cognition, is unitary. Thought of as an inspiration of wisdom transmitted from teacher to student, this notion of truth grants awareness into what is perennial and always accessible to humans because it is cognition itself. Perennialism sees truth as universal because having encountered a view of things thought to be true, one concludes it must be universally true; for perennialism, truth has ubiquity fabricated into its meaning. This does not mean there is no diversity in the traditions, it does mean, however, that neither equality nor the universality of truth requires all traditions to be identical.[12] Thus, the search for and realization of truth, as the experience of the ground of being, is what is perennial, a search that can take on many forms and involve people of diverse settings.[13]

Unlike more contemporary forms of organized religion, with their emphasis on group participation, perennialism tends to play out at the personal level of direct spiritual experience intended to transform and illuminate the individual. As many have pointed out, including Huxley, the word perennial connotes a human transformative and illuminative process that is intrinsically open to all who may have gone through such a process in the past, are going through it presently, or will go through it in the future.[14] Consequently, the process occurs perennially.

ESOTERICISM AND EXOTERICISM

As I have indicated, Platonism as a way of life plays a central role in perennial philosophy not only encouraging one to lead a virtuous life but in its recognition of a metaphysics anchored in the individual's realization of self–other transcendence. In this sense, perennialism not only commands one to lead a better, virtuous life, but it also guides the aspirant on the path to inner unity by "returning to the One." This last point is of particular importance: perennialism is inherently esoteric because those who engage in it perform a contemplative ascent not fully understood through language.

Broadly construed, esotericism is the storehouse and guardian of the mystery or secret which is the motive force of religion. The mystery perennialists speak of is hardly something unknown or unknowable; rather, it is something that is inexpressible in language.[15] Perennialists see Western philosophical traditions, with its reliance on rationality or reason, as only reinforcing predominant social tendencies toward dualism and materialism, all of which falls below the stature of human intelligence. Perennial philosophy, on the other hand, offers a way of life, a script if you will, toward inner enlightenment through higher meanings and purposes within a greater metaphysical context.

What is sought by perennialism is Ultimate Reality, which can be reached only through "mystical experience." Thus, mysticism plays an essential role in perennialism because it is through such an experience that a process is inaugurated leading to "unification" with the One, or Ultimate Reality. In practice, mysticism makes its appearance within the confines of all the revealed religions because for every religion mysticism is its inward or spiritual dimension manifested in esotericism. While it is true that Jewish mysticism is not the same as Christian or even Islamic mysticism, what is the same is that each is "one only in God."[16] It is this supraformal, divine truth that is the source for each religion because the goal of mysticism is God in all the religions.

The central role played by mysticism incorporates three essential aspects: it first concerns the doctrine of God, or Ultimate Reality as "mystical doctrine." Next, it enunciates the "mystical experience" of oneness with God, or Ultimate Reality. Lastly, it provides the path or movement that leads from mystical doctrine to mystical experience.[17] As it progresses from doctrine to experience, the mystical path also proceeds from outward to inward and from mere belief to vision. Esotericism comprises a deep—supraformal as opposed to exotericisms merely formal—structure where only those with the proper understanding can enter its confines. Here faith is essential, but unlike exoteric belief esotericism requires sincerity and total commitment; every effort must be expended toward "realization" if one is to open their soul to Divine grace.

While perennialism encompasses an esoteric metaphysical, mystical nature often thought of in terms of rites of initiation, contemplation, gnosis, universality, deliverance, and unity, it also recognizes that every religion comprises at its core a dogmatic, moral aspect, possessing an exoteric character of forms, observance, ritual, exclusivism, and salvation.[18] The difference rests primarily on the distinction between formalism and spirit. Metaphysically, the difference between exotericism's formalism and esotericism's supraformalism rests in how the end goal is sought. In exotericism, God is thought of at the level of "Being" as creator. Regardless of how deep the exotericist's belief, God and worshiper remain separate. Esotericism, on the other hand, envisions God as "Beyond-Being," or Divine Essence. As such, God and worshiper unite to form a common essence that opens up the possibility of definitive Divine Unity.[19] As Frithjof Schuon explains, "exotericism never goes beyond the 'letter.' It puts its accent on the Law, not on any realization, and so puts it on action and merit."[20] As such, the exoteric is essentially a trust in a dogmatic principle envisioned in its formal exclusiveness and in conformity to a particular ritual or moral Law.

Even though the exoteric does not derive its existence from the esoteric but from a revelation, the two do not necessarily remain separate. However, the latter is generally more intense than the former. Unlike exotericism, which is engaged in by the many, esotericism is necessarily the domain of a specifically trained few. For the average believer, exoteric dogma is a sufficient domain, but there will always be a select few blessed with the contemplative intellect necessary to infiltrate the formal dimensions of religion. As Lord Northbourne succinctly explains, "esotericism is the 'heart' of Religion, and exotericism the 'body.'"[21]

CONTEMPLATIVE ASCENT

One of the basic tenets of perennial philosophy is the concept of ascent. Not to be understood literally, it describes an inward movement toward what came before and transcends human qualities, such as the senses, reason, and the self. In other words, the movement travels from "dividedness toward unity, from dualism toward transcendence."[22] This movement from discrete individuality toward transcendence is thought of as an ascent toward perception of the intelligible realm as reflexive self-awareness of itself where the intelligible abides in itself, and is beyond being, even beyond the intellect. Thus, the movement of contemplative ascent turns away from appearance and toward reality as truth that can be subject to human cognition, but truth not in the sense of a single truth; rather, it is a much grander concept of all that precedes and transcends every multiplicity, all appearances, and everything thought of as twofold or dualistic. The truth that is sought is that which endures, is unchanging, and continuous; it is immutable.

Closely tied to a belief in contemplation, ascent emphasizes that the cosmos possesses a hierarchical order where the gods are not mortal creations, but neither are they totally out of human reach, nor are they entirely Other. Rather, they represent a dual structure of not only what is *above* human life, but what is *in* human life as well.[23] As an aspect of transcendence, the gods allow us to fluidly ascend and descend the celestial hierarchy according to our nature. If, on the one hand, we are attracted to the negative aspects of, for instance, greed and ignorance, we will inevitably descend. On the other hand, if we strive for beauty and truth it is our nature to ascend. What is important to understand is that no human initiator is necessary to launch us on our path; we participate in the divine because this is part of our intrinsic human capacity.

The hierarchy flows over from the higher to the lower such that all levels of consciousness participate in the transcendence. Perennial philosophy's adherence to hierarchical structures is an important aspect of its teachings, and it is generally understood that tradition and hierarchy are symbiotic; one does not exist without the other. Together, they constitute a chain linking civilization with the One in both a chronological and synchronic mode of time, as well as to a spiritual origin fastened to a spiritual center. Derived from the Greek, hierarchy means "scared order," and as perennialism uses the word it denotes a traditional order wherein all authority, even our socially constructed order, derives its legitimacy from the sacred center.[24]

Along with the concept of ascent, and to become a channel for the gods, one must purify oneself, which perennial philosophy refers to as theurgy, or what the Neo-Platonists thought of as "divine working" or simply the "work of the god."[25] More specifically, theurgy describes the practice of rituals that are oftentimes magical or mystical in nature. These rituals are performed to both invoke and evoke the presence of the gods with the intention of achieving *henosis* or the uniting with the divine and perfecting oneself.

Here, two operations are called forth: one must first clear the soul and then one must open the soul to God (a return to the god as *apotheosis*). The purifying action entails two complimentary actions, one belonging to the immanent world and the other pertaining to the afterlife. With regard to the immanent world, theurgy is understood as the soul becoming a conduit for god. By revealing the god within oneself through ritual practices, one reunites the cosmos with the primal timelessness out of which space and time originally emerged. The first aspect of becoming a conduit for god prepares the theurgist for the second aspect of eternity and its associated timelessness. Consequently, the theurgist does not reject the material world, but through contemplative ascent, in conjunction with the ritual and symbolic invocation of the gods, returns to its primordial and archetypal purity. Perennial philosophy is just that because its point of departure is transcendent eternity coinciding with our understanding of why we experience an overwhelming feeling in the face of greatness.

TRANSCENDENCE

As I have alluded to, absolute transcendence is another key aspect of perennial philosophy. Plotinus described it in the *Enneads* as what lies beyond intellect and knowledge, that which is totally ineffable and outside of any duality, or "the One." In actuality, however, it is unnamable, and although we can say something about it, we have no direct knowledge of it. Expressed only in the negative, we can say what it is not, but not what it is. Having acknowledged this, transcendence is articulated as light or illumination of the soul, not through some external source but by the light of consciousness as its own self-perception. Naturally, the nature of that which is beyond existence and any discursive thought entails what I have already discussed, namely, the idea of mysticism, very much a part of Christianity, but abundantly evident in Sufism in Islam, Kabbalah in Judaism, and perennialism as well. Christian mysticism urges the follower toward the exercise of mystical contemplation where one leaves behind all sensory perceptions and intellectual inclinations as well as manifestations of the world of being and nonbeing to attain that which transcends all being and knowledge. Described as a "dazzling Mystery" where one journeys into pure transcendent silence that is so illuminating as to be a kind of darkness, but a darkness beyond all light where without seeing and without knowing one knows that which lies beyond vision and knowledge. Any attachment to one's own thoughts or beliefs means the supplicant never reaches understanding and thus remains uninitiated.

While perennialism finds transcendence absolutely necessary, it recognizes distinctions between the kind of transcendence found in various forms such as Vedanta where the self (*ātmān*) is ultimately identical with transcendence (*brahman*), and the transcendence found in Buddhism where the self and other are thought of as emptiness. Regardless, perennial philosophy is perennial because of transcendence, which means that an individual is not merely an atomized figure like all others, but is something beyond being an individual, that is, beyond a subject object divide. Generally, perennial philosophy invokes a central path to transcendence reflected in various religious traditions without being limited to any particular one.

ABOVE AND BELOW

While the Platonic tradition is essential to an understanding of perennial philosophy, Hermeticism also provides a variation from which to view perennial philosophy. Hermes is the messenger of the gods and is thus associated with communications. As a winged deity, Hermes ascends and descends and asserts "that which is above is from that which is below, and that which is below is that which is from above, working the miracles of the one."[26] This aphorism confirms for perennialism that what is above corresponds to that below, and in fact unites in the One. Thus, all things either emerge from or are adaptations of the One because the One is inherent in all things. And because the One is innate in all phenomena, it is also a way of conceiving or understanding how the cosmos emerges out of or through transcendence as freedom from the self–other or subject–object dichotomy; in its essence, it is the admonition to care for others because we are all fundamentally united by the transcendence that is inherent in the cosmos.

Perennialism refers to this as wisdom, or the highest achievement of contemplative ascent. Specifically, to honor the gods is to honor the principles they symbolically represent. And one performs the rituals of honoring and worshiping the gods to either emulate them or incorporate them within. Transcendence, then, is the wellspring of wisdom. According to perennial philosophy, contemporary society has forgotten (*anamnesis*) the value of transcendence as it eschews the viability of any metaphysical context. But for perennialists, the contemplative is meant to arouse the truth by "awakening" the individual to the truth.

Hermes's *The Emerald Tablet* goes on to expand upon the One whose father is the sun, and whose mother the moon. The wind carries the One while the earth nurtures it in its belly. It is the forbearer of all "works of wonder" (*telesmi*) in the world, and its power is integral or complete (*integra*). It separates earth from fire, the subtle from the gross. It ascends above and descends below; it is the glory of the cosmos, and the strength of all strength, it infiltrates everything both permeable and solid. In the end, it is the work of the sun.[27] What this implies for perennial philosophy is that there is a clear hierarchical structure to the cosmos that stretches from above to below, from the material to the supramaterial to the transcendent. Moreover, as we have seen, all phenomena have a transcendent origin called the One.

Perennialists see the *Tablet* as a highly compact statement of their philosophical beliefs in its cosmological and alchemist construct. As Arthur Versluis reminds us, the *Tablet* "is about how transcendence is inherent in immanence, and about how we human beings can transmute and reveal the hidden perfection within nature."[28] The *Tablet* is both theurgistic and intertwined with alchemy, which is itself primarily cosmological in nature or thought of in terms of applied hermeticism.

PERENNIALISM AND SCIENCE

Most people tend to separate the concepts of contemplation, as understood by perennialists, with an appreciation of today's science. As I have indicated, for perennialists, contemplation entails mysticism, visions, and even hallucinations, but most importantly ascent and transcendence; hardly the stuff of science. In today's world we are inclined to regard science as materialistic and certainly subject to rational calculation and expression. But perennialists discount these obvious differences and argue the two are completely compatible, at least with regard to their perceived shared goal.

Perennialists believe modern science concentrates on that which is without rather than on that which is within. Science, they argue, looks to external laws, causes, functions, and effects to define its methodology, and not to the possibilities of inner or spiritual life, or even the life of the mind itself. But for perennialists, science and contemplative introspection do not have to be at odds; each seeks to investigate and understand phenomena, especially with regard to the nature of the cosmos, human reality, and universally applicable truths. The divide, it seems, is in the method undertaken and not the desired end point.

In its modern instantiation, science seeks to uncover hidden laws governing external phenomena, always with an eye to practical applications, and rarely is it devoted to awakening the individual to truth or existential transmutation. Philip Sherrard explains that:

> the social form which we have adopted cuts our consciousness to fit its needs, its imperatives tailor our experience. The inorganic technological world that we have invented lays hold on our interior being and seeks to reduce that to a blind inorganic material thing. It seeks to eliminate whole emotional areas of our life, demanding that we be a new type of being, a type that is not human as this has been understood

in both the religious and the humanist ages—one that has no heart, no affections, no spontaneity, and is as impersonal as the metals and processes of calculation in which it is involved.[29]

At odds with what they call "profane science," perennial philosophy's goal is to awaken the individual to truth, which can only be realized for oneself. As such, one's soul must be conditioned to recognize the truth and become a suitable vessel for such a transformative and illuminating experience. Perennialism's contemplation is, therefore, a very different process than scientific analysis and experimentation; yet, both are subject to logical and discursive analysis. In fact, if the mutual goal is truth, then perennialists see contemplation as advancing that goal not for any one particular individual but for all concerned. As I have already pointed out, perennialists argue that if some have experienced the truth through contemplation—here we are talking about the so-called elites who are schooled in perennial philosophy—then the truth so experienced must be true for others as well. The confluence of science and contemplation can occur through a so-called higher science that takes heed of religion and metaphysics to acquire an index of human self-knowledge that encompasses knowledge of the transcendent.

Perennialists acknowledge that contemplation requires abandoning preconceived notions about who we are in relation to others in the world. Moreover, it is not easily pursued by rational thought alone because such thought is dualistic in nature—self and other—and perennialists are far more interested in what is beyond discursive analysis. Science, therefore, cannot attain to contemplative experience because such experience is measured in terms of changes in consciousness that is beyond quantification or ordinary measurement. It is this concept of quantification that perennialists seize upon to distinguish contemplation from what they think of as profane science, which can only quantify results it cannot examine their quality. The concern for quantity over quality takes on new importance under Guénon's authorship as he condemns profane science for its adherence to the materialistic, or the primacy of the measurement of quantity at the expense of the "quality" of metaphysical inquiry.

As Nietzsche distinguished between the exoteric as seeing things from below and peering upwards, and the esoteric as seeing those same things from above and looking downward, the intent of contemplation is to obtain wisdom, not for its own sake but for the sake of all. In this regard, the view from the lower to the higher is quite different than from the higher to the lower. And, in keeping with perennialism's elitist notions, only a few can obtain the truth through contemplative ascent, which must then be passed in a downward projection pursuant to its hierarchical nature. While science and contemplation differ in their fundamental methods, perennialists see each as seeking the same ultimate goal of truth. Yet it is argued that perennial philosophy must be seen as the ultimate science because contemplation is itself both self-knowledge and simultaneously knowledge of what transcends the self. In other words, perennial philosophy must lead the sciences because it alone is concerned with the ultimate mysteries, the grand scheme of things, and the definitive goal of wisdom.

These basic considerations of perennial philosophy are, as I have indicated, melded into traditionalism, a philosophy that took root in the early years of the twentieth century under the direction of René Guénon. While Guénon encouraged many others, he is at the very origin of traditionalism, which continues to have an effect on current political discussions, especially with the alt-right movement in the United States.

NOTES

1. Marco Pallis, the translator of Guénon's *Introduction to the Study of Hindu Doctrines*, adopted the term "metaphysic" instead of "metaphysics" to describe Guénon's understanding of metaphysics. The hope was to differentiate Guénon's use from the common understanding of metaphysics as a branch of philosophic thought. Metaphysic is, therefore, not a branch of philosophy because it does not belong to any one particular philosophy or philosopher. Rather, Guénon's metaphysic should be viewed in terms such as "Universal" or the "Whole" because the absolute Whole cannot constitute a part of something else. Nor can metaphysic encompass any manner of systematization because such a system would place limits on his idea of metaphysic, which is without limitation. While Guénon did not provide a definition for metaphysic, he intended to place the concept in what he thought was its rightful place, beyond physics or all scientific knowledge. See, generally, Barbara Santos and John Giodano, "René Guénon on the Realization of Traditional Knowledge," *Prajñā Vihāra* 18, no. 1 (January–June 2017): 98–140. Throughout the discussion, I will use the more traditional form of the word as metaphysics.

2. Aldous Huxley, *The Perennial Philosophy* (New York: Harper Perennial Modern Classics, 2009), vii and 21.

3. Arthur Versluis, *Perennial Philosophy* (Minneapolis: New Culture Press, 2015), 2. In 1460, a Greek manuscript was brought to Florence and presented to the city's ruler, Cosimo de' Medici. The forgotten codex contained fourteen treatises attributed to Hermes Trismegistus, an ancient Egyptian sage. The manuscript caused immediate excitement because Hermes, identified with the Ibis god Thoth, was thought to be older than either the ancient Greeks or the Bible. The codex was entrusted to the humanist philosopher–priest Marsilio Ficino (1433–1499) to translate, and what evolved became known as the *Corpus Hermeticum*, together with works on alchemy. The *Hermeticum* became part of the canonical texts for perennialism because it was thought to predate known Western philosophy and the Christian era. However, in 1614 Isaac Casaubon (1559–1614) proved that the *Hermeticum* was not of ancient origin but should be dated from the first or third century CE, or certainly after the beginning of the Christian era. Afterward, the *Corpus Hermeticum* lost its general fascination but lived on in secret societies, such as the Freemasons and the Rosicrucians. See *The Way of Hermes*, trans. Clement Salaman, Dorine van Oyen, William Wharton, and Jean-Pierre Mahé (Rochester, VT: Inner Traditions, 2004), 9–11.

4. Harry Oldmeadow, *Traditionalism: Religion in the Light of the Perennial Philosophy* (San Rafael: Sophia Perennis, 2011), 59.

5. Lord Northbourne, "Looking Back on Progress," in *The Underlying Religion: An Introduction to Perennial Philosophy*, ed. Martin Lings and Clinton Minnaar (Bloomington, IN: World Wisdom, 2007), 18.

6. Ibid.

7. Plotinus, *Enneads IV 7*, "On the Immortality of the Soul," trans. Barrie Fleet (Las Vegas: Parmenides, 2016). See also, Dominic O'Meara, *Plotinus* (Oxford: Clarendon Press, 1993), 45.

8. A. C. Bhaktivedanta Swami Prabhupada, *Bhagavad- Gītā as It Is* (Los Angeles: The Bhaktivedanta Book Trust, 2013), IV.5.

9. Aldous Huxley, "Introduction," in *Bhagavad-Gita: The Song of God*, trans. Swami Prabhavananda and Christopher Isherwood (New York: Mentor Books, 1951), 13. Perennialists often use different terms to describe the concept of the divine, including Divine Ground, Godhead, Ultimate Reality, and the One.

10. Huston Smith, "Is There a Perennial Philosophy?" *Journal of the American Academy of Religion* 55, no. 3 (Autumn 1987): 554.

11. René Guénon, *Introduction to the Study of Hindu Doctrines*, trans. Marco Pallis (Hillsdale: Sophia Perennis, 2004), 75–76, originally published as *Introduction Générale à l'Étude des Doctrines Hindoues* by Marcel Rivière, Paris, 1921.

12. Smith, "Is There a Perennial Philosophy?," 562.

13. J. N. Ferrer identifies five forms of perennialism: First, there is a basic form that holds that only one path and one goal for spiritual development exists. Second, there is the esoteric view that, although there is one common goal among the traditions, there are many possible paths leading to spiritual development. Third, there is a perspectivist notion of perennialism that accepts the many goals of mysticism but argues that these are merely different interpretations of an identical Ultimate Reality. Fourth, there is a typological form of perennialism that focuses on the different types of mysticism that occur across traditions as diverse manifestations of a single spiritual experience, or Ultimate Reality. Lastly, there is a structuralist form that views spiritual development across traditions as unfolding through a common hierarchy of deep structures and levels. J. N. Ferrer, "The Perennial Philosophy Revisited," *Journal of Transpersonal Psychology* 32, no. 1 (2000): 7–30. See also, Steve Taylor, "From Philosophy to Phenomenology: The Argument for a 'Soft' Perennialism," *International Journal of Transpersonal Studies* 35, no. 2 (2016): 17–41.

14. Versluis, *Perennial Philosophy*, 3.

15. See Northbourne, "Religion and Tradition," in *The Underlying Religion*, 9.

16. William Stoddart, "Mysticism," in *The Underlying Religion*, 231.

17. Ibid., 232.

18. Ibid., 9. See also, Oldmeadow, *Traditionalism*, 77.

19. Stoddart, "Mysticism," 234.

20. Frithjof Schuon, *Light on the Ancient Worlds* (Bloomington, IN: World Wisdom Books, 2006), 76.

21. Northbourne, "Religion and Tradition," 9.

22. Versluis, *Perennial Philosophy*, 33.

23. Northbourne, "Modernism: The Profane Point of View," in *The Underlying Religion*, 11.

24. Northbourne, "Looking Back on Progress," 25.

25. Versluis, *Perennial Philosophy*, 39.

26. Hermes Trismegistus, *The Emerald Tablet of Hermes*, trans. Jabir ibin Hyyan (Unknown: Merchant Books, 2013), 7. *The Emerald Tablet*, also known as the *Smaragdine Tablet*, or *Tabula Smaragdina*, is an extremely compact and highly cryptic piece of the *Hermetica* reputed to contain the secrets of the origin of the universe and its transmutation. European alchemists highly regarded the text as the foundation of their art and Hermetic tradition. The original source for *The Emerald Tablet* is unknown, although Hermes Trismegistus is the author named in the text. Its first known appearance is in a book written in Arabic between the sixth and eighth centuries. The text was first translated into Latin in the twelfth century. Numerous translations, interpretations, and commentaries followed. I have amalgamated several translations to discuss its importance.

27. Hermes, *The Emerald Tablet*, 10.

28. Versluis, *Perennial Philosophy*, 61.
29. Philip Sherrard, "Modern Science and the Dehumanization of Man," in *The Underlying Religion*, 74.

TWO

René Guénon and Traditionalist Philosophy

"Those Were the Days"

Even though René Guénon was a prolific writer and thinker, especially in the field of metaphysics, few understand his work let alone his traditional philosophy. Perhaps this is due to Guénon's writing style, which William Stoddart describes as purely theoretical in character. In other words, Guénon makes no pretense to practicality; rather, his interest centers on the intellectual as doctrine and less so with method. Regardless of writing style, traditional philosophy has generally found limited acceptance. Often considered on the fringe of contemporary philosophic thought because of its penchant for a rather particularized form of antihumanism along with a heavy emphasis on the metaphysical, particularly the prominence accorded mystical revelations. However, Guénon's personality may also factor into the equation, which his friend, Whitall Perry, described as enigmatic with an "outer anonymity."

Born in the small town of Blois, France, in 1886, Guénon grew up a devout Catholic. He later moved to Paris to study mathematics at the Collège Rollin, but in 1905 these studies were abandoned to immerse himself in French occultism. At about the same time, he either dabbled in or joined several secret organizations prevalent in the early part of the twentieth century, including theosophical, masonic, spiritualistic, and gnostic societies. Guénon subsequently renounced these occultist societies as "counterfeit spirituality" and, instead, adopted a philosophy of traditional esotericism imbued with perennial philosophy. Throughout his entire mature life, however, Guénon insisted that contemporary European civilization was mired in the twin evils of materialism and decadence.

From about 1912 to the early 1930s, Guénon emerged from his occultist beginnings and associated with an intensely Catholic environment. Influences during this period of his life included, among others, Jacques Maritain, a leading advocate of "Integral Christian Humanism," who argued that secular forms of humanism were inexorably antihuman because they refused to recognize the whole person. Maritain believed that, once the spiritual dimension of human nature is rejected, we no longer have an integral, but merely partial, humanism, which simply rejects a fundamental dimension of the human person. It was also during this time that Guénon immersed himself in the study of esoteric sapient traditions within the recognized religions, especially Catholicism. However, in 1930 Guénon moved to Cairo, where he abandoned Catholicism and embraced Islam, especially the Sufic order of Shadilites. He remained in Cairo until his death in 1951.

After moving to Egypt, his writings most often appeared in *Etudes Traditionnelles*, a formerly theosophical journal that Guénon transformed into a forum for traditional thought. Toward the end of his life, he concentrated on issues concerning initiation into authentic esoteric traditions. However, Guénon espoused the conviction that a nonindividual, nonformal body of knowledge—a primordial tradition—revealed to humanity at the beginning of the present cycle of time, in Vedanta the *Kali Yuga*, but now lost, radiated outward from a central hub in a spiderlike web into the world of formal reality. Through what he called metaphysical knowledge as the fountainhead for the great religions, Guénon sought to prepare the way for the transcendent unity of all religious traditions. In his thought, humans are first and foremost metaphysicians and only later craftsmen in some art or trade.

In support of his views, Guénon attempted to give expression to many of the traditional doctrines, including Vedanta, Christianity, Sufism, Kabbalah, the Chinese tradition, mythology, Gnosticism, and even alchemy, in an effort to show their fundamental principles as manifestations of one primordial tradition. In this effort, Guénon's writings generally focus on several key themes: metaphysics as transcending all other doctrinal orders; the distinction between esoteric and exoteric initiation; hierarchy of the intellectual domain; the contrast between the traditional Orient and the modern Occident; a view of time in the Hindu tradition as cyclical and spiraling downward rather than in a progressive upward trajectory with an evolutionary view of history; and, fundamental to traditionalism, the belief in the utter decadence of the modern world.[1]

CRISIS OF THE MODERN WORLD

In a very early text, *A General Introduction to the Study of Hindu Doctrines*, Guénon adopts three central elements in his traditionalist philosophy: first, he eschews either a sociological or an anthropological approach in favor of a theological slant, especially the belief that metaphysics transcends all other doctrinal orders. For Guénon, Hinduism is the repository of spiritual truth; second, he equates Hinduism to Vedanta rather than to any of the other five *darshanas*, or philosophical schools of Hinduism; and lastly, Guénon advocates a "primal truth," or what is better known as perennial philosophy, the understanding that all religions share a common ancestry in a single perennial religion, which subsequently took several forms: Zoroastrian, Pharaonic, Platonic, and Christian.[2]

But the starting point for Guénon's traditionalism is the certainty that the modern world is in the midst of decay. In adopting Hinduism as spiritual truth, he believes that the annual cycle is essential to traditional symbolism. Applicable to both the cosmic and human orders, each phase of a temporal cycle possesses its own particular quality exerting a determinative influence on events, the speed of which is qualitative rather than quantitative. Furthermore, the four great cycles that comprise a *manvantara* are most notably signified by both their decreasing durations and increasing concealment of the primordial spirituality. The consequences of this movement are that all things take on an increasingly quantitative character at the expense of a qualitative superiority, until such time as the "reign of quantity" is conclusively established.[3]

The West, he believes, is ensconced within this reign of quantity associated with the fourth and final stage of development, the so-called *Kali Yuga*, or dark age, which has lasted for more than six thousand years and certainly predates any known classical history. Since the beginning of this cycle, the primordial truths, once abundantly available to all, are now hidden and obscured with those in possession of such truths, or as Guénon refers to them as "nonhuman"—by which he means suprahuman—becoming fewer and fewer. Although such truths can never be entirely lost, Guénon sees the modern world's materialism as imposing a veil upon these primordial truths so as to make it extremely difficult to discover. Thus, those who aspire to true knowledge must rediscover these truths even though what is hidden will eventually become visible again at the end of the present cycle and the beginning of the new.

Hindu cyclical development ostensibly rejects the modern notion of progress or any evolutionary change and instead sees only a downward trajectory. Cyclical development must proceed in such a manner, from higher to lower, or what Guénon labels a "progressive materialization," because "development or any manifestation necessarily implies a gradual increasing distance from the principle from which it proceeds; starting from the highest point, it tends necessarily downward, and, as with heavy bodies, the speed of its motion increases continuously until finally it reaches a point at which it is stopped."[4]

The Middle Ages provides the breaking point and an acceleration of the West's decline. Starting in the reign of Charlemagne (742–814 CE) and extending to the opening of the fourteenth century, a new decadence set in that continues to this day. Guénon argues that this period marks the beginning of the displacement of Christendom, with which the Western civilization of the Middle Ages was essentially identified. At the same time, it marks the end of the feudal system, closely linked to the concept of Christendom, but it also portends the rise of the political formation of nation states. Thus, for Guénon, the modern era occurred at least two hundred years earlier than most believe, with the Renaissance and the Reformation merely the product of the preceding decadence. But Guénon goes even further by saying that the Renaissance and the Reformation were not merely adjustments to traditionalism but the definitive rupture with the traditional spirit. In this view, the Renaissance, accompanied by a corresponding "intellectual regress," comes under particular scrutiny, not as its name implies as a rebirth, but as a beginning of a downward death spiral for humankind and the sciences as well as religion itself.[5]

While the change in religion is clearly marked by the Reformation—as an assault on traditional religion—the alteration in the sciences was far more complete. Guénon believes that the traditional sciences were eclipsed during this period with nothing to take their place. As we saw in our discussion of perennial philosophy, "profane" philosophy and "profane" science—by which is meant nonmetaphysical—as the negation of true intellectuality that limits knowledge to the lowest order manifested in the empirical and analytical study of facts detached from higher principles, has presented modernity with purely material and quantifiable features equating to what Guénon calls an absolute "monstrosity."[6] The blame for this abominable state of affairs lies squarely on one factor that seemingly fostered this seismic shift away from feudalism and in the direction of modernism: humanism. What Guénon laments by this term is the shift to reduce everything to human proportions at the expense of the metaphysical and the symbolic effort to turn away from the heavens under the guise of dominating the earth.[7] Humanism in the form of secularism only reduces humankind to its lowest level of attainment where satisfaction of overt desires inherent in the material side of human disposition is attained; in the end, disorder and confusion reign supreme in the modern world. Referring to the Sacred Books of India, Guénon announces that we have reached the terrible age "when the castes shall be mingled, when even the family shall no longer exist."[8]

But for Guénon, no "readjustment" like that that occurred in the Greco-Roman decadence can occur before the modern world succumbs inevitably to the bottom of the abyss. Only a total and complete renovation can impede the inescapable. Yet all is not lost: the cataclysmic event marking the makeover is, in his mind, the turn to traditionalism. Despite his dire concern for the fate of the West, the decline is, in Guénon's opinion, unavoidable because the West must enter into what he calls the general order of things—the grand metaphysical design—which is made up of the mass total of all disorders. As civilization ultimately moves from one epoch to another, it does so in darkness; yet what characterizes the ultimate phase of any given cycle is the realization of all that has been previously neglected. This state, Guénon believes, has arrived because traditionalism appraises Western sciences, with its industrial applications, as worthless or a lower form of knowledge in comparison to anyone possessing knowledge of a higher order. Again, this turn of events is inevitable because it could occur only in a stage of development lacking true intellectuality, where humans are driven by the material world. Hence, the modern world has a particular *raison d'etre*: it signals the end of the present cycle and the coming of a new traditional reign.

INDIVIDUALISM AND THE DECLINE OF THE WEST

Closely linked to Guénon's aversion to humanism is his belief that individualism negates any principle of higher authority, in other words, the denial of metaphysical principles beyond individuals. Such repudiation of higher principles reduces civilization to a purely human dimension; thus, the notion of individualism, characteristic of an antitraditional "profane point of view," generally equates to the Renaissance's use of the term "humanism." The danger of individualism is its power to negate metaphysics. The problem is that:

> what has never been seen before is the erection of an entire civilization on something purely negative, on what indeed could be called the absence of principle; and it is this that gives the modern world its abnormal character and makes of it a sort of monstrosity, only to be understood if one thinks of it as corresponding to the end of a cyclical period, as we have already said.[9]

Accordingly, individualism is the underlying determining origin of the decline of the West because it is the impetus for the development of the lowest possibilities of humankind by which is meant those possibilities that do not require a suprahuman element.

If, in fact, no suprahuman faculty exists in the West, then individualism also implies the negation of intellectual intuition and the jurisdiction of this intuition, namely, metaphysics in its true sense. Guénon argues that intellectual intuition's demise is a result of reason's dominance above all else. Here, reason or rationalism is delineated as dogmatic supremacy and the denial of anything that is either suprahuman, or of pure intellectual intuition. Because reason rejects any spiritual authority, rationalism and individuality, with their modern tendency toward simplification, are so closely allied that they are often interchangeable.[10] Yet reason is merely a human factor that Guénon views as relative. This move to rationality, or the limitation of knowledge, was but the first stage as reason was increasingly relegated to practical functions. Moreover, individualism as Guénon understands it, implies naturalism because all that lies beyond nature is beyond the grasp of the individual. Thus, naturalism and the negation of metaphysics is the same thing, and, if metaphysics is negated, then no intellectual intuition is possible, and, if this is the case, then reason itself is relative with relativism the only logical outcome of rationalism. Thus construed, individualism brought about a breach with tradition and gave rise to our modern world. As I have said, Guénon sees every traditional society espousing intellectual intuition and a pure metaphysical doctrine.

In line with perennialist thought, and as I have pointed out, Guénon considers the revolt against traditionalism to have occurred during the Middle Ages. But he is particularly concerned with the advent of Protestantism in the guise of individualism, which promoted among other things a personal relation to God, justification based on faith alone, and Holy Scripture available to all and subject to individual interpretation—"everyone a priest," according to Luther. The result, he says, is a state of anarchy and dissolution.[11] Because individualism neither allows for any higher authority than the human individual nor does it recognize any means of knowledge beyond that of individual reason, the modern world was bound to reject any spiritual authority based on the suprahuman order, "as well as any traditional organization, that is, any organization based essentially on this authority, whatever be its form—for the form will naturally vary with each civilization."[12]

Guénon is adamant that Protestantism's individualism denied the authority of the proper organization qualified to interpret the West's religious tradition. While he does not say what that proper organization was, one can legitimately conjecture that he was thinking in terms of the hierarchically structured Catholic Church that generally seeks adherence to its categorized order and denies a direct personal relationship with God.[13] It was Protestantism's so-called free criticism that resulted in the interpretation of sacred texts from private judgments, even by those who were ignorant or incompetent. Guénon analogizes religion's fall to that of philosophy, which replaced metaphysical doctrine with reason. In so doing, "the door was left open to all manner of discussion, divergencies, and deviations."[14] This resulted in a dispersion of religion based purely on certain individual's personal opinions. Not unlike philosophy, religion suffered a loss of doctrine and the disappearance of any intellectual elements. The embrace of rationalism drove religion to sentimentalism, which means that only a vague religiosity, devoid of real knowledge, remains.

EAST VERSUS WEST

Traditionalism argues, and Guénon is no different, that modern civilization exhibits a divide between what is called the East and the West. This was not always the case, however. At some time in the past, when traditional philosophy supposedly held sway in both the East and the West, no such schism existed. But when one civilization recognizes no higher principles other than the negation of principles, there can be no mutual understandings between civilizations. This, Guénon believes, occurred in the West as it abandoned its traditional past to embrace a materialist future. Only the civilizations of the East remained faithful to the traditionalist past, with the West adopting an antitraditional, materialist creed. In Guénon's thinking, the West is simply Europe and America. On the other hand, the East is slightly more complex in that it comprises three segments. The Far East is represented by the Chinese civilization and the Middle East (India) by the Hindu, but it is the Near East, represented by the Islamic, where the complexity resides. This last civilization occupies a sort of middle ground between East and West because it shares many attributes with Western civilization as it existed in the Middle Ages.

The opposition between East and West is significant not as a divergence in geographic entities but as an opposition between two types of mentalities. In earlier times—the medieval period, for instance—the Western philosophical and religious mentality was far more aligned with that of the East. During more recent centuries, that alignment ruptured and caused a reversal of the trend of human activity in the West. This brought about the development of the "Western mentality" by which is meant a modern mentality.

Guénon wants to make it very clear that he does not see traditional philosophy originating in the East and then passed on to the ancient West. Rather, he adheres to perennialism's explicit assertion that the present cycle emanates from the Hyperborean region (the extreme north) from which it migrated to both the East and the West, but now has become fully entrenched only in the East. Yet only contact with the East and its traditional philosophy, especially Hinduism through the Vedanta, can rebuild the Western tradition so keen to Guénon. And, if such a tradition were to be rebuilt in the West, it would undoubtedly be premised on a religious platform in the strictest sense and could only be Christian, specifically meaning Catholicism.

The question as to who might be capable of spearheading such a revival is an interesting problem. As with other perennial and traditional thinkers, Guénon places no reliance on the masses' capability for such an undertaking. Only an elite class, which by its very definition must be beyond all forms, can be entrusted to initiate and carry out the process. And, should a Western elite take shape, real knowledge of the Eastern doctrines would be essential to fulfilling its functions. This fixation with an elite class possessing real knowledge is significant for traditional thinking. According to this position, knowledge can come only from above and not from below because understanding must begin from the highest form of principles and descend gradually down to the lowest, or to the masses. Only a certain intellectual elite in the truest and most complete sense of the word, meaning metaphysically intellectual through intense contemplation, would be capable of such an undertaking.

CONTEMPLATION AND ACTION

One of the principal aspects of the divide between East and West is the conflict between contemplation and action. Most think that contemplation is the opposite of action. However, Guénon understands the importance of each as complementary attitudes but within a hierarchical order. Contemplation is more widespread in the East, especially in India; thus, it represents the Eastern mentality. Action, on the other hand, exemplifies the mentality of the West. Even should the West return to normal, that is, to traditional philosophy, action would continue to exist. Consequently, contemplation in the West will always be restricted to a certain elite. In other words, there would be far more *kshatriyas* (warrior class) and very few *brahmins* (spiritual, intellectual class). Guénon thinks that:

> if however the intellectual elite were effectually constituted and its supremacy recognized, this would be enough to restore everything to order, for spiritual power is in no way based on numbers, whose law is that of matter; besides—and this is a point of great importance—in ancient times, and especially in the Middle Ages, the natural bent of Westerners for action did not prevent them from recognizing the superiority of contemplation, or in other words, of pure intelligence.[15]

While both action and contemplation exist in the East as well as the West, it is the superiority of one over the other that sets the East apart from the West. But, again, Guénon asserts this was not always the case. Contemplation was once superior to action in the ancient doctrines of the West; however, the West today has lost its intellectuality by overdeveloping its capacity for action. Here, Guénon takes American philosophical pragmatism to task saying it denies the existence of anything of value beyond action, a point of view that only leads to intellectual atrophy.

To attack action, Guénon borrows a metaphysical argument from ancient Greece. Just as contemplation is superior to action, so unchanging is superior to change. Being merely a transitory and momentary modification of being, action can in no way carry its principle and sufficient reason in itself; "if it does not depend on a principle outside its own contingent domain, it is but an illusion; and this principle, from which it draws all the reality it is capable of possessing—its existence and its very possibility—can be found only in contemplation."[16] By itself change is unintelligible and contradictory; it is impossible to effect change without a governing principle from which change proceeds and which, being its principle, cannot be subject to it, and is consequently unchanging. For Guénon, it is clear that change belongs to the world of becoming: "knowledge alone gives the possibility of leaving this world and the limitations that are inherent in it, and when it attains to the unchanging—as does principle or metaphysical knowledge, that is to say knowledge in its essence—it becomes itself possessed of immutability, for all true knowledge essentially consists in identification with its object."[17] In its zeal to admit nothing higher than rational or discursive knowledge, this is exactly what the West has forgotten.

Absorbed by the thought of action, the West denies everything lying beyond it even as this type of action degenerates from the lack of any principle into a vain and what Guénon calls a sterile anxiety. The modern period shows a:

> need for ceaseless agitation, for unending change, and for ever-increasing speed, matching the speed with which events themselves succeed one another. It is dispersion in multiplicity, and in a multiplicity that is no longer unified by consciousness of any higher principle; in daily life, as in scientific ideas, it is analysis driven to an extreme, endless subdivision, a veritable disintegration of human activity in all the orders in which this can still be exercised; hence the inaptitude for synthesis and the incapacity for any sort of concentration that is so striking in the eyes of Easterners.[18]

Having focused its attention on outward action, the West oftentimes seeks change for its own sake not tied to any particular end. This type of change only devolves into a state of endless disequilibrium, which in Guénon's philosophy is indicative of the final dissolution of the present period; a further sign the concluding phase of the *Kali Yuga* is near.

Guénon notes that the same trend is true in science as well. Research for its own sake gives rise to more and more unfounded theories that soon after their debut flounder and wither away, only to give rise to another equally tenuous theory. Inevitably, science is mired in a sea of chaos in which no certainty resides. Very much in accordance with perennial philosophy, Guénon pursues a link between action and contemplation not just from the philosophical point of view but from the world of science as well.

SCIENCE: SACRED AND PROFANE

In traditional societies, intellectual intuition is the principle foundation for everything. That is, metaphysics constitutes the essential central core to which all else is joined, but in a lower hierarchical order. In this manner, a true and immutable hierarchy is maintained, or as Guénon explains, a hierarchy "is always and everywhere preserved."[19] This means that even the relative is treated as existing, but only as secondary and subordinate with different degrees of reality, depending on whether the relative domain resides nearer or further from the province of principles.

With regard to the sciences, Guénon is quite specific. Two radically different and incompatible conceptions exist. There is, on the one hand, traditional science, which existed in antiquity through to the Middle Ages and still exists in the East. On the other hand, there is profane, or modern, science known only to the West. Guénon associates metaphysics with universal and unchangeable principles of science, but he allows for differences in time and place by saying that there are periods when "readaptations" become necessary. By readaptations, Guénon means a change of form that does not impinge on the essence of the tradition. As with any metaphysical doctrine, only the expression can be modified. This is not the case with modern science, which is seen as inhabiting the realm of applications: the proliferated world of form and multiplicity, where several "sciences" study the same thing.

As an example of his lament, he points to the difference between traditional and modern science's understanding of physics.[20] In the ancient world physics, or in Greek *physis*, entailed the science of nature that deals with the most basic laws of becoming. And, for Aristotle, physics was secondary or dependent on metaphysics. Yet the modern world has used the term to describe just one particular science among all others, with each of the other sciences equally termed natural sciences. Guénon thinks this specialization arises from the modern world's analytic attitude of mind, such that science can no longer think in terms of nature in its entirety. The result is a narrowing of science that he thinks naturally impedes its outlook by accumulating ever more detailed knowledge, albeit insignificant in itself, which can never be fully assimilated. The key for Guénon, as well as traditionalism generally, is to understand that the modern world, to assure the independence of the sciences, has severed the connection of the sciences with any higher (metaphysical) principle. This robs modern science of all its deeper meaning, but more importantly, it is envisioned as traveling down a blind alley leading to a hopelessly limited realm.

There is yet another reason Guénon thinks science is on the wrong track. While he generally views modern science as pursuing ends for its own sake, he also sees the West using science not for knowledge but merely for what he calls practical applications. Thus, science becomes conflated with the notion of industry. As a result, modern science is not associated with the immutable, but with the world of change. We have already seen how Guénon derides the notion of change, but with regard to science he perceives a further ill. Constant change means that science lacks stability; no fixed point exists upon which it can ground itself; it no longer starts from the point of view of absolute certainty, but is reduced to the lesser world of probabilities and approximations. As a result, conclusions for science can belong only to the realm of conjecture or hypothesis. In contrast, traditional science has a very different character as the "indubitable consequences of truths known intuitively, and therefore infallibly, in the metaphysical order."[21] What those intuitively known and infallible truths are, however, is left unsaid.

In a somewhat curious discussion, Guénon argues that modern science represents the residue of past science that is no longer understood in modernity. He presents astrology and alchemy as two examples of ancient sciences that have morphed into astronomy and chemistry respectively in the modern world, not by a process of progress or "evo-lution," as he puts it, but through degeneration. Guénon points out that the Greeks used the terms astronomy and astrology synonymously; yet, while Greek astronomy was advanced for the time, it is undeniable that it was seriously limited. He blames the separation not on the content each displays but on the specialization forced upon science in the modern world. More importantly, he thinks only the material side—astronomy—developed independently, whereas the more metaphysical attribute—alchemy—disappeared altogether.

Chemistry, according to Guénon, fared no better. Just as astrology was forgotten as a true science, alchemy suffered a similar fate. Not only considered as a science of the cosmological domain, alchemy also encompassed the human order. One of the most typical and complete of the traditional sciences, alchemy existed expressly to permit a transposition into the purely spiritual domain giving it a symbolic value with a higher significance to its teachings. Chemistry, on the other hand, is merely a modern-day corruption, a deviation from alchemy and traditional science because chemistry today concerns itself with only the material outcome and not its vast higher meaning.

For Guénon, there are two complementary functions proper to traditional sciences. First, they act as applications of the doctrine making it possible to link the different orders of reality and integrate them into a single synthesis. Second, they constitute a preparation for higher knowledge by virtue of their hierarchical structure. This structure forms, according to the levels of existence to which they refer, so many steps of the ladder necessary to climb to the level of pure intellectuality. Modern science is incapable of such a journey, and as such it remains in the profane world, whereas the traditional sciences, through its relation to metaphysical principles, are effectively incorporated into what traditionalists call sacred science.

POLITICS: TRADITIONALISM AND DEMOCRACY

What Guénon has to say about science finds its parallels in politics, especially democratic forms of government. He takes aim at democracy and its various institutions for the simple reason that democracy endeavors to treat people equally regardless of one's origin of birth. Instead, Guénon adheres to a Platonic idea of function and class. Essentially, he sees individuals born into a certain caste or class, which ascribes a specific, preordained function. Whatever one's particular function, it is immutable; one cannot "fulfill a different function except at the cost of serious disorder, which will have its repercussions on the whole social organization of which it is a part."[22] Should disorder take hold, the repercussions Guénon speaks of are neither insignificant nor should they be treated lightly; hardly localized in nature, they will have a disruptive effect on the entire cosmic order because all things are linked by "rigorous correspondences."

Much like Plato's concern in the *Republic*, Guénon sees the possibility of disunity or the subversion of the social hierarchy within society as extremely troublesome; it destroys what he sees as the natural order that one is predestined to follow, and if society falls into disunity then chaos surely ensues. For this reason, Guénon adopts a position similar to Plato's where the guardians, as the intellectual elites, are the keeper of the traditions and the natural leaders who rule the *polis* by virtue of their birth. On the other hand, the auxiliaries are the warrior class, designated by birth as having silver mixed with their souls, trained through education in music and gymnastics and reared in a communal, communistic environment to maintain a certain kind of order embodied in the laws and traditions of the *polis*. What is quite evident, however, is the lack of interest or care Plato exhibits for the lowest class, the wage earners. Thought not to be capable of possessing knowledge beyond their specific artisan skill, they were neither educated nor allowed to reach beyond their particular function or class; to do otherwise would invite discord in the City. Unfortunately, Plato's elitism represents an oppressive hierarchy within the social structure not unlike the type Guénon advocates. This desire for hierarchical social structure and its effects assumes a central position in the discussion of social dominance theory and in Sartre's concept of group formation.

If we turn to the origin and function of the Hindu castes—highly relevant to both traditionalism and to Guénon—we find a similar pattern. In enumerating the four castes, Guénon accepts that their differentiation constitutes the basis of the social order. Referring to the *Purusha Sukta* of the *Rig Veda*, Guénon first quotes an analogy: "of the *Purusha*, the Brahmin was the mouth, the Kshatriya the arms, the Vaishya the thighs; the Shūdra was born under his feet."[23] After which, he offers an explanation:

the Brahmins represent essentially the spiritual and intellectual authority; the Kshatriyas, the administrative prerogative comprising both the judicial and the military offices, of which the royal function is simply the highest degree; to the Vaishyas belongs the whole varied range of economic functions in the widest sense of the word, including the agricultural, industrial, commercial, and financial functions; as for the Shūdras, they carry out the tasks necessary to assure the purely material subsistence of the community.[24]

Although Guénon does not specifically recognize it, because the functions of the three highest castes are fairly clear, full participation in society is strictly limited to members of those castes. In contrast, because their function is undetermined, participation by the fourth caste, the *shūdras*, is principally indirect and in effect "virtual." Therefore, their participation in society is directly related to their relation to the three superior castes. Moreover:

> to revert to the analogy of the "social organism," the part they [*shūdras*] play does not properly speaking constitute a vital function, but an activity that is in some sense mechanical, and this is why they are represented as springing, not from a part of the body of *Purusha* or "Universal Man," but from the earth beneath his feet, which is the element in which the substances of bodily nourishment are compounded.[25]

Guénon accepts the position of the lowest caste as purely mechanical, not unlike a machine used in the aid of physical labor, but surely not a "human" function. What is important to understand is that not unlike the reason for Plato's system of classes, according to Guénon the caste system in traditional societies offered a sense of stability and unity within the community: everyone knew her place—her function—within the group and performed that function and nothing else.[26] To transcend the class structure was to invite disunity within society, a result both Plato and Guénon are loath to accept. But the system also established a hierarchy within the social group structure; while everyone was important to the safety and development of the group, some were obviously more important than others. Moreover, within each class, participants were relatively homogeneous. This was true in the *Republic*, and it is equally true of traditionalism. Once this social hierarchy started to break down, with the onslaught of individualism wrapped in humanism, the advent of democratic societies with their egalitarian notions, and the mingling of the classes resulting in a loss of homogeneity, only social chaos remained.

With regard to one's function, Guénon goes so far as to say that within traditional societies functions were ruled by law, giving them a certain legal primogeniture. The argument behind this class or caste-oriented system is that some more egalitarian structures such as democracy fail to take into consideration the differences in nature between one individual and another. Yet Guénon seems not to recognize that these class systems were generally based on birth and had very little to do with merit. What seems important to him is that a traditional hierarchy within the group be maintained no matter the result. As Guénon argues:

> it is the negation of these differences, bringing with it the negation of all social hierarchy, that is the cause of the whole disorder; this negation may not have been deliberate at first, and may have been more practical than theoretical, since the mingling of the castes preceded their complete suppression or, to put it differently, the nature of individuals was misunderstood before it began to be altogether ignored; at all events this negation has subsequently been raised by the moderns to the rank of a pseudo-principle under the name of "equality."[27]

Equality, in Guénon's thinking, simply does not exist because it is contradictory to say two individuals can be both distinct and completely alike at the same time. Yet the use of the law of noncontradiction to essentially espouse an unequal hierarchical, social structure renders the concept of democratic equality rather simplistic. While it is true that the goal of modern liberal democracies is to *treat* everyone as equal, they also recognize *differences* in individuals. However, through social policies such as universal education, the goal of which Guénon disdains, and various attempts to level the playing field by offering resources to everyone, these democracies endeavor to live up to their proclaimed ideals of liberty and equality by providing the *opportunity* for upward mobility to all regardless of their class of origin. But Guénon thinks this is a subversion of the traditional structure of societies because it claims to "impose a complete uniformity on everyone."[28] However, the real reason for Guénon's apprehension goes much deeper. What he is really arguing is that the modern world, with its desire for a purely "bookish" conception of education, is concerned only with the accumulation of facts and figures where "quantity" is prized at the expense of "quality."

Guénon thinks social hierarchies are essential to traditional societies, and I should point out to modern societies as well, but he also sees everyone performing their function, a function to which one is born into. Modern democracy upends this hierarchical social structure by assuming individuals have the ability to move beyond their social class or status. What he calls "popularization," or what is really democratization, amounts to nothing less than the "pretension to put everything 'within reach of all' . . . [which] amounts in the end to a desire to bring all knowledge down to the level of the lowest intelligence."[29] The problem with democracy, Guénon says, is that it denies the natural order by recognizing that power emanates from below and that the political will is embodied in the concept of majority rule. But this, he argues, only excludes real competence, which he thinks is always a relative superiority belonging necessarily to a minority. Thus, his most decisive argument against democracy is that the "higher cannot proceed from the lower, because the greater cannot proceed from the lesser."[30] What this means is that the people, the bedrock of democratic governance, are incapable of conferring a power they do not inherently possess. True power can come only from above, which can be legitimized only by the sanction of something residing above the social order and that must necessarily be spiritual authority. Democracy illegitimately reverses the natural and true hierarchical order and seeks to make itself independent of spiritual power by granting temporal power undue authority.

Guénon also asserts that rulers and the ruled must be separated because no one can be ruled unless there are rulers. Accordingly, the very idea of democratic rule by the people is absurd and only meant to flatter the masses who are incapable of sufficient reflection to understand its impossibility. It is for this very reason that the "illusion" of universal suffrage was invented.

Disdain for the democratic ideal of rule by the majority goes a step further. While Guénon thinks that majority rule does not comport to reality, he also believes its obvious flaws rest on the premise that the opinion of the majority can be nothing more than an expression of incompetence brought about by a lack of intelligence, or just pure ignorance. Majority rule, he argues, must be likened to the law of brute force, the "same law by which a mass, carried down by its own weight, crushes everything that lies in its track."[31] It is here that the democratic conception of government with its emphasis on majority rule comes to coincide with Western materialism. The normal order is completely reversed, and the supremacy of multiplicity is substantiated, a supremacy that exists only in the material world. By contrast, in the spiritual world or, as Guénon also describes it, the universal order, unity is at the very summit of the hierarchy because unity is the most essential principle out of which all multiplicity arises.

One final point, alluded to previously, needs further clarification, and that is how Guénon considers the elite within traditionalist societies. A consequence of the democratic ideal is the negation of the idea of an elite class. Guénon analogizes his concept of an elite with the aristocracy. Few in number and possessed of an inherent and God-given authority derived from their superior intellectuality divorced from the numerical strength of democratic government, they are by nature diametrically opposed to democracy. Consequently, the guiding function of the elite is completely at odds with democracy because democracy's egalitarian dimension necessarily negates the hierarchy so essential to the concept of traditionalism and its elite, superior class.

WESTERN MATERIALISM

For Guénon, it is beyond argument that the West is exclusively materialistic. But he also envisions various meanings attached to the concept of materialism, and he desires to set out exactly what he believes is meant by the term. First, he notes that the word *materialism* originated in the eighteenth century to designate any theory that accepted the real existence of matter. This, however, is not what Guénon is referring to when he says the West is a materialistic society; rather, materialism must be considered in a much wider, more definitive context. In this broader notion, materialism represents a complete state of mind independent of any philosophical understanding. This state of mind consists:

> in more or less consciously putting material things, and their preoccupations arising out of them, in the first place, whether these preoccupations claim to be speculative or purely practical; and it cannot be seriously disputed that this is the mentality of the immense majority of our contemporaries.[32]

This wider definition coincides with Guénon's attack on profane Western science as merely the study of the sensible world. In fact, he thinks the methods employed to unlock the secrets of the sensible world are the only methods proclaimed to be scientific, which has the effect of rejecting any science not dealing with the sensible world. While science does not expressly profess its partiality to atheism or materialism, because of those prejudices, it certainly ignores what Guénon calls "certain things." While not expressed, this undoubtedly is a reference to the metaphysical laws that he holds to be immutable.

In his critique of materialism, Guénon is certainly taking aim at modern empiricism, which thinks that knowledge emanates from the experience of the senses. His dislike of empiricism seems to be centered on the conception of measurement, again a reference to quantity over quality. He believes that modern scientists conceive of things that can be measured, counted, and weighed leaving only material objects subject to quantitative analysis. As a result, modern science reduces quality to quantity and, because metaphysical "things" are by nature not subject to measurement, they cannot be the focus of scientific investigation. Moreover, in as much as no science can exist except where it is possible to introduce measurement and because the sensible order alone is subject to measurement, it follows that reality for modern science is limited to the sensible order.

Guénon's concept of Western materialism or as he sometimes refers to it as "practical materialism," rests on the premise that modern science strives to enhance the development of only industry and machinery. Yet, as humans seek to dominate matter and use it for their own purposes, they merely succumb to the slavery of machines. Science, in its enthusiasm to build ever better machines, reduces humankind to a mechanistic-like existence, devoid of metaphysical aspects. Very different from the ancient craftsman who Guénon prizes, modern workers are subject to a host of maladies, not least of which is the division of labor forcing workers to act as a single integrated body constantly repeating the same mechanical functions only to emerge as machinelike, nonhuman slaves. This idea of modern "progress" demeans the individual as it prioritizes the production of massive quantities over the more traditional approach that favors quality.

In support of his argument, Guénon sees the West mired in the dismal science of economics, which he thinks appertains as completely as possible to the reign of quantity.[33] Infatuated with the importance economic factors assume, both in the lives of individuals and of society as a whole, the only social distinctions that have survived are those based on material status and wealth. Such a reliance on economic factors, Guénon argues, fails to bring people together; rather, they have the opposite effect. For Guénon, matter is essentially multiplicity and division, and, as I have pointed out, this results in struggles and conflicts. Once again, the culprit lies in the humanitarianism brought about by the demise of the traditional order. Humanitarianism, egalitarianism, compulsory education, and universal suffrage find their expression here as the usurpation of the feudal system and the disruption of a higher unity of medieval Christendom that eventually gave rise to the nation state. But, equally insidious is the modern world's denial of any spiritual authority allowing practical materialism to thrive.

Guénon reserves one aspect of economics with its industrial priority to special scrutiny. Oddly, the world of invention takes on significant importance for Guénon's critique. He thinks the vastly growing number of modern inventions presents an ever-increasing and most dangerous situation because they bring into play forces whose real nature is quite unknown. This ignorance is the best proof of the utter worthlessness of modern science as a source of knowledge.

Guénon also questions the supposed benefits modern inventions bring about. In his mind, the so-called progress associated with inventions is merely illusory, for the simple reason that some people do not need such things. While Guénon does not say, the "some people" he refers to are the masses of society who should, in his mind, perform their function and be content to do so. That function does not require an expenditure of money on machines or technology such as the latest smart phone or fitness tracker, or for that matter something as basic as an automobile, to make life more productive and enjoyable. As Guénon sees it:

> the modern West cannot tolerate that men should prefer to work less and be content to live on little; as it is only quantity that counts, and as everything that escapes the senses is held to be non-existent, it is taken

for granted that anyone who is not in a state of agitation and who does not produce much in a material way must be "lazy."[34]

The idea that humans have progressed through what Guénon refers to as "material welfare" comes under particular attack. He questions whether humans are really happier today with swifter means of communication and other such modern conveniences. Rather, he thinks that technology, although he does not use that term, only brings about a "more agitated and complicated manner of life."[35] In other words:

> modern civilization aims at creating more and more artificial needs, and as we have already said, it will always create more needs, than it can satisfy, for once one has started on this path, it is very hard to stop, and, indeed, there is no reason for stopping at any particular point.[36]

This plethora of material goods causes humans to struggle in every possible manner to obtain material satisfaction; turning wants into needs lends itself to the never-ending spiral of the more you have, the more you want to have. Satisfaction of wants eventually becomes an obsession caused by the disequilibrium of the materialist modern world.

One of the upshots of this materialism is an inevitable envy that eventually results in hatred felt toward those who possess wealth by those who do not. Surprisingly, Guénon attributes this resentment to modern civilization's adoption of democratic ideals with its mantra of equality, when, in fact, he says all the people see is inequality in the most material order of things, the order most sensitive to their existence. Yet the inherent inequality of strict class hierarchy Guénon advocates never enters into the discussion. In other words, everyone should not only adhere to their particular class but happily comply with its strictures.

One of the key points for Guénon is materialization's effect on Western culture. In a very interesting concept, Guénon argues that the conformity to materialistic concerns, undoubtedly reached in the modern period, results in a certain "solidification" used in the sense of materialization, but with an emphasis on the notion of solidity, density, and impenetrability.[37] To approach this realm, humans must have "lost the use of the faculties which in normal times allowed [them] to pass beyond the bounds of the sensible world, the loss being due to the existence of 'materialization' or 'solidification.'"[38] Guénon utilizes this concept of solidification of the world to indicate the general direction in which changes occur; thus, solidification of the world confers on all things an aspect corresponding to the way in which things appear according to mechanistic or materialistic conceptions. While he thinks that the solidification of the world has already occurred, he also reasons that this results in "fissures" or "pathways" in the "Great Wall" surrounding the world and protecting it from destructive influences emanating from inferior yet subtle domains. Thus, the wall is primordial in his thinking. It was always there operating in the symbolic domain and acting as both a protective barrier and as a limitation; it both keeps the malefic out and refuses to let those within depart. However, and this is the essential point, the wall's principal purpose is to ensure an adequate defense against the potential onslaught of those who seek to attack from below, or the inferior races. Thus:

> the advantages [of the wall] are incomparably the more important, for it is on the whole more useful to anyone who happens to be enclosed within its perimeter to be kept out of reach of what is below, than it is to be continuously exposed to the ravages of the enemy, or worse still to a more or less complete destruction.[39]

The fissures Guénon refers to only occur at the base of the wall, and because modern materialism has severed all ties to the higher realm, there are no "forces" able to intervene in order confront the inferior herd and turn them away. In fact, the present-day mentality is wholly incapable of perceiving the actual threat looming before their very eyes. Only an elite can save those enclosed within the wall, a subject that is part of Guénon's solution to the social problem.

The use of the symbolism of the wall takes on added importance when the discussion turns to social dominance theory and to Sartre's theory of group formation. Both discuss the concept of the wall with similar outlooks, yet decidedly different connotations than Guénon, and even though walls have been built since humans first organized themselves into groups, the issue takes on new significance as President Trump extols the virtues of a wall on the border between the United States and Mexico, a topic I shall return to later.

THE SOLUTION TO THE SOCIAL PROBLEM

After cataloging the ills of the West, Guénon discusses what he says is the deleterious effects of the encroachment of the West upon the East. This intrusion is the advent of Western materialism in all its semblances. At the time, Guénon thought that many in the East had become completely westernized by forsaking their traditions and pursuing the aberrational ideals of the modern outlook. While not the majority view, Guénon thought this antitraditional movement had the ability to gain favor resulting in mass confusion, the characteristic of the final stages of the *Kali Yuga*.

Guénon is emphatic, however, in his belief that the modern outlook is purely Western and those who espouse such views must be thought of as Westerners even though they may have been born in the East. This is so because to any Easterner the modern view is utterly foreign and can never be assimilated. But, according to Guénon, it is quite logical to think that the ideas propagated by the West will eventually turn against it because those ideas are rife with division and ruin. Thus, it is though the West's very own ideas that its downfall will be brought about, and Guénon certainly has no sympathy for such an end because he thinks it is of the West's own making. In the downfall of the West, which I think Guénon believes will be at the hands of some cataclysmic or apocryphal event, the question arises whether the East will succumb as well. While a downfall may come, the crisis in the East will be more transitory and superficial than in the West simply because the spiritual power inherent in tradition will triumph over material power. Guénon fervently believes, "the traditional spirit cannot die, being in its essence above death and change; but it can withdraw completely from the outward world, and then there really would be the 'end of the world.'"[40] This eventuality is, Guénon adds, by no means unlikely in the not too distant future.

So where does the solution to the problem lie? For Guénon everything begins with knowledge that he thinks resides at the most remote point from the practical order. Yet knowledge, and here as in all aspects of his thinking knowledge equates to the metaphysical realm, is far more potent than the profane knowledge of, for instance, modern science that Guénon disparages. The modern world is based on the negation of traditional values and suprahuman truth, and if humans were to understand this, the modern world would cease to exist. Consequently, through knowledge change can be brought about without the intervention of a catastrophic event.

More specifically, Guénon thinks that a small cadre of powerfully established elite, steeped in the intellectual traditional, could guide the otherwise ignorant but malleable masses who would obey its directions. Guénon envisions the following:

> the elite still exists in the Eastern civilizations, and, granting that it is becoming ever smaller due to modernist encroachment, it will nevertheless continue to exist until the end, because this is necessary for the safe-guarding of the "ark" of tradition—which cannot perish—and for the transmission of everything that is to be preserved.[41]

The question then must be asked, because the elite of which Guénon speaks of no longer inhabit the West, where will they come from? The answer seems to be within the Catholic Church. The Catholic Church is the only Western institution that exhibits a traditional character and that has preserved a doctrine that could serve as a basis for the transformation of the West. Because Catholicism embodies the true sense of the ideal of universality, the need is to implement or "re-establish what already existed prior to the modern deviation, though with the adaptations called for by the conditions of a different period."[42]

The topic of an elite class leading the way for Western redemption and spiritual renewal is endemic to Guénon's traditional philosophy. It is the natural extension of a political theory that rests on a social hierarchy dominated at the top by those he calls suprahumans. Yet this nostalgia for a past time of "greatness" is mired in a type of melancholia for a period that never existed, or if it did exist it was probably not as Guénon envisioned. Human memory always has a habit of producing a past that is more glorious than the present, especially when confronted with the vicissitudes of the future. As T. S. Eliot once remarked, humankind cannot bear too much reality, and it is doubtful whether it can bear the reality of being told so. The 2016 Trump campaign slogan, "Make America Great Again," was the type of political verbiage vague enough to be both positive, and at the same time lack any specific meaning. MAGA does not just appeal to people who heard it as a racist "dog whistle," but it also enticed those who felt a loss of social status as other groups around them become more empowered. Underlying these concerns is an overriding feeling for a long-lost past that existed prior to the present decadence. What the present decay entails can be difficult to discern; suffice it to say that whatever the decline consists of, the past was inevitably better.

Guénon's traditionalism is merely the starting point. For a more expansive discussion of traditional philosophy and its ramifications on the present political scene, I want to turn to Julius Evola who inserted himself into the politics of his time to a far greater extent than Guénon.

NOTES

1. Oldmeadow, *Traditionalism*, 15–16. See also René Guénon, "*Sanātana Dharma*," in *The Essential René Guénon: Metaphysics, Tradition, and the Crisis of Modernity*, ed. John Herlihy (Bloomington: World Wisdom, 2009), 108–16.
2. See, generally, Guénon, *Study of Hindu Doctrines*. See also Oldmeadow, *Traditionalism*, 15; and Mark Sedgwick, *Against the Modern World* (Oxford: Oxford University Press, 2004), 22–23.
3. René Guénon, *The Reign of Quantity and the Signs of the Times*, trans. Lord Northbourne (Hillsdale: Sophia Perennis, 2001), 42–43, originally published as *Le Règne de la Quantité et les Signes des Temps* by Les Éditions Traditionnelles, Paris, 1945.
4. Rene Guénon, *The Crisis of the Modern World*, trans. Marco Pallis, Arthur Osborne, and Richard Nicholson (Hillsdale: Sophia Perennis, 2001), 7–8, originally published as *La Crise du Monde Moderne* by Éditions Gallimard, Paris, 1927. See also, Guénon, "Some Remarks on the Doctrine of Cosmic Cycles," in *The Essential René Guénon*, 117–23.
5. Guénon, "Civilization and Progress," in *The Essential René Guénon*, 68–74. Guénon explains that the intellectual regress has reached such epic proportions that Westerners no longer understand the concept of pure intellect and, because of this ignorance, they exhibit only contempt for Eastern civilizations as well as the European Middle Ages. Indeed, ignoring all pure and supra-rational knowledge opened the door to not only positivism and agnosticism but sentimental and "voluntarist" theories seeking the infra-rational. Ibid., 68–69.
6. Guénon, *Crisis of the Modern World*, 16.
7. Ibid., 17.
8. Ibid., 18.
9. Ibid., 55.
10. Guénon, *Reign of Quantity*, 90.
11. Guénon, *Crisis of the Modern World*, 60.

12. Ibid., 60–61.
13. Ibid., 63. See, generally, Michael Massing, *Fatal Discord: Erasmus, Luther, and the Fight for the Western Mind* (New York: HarperCollins, 2018); and Carlos Eire, *Reformations: The Early Modern World, 1450–1650* (New Haven, CT: Yale University Press, 2016).
14. Guénon, *Crisis of the Modern World*, 61.
15. Ibid., 35.
16. Ibid., 37.
17. Ibid., 37–38.
18. Ibid., 38.
19. Ibid., 42.
20. Ibid., 43–47.
21. Ibid., 47.
22. Guénon, *Reign of Quantity*, 58 and 64.
23. *The Rig Veda*, trans. Wendy O'Flaherty (Harmondsworth: Penguin Books, 1981), 29–32 [§10.90 verse 12] (translation altered). This is the first instance where there is reference to four social classes, or *varnas*, in Indian civilization.
24. Guénon, *Study of Hindu Doctrines*, 154–55.
25. Ibid., 156. By Universal Man, Guénon means the correspondence between the cosmic and the human orders, which find their natural expression in the organization of the individual are also be realized in an appropriate manner in the organization of society.
26. Guenon, *Crisis of the Modern World*, 69.
27. Ibid., 70.
28. Ibid.
29. Guénon, *Reign of Quality*, 82. A little later in the same section, Guénon argues that it is not possible to put the *Vedanta* within the reach of the common person because not only was it never intended to be within such reach but, as he says, it is all the more certain today that the common person has never been more uncomprehending. Ibid., 84.
30. Guenon, *Crisis of the Modern World*, 73.
31. Ibid., 76.
32. Ibid., 82.
33. Guénon, *Reign of Quantity*, 107.
34. Ibid., 92.
35. Ibid., 93.
36. Ibid.
37. Guénon, *Reign of Quantity*, 115.
38. Ibid.
39. Ibid., 173.
40. Guénon, *Crisis of the Modern World*, 99.
41. Ibid., 109.
42. Ibid., 112.

THREE
Julius Evola's Traditionalism

Julius Evola was born into a Sicilian family of minor nobility in May 1898. Even though his family life revolved around a strong, dogmatic Catholic upbringing, his early development would be characterized by successive intervals of personal change. While still quite young, Evola entered into the circle of rebellious poets surrounding the Futurist movement of the avant-garde poet Filippo Tommaso Marinetti. This group influenced Evola with new directions in art and fashion as well as oriental wisdom and the mystical works of Meister Eckhart. In the Great War, Evola served as an artillery officer but saw limited action. After the war, he was drawn to occult teaching and occasional drug experimentation. These new activities deepened Evola's despair, only exacerbating his already held belief in the insignificance and illusion of everyday existence with its continual desire for something that can never quite find fulfillment.

In the early 1920s, Evola encountered the Dada movement and its founder Tristan Tzara, who, while still ensconced in the avant-garde art movement, wanted to establish a revolutionary vision of the world through absolute liberation by reversing all known logical, ethical, and aesthetic categories. Evola's attraction was largely centered on his desire for self-liberation through art transcending into a higher plane of freedom.

A more philosophical introspection, lasting until about 1927, followed on the heels of his Dada period. Three of his books emerged from this period, all of which show the influence of Frederick Nietzsche (1844–1900) and Max Stirner (1806–1856). Also, during this period, Evola made contact with theosophy, which he eventually condemned.[1] But it was probably politics that attracted Evola's interest most of all. Thinking that the New Order of Italian Fascism lacked a spiritual foundation, he sought to reignite the patrician ideals of the ancient Roman Empire to counter fascism's more plebian, bourgeois, and bureaucratic leanings. As Guénon did before him, Evola believed in the principles of hierarchy and the need to anchor everything in the transcendent as the supremacy of spiritual thought. During the Second World War, Evola tended to write articles, but in 1944 he moved from Rome to Vienna to study the SS-confiscated archives of Freemasonry and other magical groups. While there, he suffered severe wounds from an air raid that left him paralyzed for the rest of his life. After the war, he returned to Rome and was arrested in 1951 on charges of "glorifying Fascism." A lengthy trial ensued, which acquitted him of all charges. Evola died in 1974.

Evola's name is oftentimes linked, along with that of Guénon, to the founding of traditionalism. While others provided shape and form to the movement, Evola gave it meaning, and, while Guénon was more ethereal and an abstract a thinker, Evola was certainly less so. He became acquainted with traditionalism in the late 1920s, but it was not until the early 1930s that he recognized its true importance. In 1934, Evola published what he refers to as his main work, *Revolt against the Modern World*, in which he envisions the political domain as hierarchical, heroic, ideal, antihedonistic, and even anti-eudemonistic.[2] Aside from Guénon and Nietzsche, another nineteenth-century thinker, Johann Jakob Bachofen (1815–1887), was of utmost importance to the development and trajectory of Evola's thought. While Nietzsche provided the idea of the Absolute Individual and the *Übermensche*, Bachofen laid the groundwork for Evola's binary typology of uranic masculine (pertaining to the heavens) and telluric feminine (pertaining to earth) civilizations. In the former, "the highest principle of the universe is embodied by the celestial and luminous element personified by male divinities; in the latter, it is embodied by the principle of life and fecundity personified by the Great Goddess— by the Magna Mater."[3] Bachofen also provided Evola with the concept of the progression of human society from early matriarchal (sensuous) to patriarchal (spiritually pure) societies. Evola, however, reversed Bachofen's binary positing that telluric (female) and uranic (male) qualities are opposites and that Western civilization's decline can be traced from uranic to telluric (male to female).

As with Nietzsche, Evola emphasized action as uranic, which he associated with the Hindu *kshatriya*, or warrior caste, a caste he personally identified with. While Guénon thought spiritual authority superior to its temporal counterpart, in Hindu terms, the *brahmin* superior to the *kshatriya*, Evola thought quite differently. He was of the view that both castes were originally one and separated only in the decline from primordial tradition. This decline produced what Evola viewed as a "desacralization of existence": first, individualism and rationalism; then collectivism, materialism, and mechanism; and, lastly, an opening to the forces that are not ascendant to humans but rather below them. At the same time, Evola saw what he termed the "law of regression of castes" operating with power passing in a downward direction from the priestly and military castes (highest) to the merchant caste (bourgeois democracy), and finally to the serf caste (proletariat and lowest). In Evola's mind, the primordial sacred caste was uranic and also pre-Christian, while Christian Catholicism, with its allegedly nontraditional conception of a personal god, was telluric and characteristic of modernity.

Evola also differs from Guénon in the solution he offers. For Guénon, the transformation of the individual through initiation under the influence of an elite is the means to transform the West as a whole. Evola, on the other hand, was never as specific, but he did call for self-realization through the reintegration of humankind into a state of centrality brought about by uranic action as the Absolute Individual. Transformation here should be thought of as more in line with consequences than with means.

With regard to fascism, which Evola's name is often associated, both the Italian Fascists and Germany's National Socialists rejected Evola's traditionalism.[4] For several years in the 1930s, Evola sought to influence both Italian and German fascism. In each instance, however, he was largely rebuffed in his efforts probably because he espoused a far different position than either of the two fascist regimes. As John Morgan points out, Evola embraced a political philosophy tethered to the political advancement of a traditionally minded individual. Because he recognized modern politics as repugnant, he sought to bring the political affairs of the community in line with the values and teachings of traditional belief.[5] As he reflected on his own position, Evola saw his political goal as:

> to defend ideals unaffected by any political regime—be it Fascist, Communist, anarchist or democratic. These ideals [traditionalism] transcend the political sphere; yet, when translated on the political level, they necessarily lead to qualitative differences—which is to say: to hierarchy, authority and *imperium* in the broader sense of the word as opposed to all forms of democratic and egalitarian turmoil.[6]

This goal was never embraced by either fascist regime. In fact, Himmler's SS (*Schutzstaffel*) made it clear that, as a whole, they were not favorably inclined toward him and, after 1938, sought to curb his public activities in Germany and prevent any "further penetration into leading offices of the party and the state."[7]

Other factors also distinguished Evola's politics from both Italian Fascism and National Socialism. Each regime sought the support of the masses, including the lower classes, for their political existence, a position Evola rejected. Not that either regime was democratic in nature; they were totalitarian dictatorships as is customary for fascist political thought. However, each sought to enlist popular support, which was anathema to Evola's envisioned rule by aristocracy of the traditional world, by which he generally meant the authoritarian, hierarchical reigning force of the patrician Roman Empire. As he denounced the primacy of politics over ideals, he argued that only genuine ideals—by which he meant those of tradition—were to be placed at the forefront, and it was only on the basis of those ideals that a political system transcending one considered totalitarian could be promoted. For him, the fascism of his day fell short of these expectations: "for the irreducible enemies of all plebeian politics and 'nationalist ideology,' of all political plots and party spirit . . . Fascism is not enough. We would like a more radical, intrepid Fascism: a truly absolute Fascism, founded on pure energy and subject to no compromise."[8]

In the end, both fascist regimes were in many ways political parties in search of a philosophical foundation. Evola, on the other hand, possessed a philosophical foundation—traditionalism—that he felt needed only a political environment to flourish.

RACE AND RACISM

Evola delved into the issue of race and racism at great length in both newspaper and magazine articles as well as in his other longer writings. While he is often associated with racist views, he believed his understanding of race was deeply intertwined with his entire worldview, and in that sense it was inextricably tied to his thoughts on transcendence as "spirit." As with much of his thought, it is not really possible to understand his political positions, including his writings on race, without placing significant weight on his spiritual realism.

After being rebuffed by both major fascist regimes, Evola determined to alter course from infiltrating a political movement to commandeering a cause—race. Between 1936 and 1941, he published articles and several books, which he referred to as his "work on the rectification of racism." These writings, among other things, articulated his political and social perspective on racism as an expression of both an anti-egalitarian and antirational approach. It emphasized what he believed was a clear differentiation between the races, and it juxtaposed racism to Enlightenment's identity with equality, dignity, and human freedom. Although not outright rejecting a biological approach to race, he attacked the racial policies of both the Italian Fascists and the Nazis by advocating a spiritual definition that elevated the racial idea above the biological determination, or the strictly nationalistic concept of folk (*Volk*) and nation (*Volksgemeinschaft*).[9] Far more complex than mere biology,

> it is only if race is considered as existing not only in the body, but also in the soul and in the spirit, as a deep, meta-biological force which conditions both the physical and the psychical structures in the organic totality of the human entity—it is only if this eminently traditional point of view is assumed—that the mystery of the decline of races can be fathomed in all its aspects.[10]

The meta-biological and psychical structures Evola speaks of are likely to become "neutralized" when the inner moral and spiritual dimensions of an individual are absent. Analogous to an infection, the intermingling, or "crossbreeding," of the races has a fatally degenerative effect when one race is already in the throes of disease.[11] Evola argued that this is especially true with regard to inferior races, including Jews. However, even though he thought Jews were, indeed, infected, Evola admonishes us not to understand Aryan and Jew solely in the biological terms claimed by the Nazis and later the Italian Fascists, but as denoting typical attitudes that are not necessarily present in all individuals of Aryan or Jewish blood. The real enemy is not Jews, biologically defined, but global subversion and antitradition.

In his discussion of race, Evola expounds upon what he terms two heroisms. In actuality, however, he really wants to distinguish between his concept of a "super-race" and everyone else. In traditionalism's eyes, humans are not reducible to purely biological, instinctive, hereditary, or naturalistic determinations. On the contrary, the distinctive feature of humankind—at least some members of humankind—is their participation in a supernatural, super-biological endeavor.[12] Those who are not participants in such super qualities are labeled "races of nature," whose characteristics are more akin to animals than humans. These races of nature exhibit a herd mentality together with a predominant collectivist element, which Evola variously derides as "the race of the bourgeois," "petty conformists," or "right-thinking man." While the feeling of race and blood may be quite strong among these groups, it always represents something subpersonal, completely naturalistic, and similar to "the dark 'totemism' of savage populations."[13]

In other races, however, this naturalistic element is a vehicle of a superior, super-biological sphere that inevitably is incarnated into the tradition of such races. Among these groups, there is a foundational "race of spirit" underlying the race of body and blood.[14] Quite unlike the petty bourgeois personality, however, the race of the spirit possesses an elemental, nonhuman aspect of the heroic experience (meaning combat in war) that both transfigures and elevates their personalities into a transcendent way of being. This transfiguring mystical value, connected to an inner rebirth through heroic action, is for Evola the "Aryan conception of 'victory.'"[15] It must be understood that Evola equates war with a Manichean struggle between two diametrically opposing metaphysical forces. On one side of the battlefield are gathered the armies of the Olympian and luminous principle, uranic in nature and imbued with what he calls, solar truth. Arrayed on the opposite side are the raw forces of the titanic, telluric element, barbaric in nature representing the demonic-feminine principle of chaos. Not only is Evola symbolically cloaking the struggle of war with diametrically opposing metaphysical forces, those same forces apply to the more concrete forms of everyday existence as well.

Evola offers two solutions to what he terms the "practical tasks of racism." The first such task is in the form of *passive* defense, which essentially means, to avoid the danger of mutation, the superior races should be sheltered from all external actions, such as mixing with other races and what he calls "unsuitable forms of life and culture."[16] In a sense, Evola is invoking Guénon's concept of the Great Wall, designed to keep inferior, undesirable elements from encroaching upon the superior races contained within the barrier. In contemporary Europe, we see vestiges of Evola's concerns in countries, such as Hungary, who sealed off its borders to Muslim refugees fleeing the war in Syria. In 2015, Hungary's far right prime minister, Viktor Orbán, ordered the building of a protective barrier to stem the tide of immigrants attempting to enter the country on their way to Germany. In his more recent public statements, Orbán admitted that he did not want Muslim immigrants to infiltrate Hungarian society. In fact, he advocates the creation of an anti-immigration "axis" in Europe that would ally themselves with similarly minded countries, such as Italy and Poland (both have far-right governments) to alter the European Union's direction. Orbán ultimately sees two civilizations: "one mixed Muslim-Christian in the west and one *traditional*, in central Europe."[17]

More difficult than the first, the second task is *active* resistance or the exaltation of one's inner race revealed in the overcoming of the inertia of spirit epitomized by pursuing the easiest path of least resistance. Not unlike other writers at the time, Evola believes the highest instrument of inner awakening of race is physical combat, with war its utmost expression. He also sees the political ideals of pacifism and humanitarianism, phenomena he associates with internationalism (globalism), democracy, cosmopolitanism, and liberalism, as driving toward subracial leveling that impedes heroic activity at the hands of a few surviving and not completely deracinated people.[18]

In putting a concrete meaning to his practical tasks of racism, Evola asserts that racism is a sort of barometer showing what he calls the "quantity" of race. "*To say yes or no to racism is not merely to differ intellectually, it is not something subjective and arbitrary*. The one who says yes to racism is the one in which race still lives," even though the distinction between the races has been stifled through "ethnic waste," crossbreeding, bourgeois weakness, and the degeneration of intellectual effetism.[19] In today's world, we see former Counsel to the President Steve Bannon, a reader of Evola, calling on members of France's National Front Party (*Rassamblement National*) to "let them call you racists. Let them call you xenophobes. Let them call you nativists. Wear it as a badge of honor."[20] For Bannon, it seems racism needs to be resurrected from its murky confines and not only placed at the center of the political agenda but emphatically embraced. Certainly, for Evola, and for Bannon as well, true racism resides in the "classical spirit," embedded in the Aryan-Nordic race, which is rooted in the exaltation of everything that has form, face, and individuality, as opposed to what is formless, vague, and undifferentiated.

RACISM AND HIERARCHY

Throughout the discussion, I have alluded to the hierarchical system so dear to perennialism and traditionalism, and which also plays a significant role in Evola's racism. The starting point for any discussion of class or caste structure is Evola's general outline of ancient Aryan social hierarchy, exemplified in what he calls both the Indo-Aryan and Nordic-Romantic Medieval civilizations. In each, the system of hierarchy was divided into four parts. At the top resided the exponents of spiritual authority. The second caste, the warriors or nobles, were subordinate and subject to that spiritual order. The bourgeoisie came next, and they were followed by the class of wage earners, or what Evola refers to as the modern-day proletariat. Obviously, in each instance, the division revolves around function.

Evola equates this hierarchical structure to types of historical civilizations corresponding to the four castes distinguished according to whether they are guided by the various truths, values, and ideals of the respective spiritual leaders, or of the warriors, or of the bourgeoisie, or of the slaves. The appropriately Aryan element had its locus in the two superior castes, while in the two inferior castes another blood, coming from subjugated aboriginal peoples, predominated.[21]

In addition to this hierarchical ordering, Evola argues that humankind has endured four phases of development, which he characterizes as conditions of ethical conflict. Starting with the class of spiritual authority, he associates an ethics in the form of a supernatural justification of supreme value. This superior caste, however, gave way to a warrior class whose ethics were already secular in the form of fidelity, honor, and loyalty. Along with the move from spiritual to warrior authority, the sacred content of heroic experience of war also shifted to a mere veiled and symbolic glimmer of an ascending and metaphysical struggle; the struggle now is in the pursuit of honor and glory. Bourgeois ethics follows the warrior period with an ideal of economic prosperity based on capitalistic exploitation. During this phase, the warrior was supplanted by the soldier in the form of the *citoyen* induced by the pathos of war and myths, such as *élan vital*, to take up arms in a fight for "freedom" as a struggle against tyranny and defense of nationalistic honor. In the final phase, the civilization of the slaves, war transformed into worldwide revolution with ethical values reflected in materialism, and the supreme value of work in its collectivized and deconsecrated form. In Evola's understanding, every phase is a usurpation and degradation from the previous higher stage, but it also incorporates fatal consequences: "this process almost always presupposes the infiltration of socially and racially inferior elements. In the case of Western bourgeoisie these elements have been supplied by Hebraism."[22]

Within Evola's strict hierarchical system, the Aryan-Nordic (white) race claims superiority to all others.[23] Even with regard to his own Italian heritage, Evola declared the concept of "Latinity"—an issue of great importance to Italian Fascism—to be unfitting for the Italian people in its entirety. Evola argued that in comparison to the lower Mediterranean race, the higher Nordic is the race of active men who perceive the world as presented to them as material for possession and attack. Essentially, it is the strong, silent hero, much like in the Greek tragedies. On the other hand, the Mediterranean soul, typified by its vanity, seeks to show off in a noisy, and over exaggerated manner emblematic of modernity. Evola's position was thought to be so incendiary that the Italian Department of Foreign Affairs withdrew his passport in 1941, only to have it reinstated after Mussolini's intervention.

In support of his hierarchal structure, Evola looks specifically to the *Bhagavad Gita*, a portion of the *Mahabharata*, as indicative of the spirituality of the Aryan races, which he says migrated to Asia from its Hyperborean origin. The *Gita* portrays an epic battle fought between warring factions of an extended family. Overcome by humanitarian and sentimental scruples, Arjuna, the warrior prince of the *Gita*, is not able to fight his enemy which includes his own family. The God Krishna admonishes Arjuna to "not yield to this degrading impotence. It does not become you. Give up such petty weakness of heart and arise."[24] Krishna exalts Arjuna to fight and be killed on the battlefield and thus attain the heavenly planets, or conquer and enjoy the earthly kingdom. In either case, Arjuna must get up with determination and fight. The purity of heroic action is clear: it must be incurred for itself, beyond any personal gratification; Arjuna must fight for the sake of fighting because he desires the battle.[25] For Evola, the higher life manifests itself through death and destruction, but for the one who overcomes it, it is liberation. To follow this path is to realize wisdom through sacred heroism, which leads to restoration, awakening, and resumption of what lies at the origin of tradition and which has survived in the depths of the race of the Aryan spirit.

REVOLT AGAINST THE MODERN WORLD

Revolt against the Modern World begins its discussion with the world of tradition and ends with an analysis of the genesis and face of the modern world. Not unlike Guénon, Evola evokes what he calls the fundamental doctrine of the spirit of tradition: on the one hand, an inferior, mortal, physical order of things of *becoming*, and on the other hand a superior, immortal metaphysical order of things of *being*, which are present in any traditional philosophy. Thus, any person of tradition is aware of the existence of a dimension of being much greater than what present-day society refers to as reality.[26]

Contrary to the person of tradition, modern individuals develop an understanding in relation to the world of physical bodies through their direct and immediate experiences, what Evola and Guénon term materialism. According to Evola, this is so regardless of spiritual beliefs. As a result, modern human's experience is incapable of extending to the nonphysical metaphysical realm. The experience of the traditional world reached well beyond these physical limitations to include the invisible as an element as real and, indeed, more real than that provided by empirical sense data alone. Moreover, the traditional world believed spirituality to be beyond life and death. Thus mere living is meaningless unless it approximates the higher world or that which is "more than life," which seeks to break the bonds of the human condition. As Evola summarizes:

> the traditional world knew divine kingship. It knew the bridge between the two worlds, namely heroic action and contemplation; it knew the mediation, namely, rites and faithfulness; it knew the social foundation, namely, the traditional law and the caste system; and it knew the political earthly symbol, namely, the empire.[27]

Within each traditional society, there are beings who, "by virtue of their innate or acquired superiority over the human condition, embody within the temporal order the living and efficacious presence of a power that comes from above."[28] Evola calls some of these types of beings the *Pontifex*, or builder of bridges connecting the natural and the supernatural worlds.[29] Unsurprisingly, the *Pontifex* is equated with a monarch. Accordingly, the true ruler personifies the life transcendent to ordinary life. In other words, monarchs are of divine (extra temporal) origin meant to rule under the *Ancien Régime*'s mantra of the divine right of kings.

Evola reasons that in the world of tradition the most important foundation of authority and the right of kings—the reason they are to be feared, obeyed, and venerated—lies in their transcendent and nonhuman, metaphysical quality. This metaphysical character of the sovereign's authority formed traditionalism's view of the absolute ruler as the natural order of things, often associated with the solar symbol. In the king, the people were expected to see the same glory and victory proper to the light emanating from the sun, which with the coming of daylight conquers darkness. It is for this reason that French King Louis XIV enjoyed the title "*Roi Soleil*" (the Sun King).

With regard to traditional society's view of the law and the state, Evola links both to the transcendent quality of the ruler. By virtue of embodying a higher ideal and power:

> the true state constitutes something altogether different from a mere union, from any kind of association artificially constructed or based on natural law, from any human aggregation founded on social, economic, biological, utilitarian or happiness-seeking principles. *Authority*, thus conceived, also represents the necessary condition for the stability, firmness and unity of any socio-political organization.[30]

Strictly construed, the political realm is defined by the hierarchal, heroic, ideal, and antihedonistic values of the warrior caste. Thus the true political order, and consequently the state itself, lies in its anagogical function in arousing the peoples disposition to act, to think, to live, to struggle, and, most importantly, to sacrifice for something beyond themselves. As he says, transcendent realism is the presupposition of the traditional forms of the law, meaning that only a law with divine character traced back to its nonhuman tradition can be regarded as an objective, absolute law. As such, the concept of law, "has an intimate relationship with the notions of truth, reality, and stability inherent to 'that which is.'"[31] What was absurd for the traditional world was to think that any human-made law could carry the weight accorded those of divine origin.

Evola's doctrine of the two natures is also reflected in the relationship between the state and the people. The modern notion that the state derives its authority from below, that is, the people, is again an absurd and regressive notion for traditionalism. In fact, the *demos'* substance is always demonic in the amoral, non-Christian sense of the word; it forever requires a catharsis or liberation prior to its acting as a unified force. Once this direction occurred, the downward spiral commenced leading inevitably to the collectivistic world of the masses culminating in radical democracy. Contrary to this view and according to the traditionalism's interpretation:

> the state was related to the people, just as the Olympian and Uranian principles are related to the chthonic and "infernal" world; or as "idea," "form," . . . are related to "matter," [and] "nature" . . . or as the luminous, masculine, differentiating, individualizing, and life-giving principle is related to the unsteady, promiscuous, and nocturnal feminine principle.[32]

Evola's discussion highlights the main principle upon which the differentiation between the people and the hierarchy of the traditional castes is established not in the political or economic realm, but in the spiritual. This authentic system of state and law entailed a supernatural formation not necessarily manifest in any visible manner, but nonetheless still present.

Connected to the concept of divine right as the cornerstone of the traditional state were two additional elements: rites and faithfulness. Both of these linked particular components and activities within the social order to the center—the monarch—and allowed ordinary individuals to partake in the transcendent influence emanating from the sovereign. The rite was the glue binding together traditional organizations conceived in their nonnaturalistc dimensions. First, as a prerogative of the king, then of the aristocratic and priestly classes, and finally of the head of the household, the rites were strictly construed leaving little room for arbitrary or subjective interpretation.

Once the meaning and relevance of rites to the traditional order are clarified, Evola establishes two very significant points. He states that there are two elements within traditional civilizations, or of the castes characterized by a uranic consecration: first, there is a materialistic and naturalistic element, which consists in the transmission of something related to blood and race as a vital force originating in the subterranean world that combines with elementary, collective, and ancestral influences. Thus, for the traditional world, the material and natural elements of blood and race become a generative force assuring the hierarchical structure's future against those who do not share the common blood. The second element is not of the material world, but from above, which is conditioned by the transmission and domination realized within the substratum of the first element. This latter element is of a higher quality that constitutes and originates the royal bloodline, the state, the city, and the caste system according to certain supernatural dimensions acting as a type of Platonic "form" to work and shape what would otherwise be chaos.

A more present-day example of Evola's concern with the generative force of race and blood was the rally in Charlottesville, Virginia, by the alt-right white nationalist group, Unite the Right. There to ostensibly protest the removal of a commemorative Civil War statute, the few hundred protestors, many of whom were dressed in white, were more interested in carrying tiki torches reminiscent of Nazi marches in the 1930s while chanting Nazi era slogans such as "Blood and Soil." Originating in the conservative ideal of promoting German nationalism in the late 1800s and early 1900s, the slogan *Blut und Boden* combines the nationalistic desire of a white homeland with aspects of race and place as the symbolic adhesive binding the German people together.

As a further example of what he has in mind, Evola points to the Indo-Aryan civilization. In this civilization, the *brahmin* caste did not occupy the top of the social hierarchy by virtue of its strength or wealth. Rather, the rite of sacrifice as its privilege determined the *brahmins'* status in relation to the other castes. The rites conferred upon those who controlled them some kind of frightful, yet valuable psychic power; a power that would exist in that person forever and pass unabated through the bloodline from generation to generation. All that need be done to activate such an innate power was the rite of initiation.[33] For Evola, in this divine dimension, only blood counts. The state, the community, the family, bourgeois feelings, duties in the modern sense of the word is an entirely human fabrication.[34] Evola also argues that the rites have little to do with the modern-day notion of religion. Rather, they are associated with the idea of perception or pure power illustrated by the Roman concept of *numen*. Unlike the notion of god, the *numen* is not a person or a being, it is a sheer power capable of producing effects, and of acting and manifesting itself. Such powers are, at the same time, transcendent and imminent, stunning and frightening, and constitute the substance of the original experience of the scared.[35] The rite itself is merely a technique or determining action upon invisible forces. Consequently, the officiating priest is simply a person whose qualifications ensured the results pursuant to this technique. Evola explains that:

> what was at stake was to be able to understand such relationships so that once a cause was established through a correctly performed rite, a necessary and constant effect would ensue on the plane of "powers" and invisible forces and states of being. Thus, the law of action reigned supreme. But the law of action is also the law of freedom; no bond can be spiritually imposed on beings who neither hope nor fear, but rather act.[36]

It is important to emphasize Evola's use of the law of action. Equated with freedom, action becomes a leitmotif for traditional philosophy, yet, later, just like Guénon, he admonishes the West as consumed with the spirit of action at the expense of contemplation, a wholly Eastern attribute.

Blood and ethnic purity are certainly factors that assume great importance in traditional civilizations, but we should not lose sight of the fact that Evola rejects the idea employed by modern racist ideologies at the time that understood human blood and ethnic purity merely at the biological level. For Evola, the blood registers the effects of the deepest forces of life that is performed and refined so that through several generations, realizations similar to the original ones may be prepared and developed in a natural and spontaneous way. But merely being born into a superior caste is not enough; it is necessary for the virtual qualities conferred upon a person at birth to be actualized by a process of initiation. Thus, Evola argues that "both the higher castes and traditional aristocracies, as well as superior civilizations and races . . . cannot be explained by blood, but *through* the blood, by something that goes beyond blood and that has a metabiological character."[37] The result for traditional societies is somewhat catastrophic when this ideal breaks down:

> when the last residue of the force from above and the race of the spirit is exhausted, in the new generations nothing else remains; there is no

longer a riverbed to channel the current that is now dispersed in every direction. What emerges at this point is individualism, chaos, anarchy, a humanist hubris, and degeneration in every domain. The dam is broken. Although a semblance of ancient grandeur still remains, the smallest impact is enough to make an empire or state collapse and be replaced with a demonic inversion, namely, with the modern, omnipotent Leviathan, which is a mechanized and "totalitarian" collective system.[38]

THE DOCTRINE OF THE CASTES: "UNITY" WITHIN SOCIETY

Evola looks to the caste system as embodying one of the main features of traditionalist sociopolitical order. As such, it represents victory over chaos and the embodiment of the metaphysical ideals of stability and justice. To be born into a particular caste meant conformity to that caste, which was considered the foremost duty of all individuals. Consequently, the activities of those at the bottom of the hierarchy, the slaves or workers (*sūdras*) were subordinated to those activities of the bourgeoise (*vaishya*); in turn these castes came under the control of the warrior nobility (*kshatriya*) who were themselves subject to the authority of the representatives of the spiritual authority and power (*brahmin*). By acknowledging one's own nature, traditional humans knew their rightful place, their function, and even the correct relationship with both superiors and inferiors. Importantly, the "true" hierarchical structure did not evolve from human nature but originated as a natural law the absolute meaning of which has two related aspect. First, that which is above is superior to that which resides below. The second aspect follows quite naturally: there exists a spiritual elite.[39]

While many, including those in the contemporary world, find the caste system arbitrary and unjust, Evola argues that this could not be further from the truth. The closed caste system was based on two fundamental principles: first, traditional humans considered everything visible and worldly as the mere effects of higher order causes. To be born male instead of a female, or in one caste over another, or in one race as opposed to a different race was not the result of pure chance. In other words, in traditional societies birth did not determine nature; nature determined birth. Thus, a person is endowed with a certain type of spirit by virtue of being born in a certain caste, but at the same time, one is born into a certain caste because one possesses a certain spirit. The differences in the castes were thus far from being artificial, arbitrary and unfair when seen as the reflection and the confirmation of preexisting, deeper, and more intimate state of affairs. Moreover, Evola asserts that within traditional caste society, no one caste was considered superior to another.[40]

While Evola does not attribute this conclusion to any particular traditionalist society, it is hardly the case that Plato's wage earners, the lowest of the classes in the *Republic*, found themselves on equal footing with the auxiliaries let alone the guardians. One might also point out that Socrates feels compelled to resort to a "Noble Lie"—that the guardians souls were mixed with gold, the auxiliaries with silver, and the wage earners with base metals—to cement the relations between the classes. His fear is that one born into an inferior class may believe himself to be equal to the ruling guardians. For Socrates such upward mobility destroys the unity of the City. However, Evola argues that in traditional society there was no aspiration to go from one caste to another because every function was considered equal:

> in this regard, by being in their own caste, in faithfulness to their own caste and to their own nature, in obedience not to a general morality but to their own morality, or to the morality of their own caste, everyone enjoyed the same dignity and the same purity as everyone else; this was true for a *sūdra* as well as for a king.[41]

Everyone performed their particular function within the social order, and here order and unity are extraordinarily important. Evola points to the Hindu notion of *dharma*, one's particular nature to which one is faithful, as originating from the root *dr* (to sustain or uphold) and expressing the concept of order, form, manner of being, and cosmos so important for traditional societies seeking to overcome chaos and becoming.

In a similar discussion, Guénon goes so far as to say that the same idea applies both to a single as well as to an organized collectivity. But most significantly, he thinks it denotes conformity with the essential nature of human existence, which comes to fruition in an ordered hierarchy, and consequently it is also the "fundamental equilibrium or integral harmony resulting from this hierarchical disposition, which is moreover precisely what the idea of *'justice'* amounts to."[42] Guénon is, in effect, following in the footsteps of Plato's inauguration of a hierarchical class system in the *Republic* to give the city a sense of order or unity, concepts he thought paramount to the success of any society. For Plato, justice is performing your function and minding your own business, that is, doing one thing and only one thing and, if you are a wage earner, not entertaining thoughts of becoming something you were neither born into nor possessed the inherent nature for. In fact, not minding your own business and meddling among the classes was not only an act of injustice, it was the most extreme evil doing that would cause the greatest harm to the City.

To ensure the viability of the castes, it was considered "impure" to cross the line into a higher caste. Simply put, mixing of gold and base metals alters or contaminates both metals; neither retains their original quality nor their metallic luster. Consequently, mixing of the castes subverted the natural, traditional order. According to Evola, when everyone attends to their own function:

the anarchy of "rights" and "demands" did not arise until the inner spiritual orientation died out and the action performed in purity was supplanted by one motivated by materialistic and individualistic concerns, and by the multiform and vain fever brought about by the modern spirit and civilization that has turned economics into a guiding principle (daemon) and a destiny.[43]

Yet the question still remains: if, as Evola would have us believe, each of the castes' functions were equal, why did Plato feel it necessary to introduce the Noble Lie to the City?[44] After all, Plato thinks it is imperative to inculcate the idea that each of the classes' souls is mixed with some metal. If the members of each particular caste come to believe in the lie, then they will inherently accept as true that they belong to their particular class, and not desire to venture into any other class. Obviously, Plato thought that the social hierarchical structure might give rise to dissension within the City, so he was willing to found his ideal city on the basis of a lie.

Beyond the class system, Evola thinks that when the inner strength of a *fides* is vanquished, then all activity is defined in relation to its materialistic character. In a paradoxical manner, he argues that this gives rise to slavery because work characterizes the condition of the slave, and not the other way around. In other words, when activity in the lower strata of the societal hierarchy no longer retains its spiritual meaning, then no action can occur, only work remains. Thus, the material aspect takes over from the higher form with the consequences that work is looked upon as degrading and unworthy of any human being. Work, then, is seen as something only a slave could perform and the only *dharma* possible for a slave is work. As Evola points out, the ancients did not despise labor because it engaged in slavery; rather, it scorned labor, therefore, it scorned the slave. While this may be partially true, if one removed the slave from labor, the slave still remained.

ASCETICISM

Having explained the spirit that animates the traditional caste system, Evola directs his attention to the implementation of the realization of transcendence. Those who are above the caste and are free from the "form" by renouncing the illusory center of human individuality are called ascetics. They turn toward the principle from which every form proceeds, but not as other members of the social hierarchy with faithfulness to one's own nature and devotion to the hierarchy but by direct action. While pariahs—those without a caste, or who have lapsed, or have eluded the form—are subject to scorn and ridicule, the ascetic is venerated as above the caste. Evola explains that "asceticism occupies an ideal intermediary state between the plane of direct, Olympian, and initiatory regality and the plane of rite and of *dharma*."[45] The use of the term Olympian is meant to underscore the true superiority of the Aryan races manifested in the calm domination of the spirit over the soul and the body. Unlike Guénon's criticism of Western action in lieu of contemplation, Evola places great emphasis on action for the esthete. However, what Evola means by action must be understood in heroic terms. While the path of ascetic contemplation is mostly an inner-directed journey in which the ideal of detachment and an orientation toward transcendence predominates, action is an immanent process aimed at awakening the deepest human forces causing a so-called "superlife" of absolute intensity to emerge in the form of a heroic life.

Even though heroic action is paramount, Evola also understands that a second, crucial aspect of asceticism is the path to contemplation. Here, asceticism of contemplation comprises the integration of a knowing faculty (divorced from a sensible reality) with a neutralized individualism together with the progressive "stripping" of the center of consciousness. Thus, ascetic contemplation is no longer tethered to conditionings, including all determinism either real or imagined. This type of contemplation recognizes the universal as knowledge and knowledge as freedom and opens the world to the seeker through enlightenment and vision. The ascetic's detachment from the material world implies a renunciation of the desires of the profane world. One's natural nobility, consciously willed through an animated inner strength of a virile and aristocratic type, leads to renunciation for ascetic contemplation rather than any desire to escape temptation as in Christian asceticism.

Evola argues that the opposition between action and contemplation was unknown in the ancient Aryan world. Rather, they were two distinct paths to an identical spiritual realization. However, the Aryan-Western races have experienced a precipitous decline, and today they only recognize a secularized and materialized form of action devoid of any contact with the transcendent. Similarly, contemplation is merely a confused culture and a lifeless faith.

Much like the recent political slogan, "Make America Great Again," Evola sees himself undertaking an essential task of reversing the trend of decline by seeking to inspire the faithful to a Vico inspired *ricorso* or renewal, a return to the origins as recovering the ancient Aryan conception of action.

RELATIONS BETWEEN MEN AND WOMEN

To round out an understanding of traditional life, we must turn to the relationship between the sexes. Not surprisingly, Evola returns to the traditional worldview that realities correspond to the symbolic, while actions are aligned to rites. From these two concepts the relationship between man and woman is best understood.

Traditional symbolism conferred a supernatural principle to masculine character, and the principle of nature and of becoming to the feminine character. Thus, the "One," which is "in itself" and complete and self-sufficient, is regarded as masculine; the "dyad," the principle of differentiation, the "other-than-self," and the principles of desire and movement are regarded as feminine.[46] While the two principles seem to be in opposition, Evola believes in the traditional world the two are transformed or synthesized into a single element where each retains their particular function.

Within traditional societies, the law is not oriented toward equality but is based on the will to order. Men and women are of two distinct types, and those born male must realize their masculinity and act accordingly, while those born female must likewise realize their femininity. More importantly, each must overcome any mixing and promiscuity of what Evola calls their vocations.[47] In Evola's idealized world, the masculine or warrior hero-ascetic, who represents the two fundamental types of pure virility, must follow dual paths to the goal of being "a principle to oneself": heroic action and contemplation. In symmetry to the masculine, the feminine must also pursue two paths: she must realize herself as a woman, and rise to the same level as the warrior-ascetic male only in the form of a lover and mother.

The practical implications are important for Evola. As I have already discussed, a correlation exists between the disappearance of any preexisting principle of authority and the rise of individualism in the form of humanism. While this interrelation is already prevalent in the political sphere, it is now revealed in the domestic realm: the modern family.[48] Consequently, Evola argues that the concept of family in the modern world no longer has any higher meaning beyond that of the individual. In times past, and thought of in terms of an organic heroic character, the family presented a unity premised upon the absolute authority of the *pater* as lord or sovereign whose role in the modern world has degenerated to that of a mere instrument of "mindless propagation."

Evola refuses to recognize that in ancient Greece, and in the Roman times so dear to him, only males were considered as true citizens. Greece generally recognized women and children as property, as did Rome. In fact, Roman law conferred the right, in certain circumstances, to dispose of family "property" in any manner the head of the household (*paterfamilias*) deemed appropriate. While some alt-right adherents may approve of this type of treatment of women and children, it remains a draconian tradition.

Again Evola's idealized notion of the relations between the sexes and family life came undone with modernity. The blame, it appears, falls directly on the modern world's emancipation of women brought about through the decline of the caste system and the subsequent rise of human rights with their emphasis on the dignity of all humans, which only preserved a "sense" of the traditional relationship between the sexes. In the modern world, where the idea of the ascetic or warrior no longer abounds, it was only a matter of time before women rose up to assert their own personalities and "freedom" according to anarchist and individualist meaning of these terms (Evola does not elaborate on what he means by the terms anarchist). In Evola's thinking, the feminism that sought to eradicate the slavery of women only devised a personality imitating the male personality, which resulted in a fundamental lack of self-esteem as well as an inability to function as a real woman and not as a man. This led to an ambiguity in human relations; in the deepest recesses of their souls, humans are neither men nor women, but either masculine females or feminine males.

In the end, the degradation of the relations between the sexes only hastened the decline—in both their numbers and in their purity—of the superior races, by which he means the Western, Aryan-Nordic (white) races. While the earth's population has increased, the opposite is true for the superior white races with supposedly catastrophic results: "the deterioration of the population affects only those stocks that should be considered the bearers of the forces that preside over the demos and the world of the masses and that contribute to any authentic greatness."[49] Not unlike white nationalist chanting such slogans as "Jews will not replace us," Evola believes the superior Western races have been agonizing for centuries, fearing that the increasing growth in world population is tantamount to a "swarming of worms on a decomposing organism or as the spreading of cancerous cells."[50] Similar to Guénon's alarm, the culprit is the mixing of the castes with the inevitable coming to power of the inferior social strata and races.

The alt-right has adopted the theme of the decline of the white race, which it labels the "Great Replacement." A conspiracy theory, originating from the French writer Renaud Camus, this scheme is twofold. On the one hand, due to massive immigration and higher fertility rates, the populations of non-European origin are likely to numerically surpass the populations of the "Originating" (white) populations in Europe and America. At the same time, those "invading" inferior populations seek to impose their culture and religion on the continent and America. On the other hand, this "Great Replacement" is covertly advocated with the complicity of a so-called substitute power, that is, a capitalist ruling elite, better known as globalists, who organize voluntary massive immigration to build a new "exchangeable" human race free of any national, ethnic, and cultural specificity. Jewish financier and liberal philanthropist George Soros is often the target of such conspiracy theories. Various public personalities like Tucker Carlson and Laura Ingraham of Fox News and even President Trump have waded into the theory with their followers, but Steve King, an alt-right sympathizer and member of Congress from Iowa, embraced the theory by tweeting: "Wilders understands that culture and demographics are our destiny. We can't restore our civilization with somebody else's babies."[51] The recent mass shooting in New Zeeland by Brenton Tarrant was preceded by a manifesto posted online with the title "The Great Replacement." The lengthy document is essentially a rant about birth rates and the need to eradicate nonwhites from Europe and America.

While some studies do show that whites are dying off at a greater rate than their birth rate, even if the white population of the United States becomes a minority, it is unlikely that the power structure will alter significantly in the short term. This is especially true with regard to economic power.

THE STORY OF TRADITIONAL CIVILIZATION: THE DOCTRINE OF THE FOUR AGES

While modern thinkers, especially since the Enlightenment, generally espouse the theory of human progress in one form or another, the opposite is true of traditionalism, which eschews the notion of progress in favor of regression: from originally higher forms, humans digressed to states increasingly dominated by mortal and contingent influences. This inverted process began in a very distant past and is narrated in the organic doctrine of the four ages, according to which, the modern world is the result of a process of gradual degradation and decadence through the four cycles or generations. While there is no substantiation for Evola's accusations, it is worthwhile to understand what he has in mind and how myth is an important element of traditionalist thought.

Evola points out that many civilizations espoused a form of the doctrine of the four ages ranging from the Greco-Romans, the Hindu, the Persians, and the Chaldean versions. For the Hindus, the four stages are really cycles: *Satya Yuga, Tretā Yuga, Dvāpara Yuga,* and *Kali Yuga*.[52]

The so-called Golden Age corresponds to an original, primordial civilization that was naturally and totally in conformity with the traditional spirit. Historically, this period is associated with the highest function of regality: symbols of polarity, solarity, height, stability, glory, and the life of a higher order. This first era is the domain of Being with its attendant transcendent truth where purity of heart, justice, wisdom, and adherence to the scared institutions abounded in every caste.[53] During this period, mortals lived as if they were gods where old age never came about. Thus, it is recognized as the era of the Living in the eminent sense of the word. When this cycle ended, the inhabitants of the original period continued to live on earth, albeit, in an invisible manner.

The source of this original, traditional civilization is rooted in the mythical symbolism of the pole as its utmost importance. Characterized as an island, or some other form of elevated ground symbolizing spiritual stability as opposed to the contingency of the waters, this polar symbolism applied to the supreme center of the world and assumed the character of an archetype.[54]

According to traditionalism, in a period predating history that corresponds to the Golden Age as the Age of Being, the symbolic island or polar land actually existed in the Artic region. This region was inhabited by a population, known as Hyperborean, who possessed nonhuman (what Guénon refers to as "supra-human") spirituality and who established the race exemplifying the uranic tradition in a pure state. The demise of this land occurred at the hands of a cataclysmic climatic change associated with a tilting of the terrestrial axis.[55] A new ice age descended on the region and forced the migration of the people, thus ending the first cycle and inaugurating the new cycle.

The second or Atlantic Cycle, witnessed the Northern, primordial race migrating in two separate directions: the first wave from north to south and the second from west to east. The first wave initially occupied North America and the northern parts of Eurasia. Thousands of years later a second wave originating from the first wave migrated to Central America and eventually to an island situated in the Atlantic that most likely was the mythical island of Atlantis. In each case, the Hyperborean established a new civilization modeled after their original polar habitat. From their Atlantic home, the races of the second cycle spread to the American, European, and African regions. The domination by Hyperborean was complete:

> from north to south and from west to east, through diffusion, adaptation, or domination there arose civilizations that originally shared, to a certain degree, the same matrix, and often strains of the same spiritual legacy found in the conquering elites. Encounters with inferior races, which were enslaved to the chthonic cult of demons and mixed with animal nature, generated memories of struggles that were eventually expressed in mythologized forms that always underline the contrast between a bright divine type (an element of Northern origins) and a dark, demonic type. Through the institution of traditional societies by the conquering races a hierarchy was established that carried a spiritual, ethnic, and racial value.[56]

Evola then separates two distinct migrations of the polar north. The first major group became differentiated through variation without mixing, that is, mixing with the inferior indigenous population and thus diluting their Aryan purity. The second group became differentiated through their interbreeding with the aboriginal Southern races, including what he refers to as proto-Mongoloid and Negroid races. This north to south migration resulted in a degenerate civilization that Evola elaborates on with some specificity.

As I have pointed out, the Hyperborean were characterized as the luminous principle of immutability and centralism typically denoted as "Olympian." As such, they were tied to the Hyperborean god Apollo who represents the sun itself as the dominating and unchanging source of light, and not merely the celestial path of ascent and descent over the horizon.[57] However, it is the winter solstice that provides Evola with a significant point of departure between the Northern Hyperborean and the Southern indigenous populations.

While the winter solstice is the shortest day of the year and, consequently, the day with the least amount of light, Evola says that this particular symbol does not appear in the traditions of pure boreal societies. However, it does appear in the Southern civilizations and takes on a central meaning. It is a feminine, telluric, symbol portrayed as the Mother, the Earth, or the Waters; all three symbols are related to each other because Mother Earth generates the Waters. The real importance is, however, the relationship between the two principles—Mother and Sun—that gives meaning to the symbols. "The first of which still retains traces of the 'polar' tradition, while the second characterizes a new cycle . . . and a mingling (which is already a degeneration) of North and South."[58] In other words, when the center consists of the solar male principle conceived as a cyclical life of ascent and descent advancing through winter to spring—the symbolic death to rebirth analogy—and while the identical immutable principle is identified with the Universal Mother and with the Earth designated as the eternal principle of life, then the civilization espousing these latter beliefs is truly decadent. Evola is content to conclude that the themes of the Mother, the Waters, and the Earth in the symbolic form of Mother Earth all originate in the South. In opposition, are those civilizations that revere the sun as uncreated and unparalleled pure light. These are the civilizations that practice the highest, purest, and most ancient spirituality as the cycle of uranic civilizations.

Evola's point is that in the South the object of everyday life was not the solar principle but the fertility of the Earth, essential for the preservation of life. Thus, the emphasis shifted in these civilizations toward Mother Earth as the sustainer of life with the chthonic deities encompassing the goddesses of vegetation, the harvest, and animal fertility. While the Northern Light, through its solar and uranic symbols embraces a virile, warrior spirituality consisting of a harsh will to dominate and establish order, the Southern traditions exhibit a predominance of the chthonic theme and pathos of death and rebirth, which Evola equates to promiscuity, escapism, abandonment, and naturalistic pantheism.[59]

The civilization of the Mother, preeminent in Southern civilizations, is a transposition into the metaphysical view of the woman as the supreme generator of life, and humans as merely conditioned, subordinated, and lacking life.⁶⁰ Even in death, the southern civilizations where the feminine telluric cults prevailed, burial was the ordinary funerary rite, while cremation was practiced among the Northern, Aryan civilizations. Accordingly, the fate of the individual was not to be purified by fire of all earthly residues to ascend to the heavenly domain but to return to the depths of the earth and become dissolved into the chthonic matter as the source of eternal life.

THE WESTERN WORLD

Within the Western world, Evola argues that the solar spirituality of the Hyperborean is located in the Aryan civilizations. What Evola means by Aryan is, perhaps, different than National Socialists' (Nazi) beliefs in that Evola thinks the classification should not correspond to merely biological or ethnic concepts, but to what I have already mentioned, the "race of the spirit."⁶¹ While both Evola and the Fascist regimes believed Aryan civilizations embodied a white race, Evola placed the idea of spirit at the forefront to emphasize a heroic tendency toward inner liberation and reintegration in an active and combative form. The Aryan race of spirit is illustrated as Evola takes us through three types of civilizations, the first two are cycles of decadence and the last is known as the heroic cycle.

First, the titanic, which refers to the spirit of the materialistic and violent race that ceased to recognize the authority of the spiritual principle associated with the priestly symbol or to the spirituality of the feminine brother, that is, Cain and Abel.⁶² The second type of civilization upheld the feminine primacy through the Aphrodistic principle where the *hetaera* (in ancient Greece, a courtesan or mistress) replaced the Mother. The divine male, subjected to the magic of the feminine principle, is reduced to an earthly demon of deficient and dark power. The third form of civilization is the race of heroes to whom the possibility of attaining immortality is bestowed. This type of civilization attempts to restore the tradition of origin on the foundation of the warrior principle. Next, Evola traces these civilizations from a "historical" point of view through to the ancient Greek and Roman societies, understood as the Heroic-Uranian Western Cycle.⁶³ The decline from these civilizations and the advent of the modern period rests primarily on the rise of Christianity.

With no equivocation, Evola declares that Christianity marked the beginning of an unprecedented decline from traditional civilization.⁶⁴ The sacral, patrician, and virile Rome that Evola so extols increasingly came under the influence of what he refers to as "Asiatic" cults as a return to the symbols of the Mother and of the most spurious forms of the mystical and pantheistic cults of the Southern deities. Even the sacred idea of *imperium* is reduced to a mere symbol, but worst of all, the distinction between Roman citizens, Latin citizens, and the masses of other citizens was abolished, and Roman citizenship was extended to all. The mixing of the races together with the subversive influence of Christianity added to an otherwise volatile combination with inevitable and diabolic results.

In regarding Jesus as savior, Christianity broke from the "Law" of Jewish orthodoxy and took up several themes typical of the Semitic soul. These themes were proper to an inwardly divided soul and provided fertile ground for antitraditionalist sentiment. Christianity appealed to the irrational part of being while sowing disdain for the heroic, sapient, and initiatory path. In Christianity we no longer encounter the pure religion of the Jewish Law nor a true initiatory Mystery, but rather humans felt redeemed through the feeling of grace imbued with a new sense of hope, recused from both earthly cares and sins of the flesh, and offered a death-evading life everlasting. All of this represented a predominance of pathos over ethos. God was no longer thought of as a symbol of an essence not subject to passion and change, and at the same time, God ceased to be the God of the patricians who was carried in front of the heroic legions and became embodied in the victorious warriors. Significantly, and in contrast to the heroic ideal, the Christian God proclaimed equality among human beings with love its supreme guiding principle.

Evola equates equality with the Southern, non-Aryan influence that presents itself as a worldview linked to a variety of "natural law," present in the more decadent times of Roman law. Antithetical to the heroic ideal bestowed upon a differentiated being within a social hierarchy, Christian egalitarianism with its fundamental beliefs in love, brotherhood, and social community became the mystical and religious foundation of a social ideal adamantly opposed to pure Roman law:

> instead of *universality*, which is authentic only in its function as a hierarchical peak that does not abolish but presupposes and sanctions the differences among human beings, what arose was the ideal of *collectivity* reaffirmed in the symbol of the mystical body of Christ; this latter ideal contained in embryonic form a further regressive and involutive influence that Catholicism itself, despite its Romanization, was neither able nor entirely willing to overcome.[65]

Christianity, it seems, universalized, rendered exclusive, and exalted the way in which the truth and the manner in which that attitude applies only to the lower forms of human society for whom the exoteric forms of tradition were devised. Without doubt, Evola believes this is characteristic of the cycle of the Dark Age, or *Kali Yuga*.

As Christianity developed, it brought about the decline of the medieval world's feudal structure and inaugurated the rise of nation state, a decidedly antitradition occurrence. The political assumed a new secular and material role steeped in humanism, liberalism and rationalism. Dualism prevailed, which bifurcated the *civitas diabolic* and the *civitas dei* with

Christ designated the leader of the higher spiritual world, which represented a direct attack on the nature of traditional sovereignty in Imperial Rome. Moreover, the advent of lay judges and bureaucratic functionaries together with a tendency toward the antifeudal centralizing of power further eroded the traditional structure. Evola pays great attention to the medieval social construct of feudalism. He believes it characterizes the majority of the great traditional eras:

> in this type of regime the principle of plurality and of relative political autonomy of the individual parts is emphasized, as is the proper context of that universal element, that *unum quod non est pars* (one that is not a part) that alone can really organize and unify these parts, not contrasting but by presiding over each one of them through the transcendent, superpolitical, and regulating function that the universal embodies.[66]

The feudal system allowed royalty to work hand in hand with the aristocracy such that the royal function did not hinder the autonomy of the particular principalities, but fostered a single nationality. However, when the *dignitas*, which rules beyond the multiple, temporal, and contingent, fell into decline, the principalities began to assert their own fiefs absolute authority, which was more typical of the Empire. At this juncture, a new and subversive element was introduced to the political: the nation state. When this occurred, a variety of free cities, communes, republics, and other political entities established their own independence and rebelled against imperial authority.

The inevitable decline brought with it a deterioration in chivalry as the ideal human type molded upon purely ethical and spiritual values. Indeed, even the concept of royalty in general became increasingly secularized, with the king assuming the stature of a mere head of state. But Evola also takes pains to point out that the deconsecration of the ruling class and their subsequent subordination to the Empire deprived the community of any higher principles. As a result, royalty was unavoidably pushed into the orbit of the lower castes who were destined to prevail. Evola explains that "whenever a caste rebels against a higher caste and claims independence, the higher caste unavoidably loses the character that it had within the hierarchy and thereby reflects the character of the immediately lower caste."[67] Why the allegedly superior caste ultimately succumbs and is absorbed into the lower more inferior caste is never explained. This anti-aristocratic movement, however, turns the people of the nation into a social collective structure rather than a hierarchical one, so important to traditional beliefs. Eventually, the sovereignty of the hierarchical state is usurped by popular sovereignty where all laws and authority assume legitimacy as the free expression of the "people" who are thought of in terms of autonomous, sovereign individuals. The result is a decadent collectivized society in the form of a democratized liberal state.

Evola makes it clear, however, that causes do not just emanate from above, those from below also abound. In all traditional societies, a dynamic is present that assumes forces of chaos, inferior impulses, and what Evola calls "lower social and economic strata that are dominated and restrained by a principle of 'form.'"[68] In simple terms, there is an ongoing tension between the superior, connected to the supernatural's attempt to lift up the inferior, while at the same time the inferior, connected to the masses or *demos*, seeks to bring the superior down to its level. One can envision, then, with the emergence of lower strata liberation movements in the form of revolt or revolution or even a weakening of the representatives of the superior ideal, a degeneration occurring at the top of the hierarchy. According to Evola, liberation movements from below destroy the unconditional (blind) faith in civilization's spiritual foundation and ushers in the rising tide of inferior races.

Evola also sees the advent of liberation movements turning the absolute ruler into a mere political leader subject to normal political challenges. Accordingly, a certain "bad" freedom emerges that destroys and denies every principle of true authority, and anoints the merchant class and organized labor with omnipotent power.

To follow Evola's trajectory of Western decline, we must also understand that what we have been talking about thus far are characteristics of the modern world in general. In more specific terms, Evola sees these nefarious influences accelerating to the point where civilization reaches the stage in which various forces of decadence, which were present but oppressed in previous times, finally reach their full measure. The main perpetrator leading to the emancipation of this new civilization is something I have discussed before: humanism. Civilization will, henceforth, limit itself to the human dimension, an experience that begins and ends in this world and on this earth. Thought of in terms of individualism, modern humanism constitutes an illusory center separate and apart from the true center of the metaphysical. Modern phenomenon thus presents us with a radical unrealism and inorganic character where Being is replaced with the will, the self, and an ego accompanied by a body.

Evola's unrealism means the loss of the initiatic tradition in religion, which is the only means to ensure the objective participation of humans in the superworld. The modern world's spirituality, with its associated immortality of the soul regarded as a privilege belonging to everyone, contributed to the loss of understanding of the necessity of initiation as the only operation able to free an individual from all conditionings of a mortal existence. In its place, rose the mystery and redemption of Christ, through death and resurrection, applied to the merely religious plane of faith. The mysteries of Christ were thought of in terms of a moral standard as a way to lead a life in view of the sanctions awaiting the immortal soul in the afterlife.

Humanism in the form of individualism, especially within the Protestant theory of personal interpretations of scripture, also brought with it a second demonic effect, rationalism, which created the opportunity for:

> the single individual who got rid of the dogmatic tradition and the principle of spiritual authority, by claiming to have within himself the capability of right discernment, gradually ended up promoting the cult of that which in him, as a human being, is the basis of all judgements, namely the faculty of reason, thus turning it into the criterion of all certitudes, truths, and norms.[69]

Interspersed with the notion of rationalism are a host of conspiracy theories. Evola postulates that beginning in the Renaissance, rationalism became differentiated and assumed. From its speculative origins, rationalism adopted an aggressive stance that generated the Enlightenment, Encyclopedism, and antireligious and revolutionary criticism. This aggression negatively affected initiatic organizations, such as the Illuminati and Masons. Those who claimed the sovereign power of reason displaced the superiority of dogma that supposedly granted the initiate spiritual enlightenment.

Much like today's conspiracy theorists, Evola offers no substantial proof of rationality's intrigue against traditional organizations, yet it is one of traditionalism's major themes. Moreover, for various reasons, alt-right adherents seem to espouse an endless stream of conspiracy theories designed, for the most part, to undermine trust in public institutions and officials. These theories run the gamut from the incredulous allegation that Hillary Clinton and other Democrats operated a child sex ring out of the Comet Ping Pong Pizzeria in Washington, DC, to the type of conspiracy designed to offer proof of a "deep state" intrigue, such as the "birther" issue revolving around former President Obama's origin of birth, or to the organization known as QAnon, which alleges the existence of a deep state conspiring to remove President Trump from office. The common theme of these conspiracy theorists seems to be the internet that connects often outrageous allegations with a ready audience unfazed by the lack of facts but willing to take matters into their own hands, as Edgar Welch did in December 2016. Armed with an assault rifle, Welch traveled from North Carolina to "self-investigate" the child sex ring operating in the Washington pizza parlor. After firing several shots into the restaurant, Welch was arrested. However, even when confronted with the actual facts, Welch refused to reject the conspiracy as "fake news."

The revolt of individualism meant that all consciousness of the superworld vanished as the material world replaced the superworld as all-inclusive and certain. Indeed, science adapted to the new circumstances by concerning itself exclusively with physical dimension such as mathematical relations, laws of consistency, hypotheses, and abstract principles. In Evola's judgment, the reign of rationalism and scientism unavoidably gave birth to technology and machines.

Rationalism also meant the degradation and democratization of knowledge in the form of science based entirely upon the establishment of uniform criterion of truth and certainty grounded in the soulless world of numbers and a "positivist" system indifferent toward anything presenting a qualitative and symbolic approach. In the modern world, this process of disintegration continues to this day. As a result, modern humans experience a regression from the personal to an anonymous, pure chaotic realm of quantity. A new collective form arises based on the conditions of material existence and a social life dominated by the impersonal and egalitarian system of public powers that eventually overtakes individualism:

> moderns tried to replace the unity that in ancient societies consisted of living traditions and scared law with an exterior, anodyne, and mechanical unity in which individuals are brought together without an organic relation to each other, and without seeing any superior principle or figure, the obeying of which would mean consent, and submission to which would represent an acknowledgement of elevation.[70]

The road of decadence, taken by modern society in its denial of traditional principles, leads to the upending of the castes with deleterious effects. As Evola describes it, humankind has inexorably moved from sacred leaders, to warrior aristocrats, to merchants, and finally to serfs.[71] I have already described Evola's fascination with a mythical, divine royalty embodying two great powers—spiritual and temporal—that he oftentimes labels "Olympian sovereignty." It is from the height of this spiritual virility, what he labels the "Light of the North," that the West has gradually deteriorated to a casteless, utter chaotic decadence called the modern world.

While I have generally discussed the historical Hindu periods, Evola ties those periods to what he describes as the historical descent of the West, which occurred over three primary epochs. Roughly similar to Book VIII of Plato's *Republic*, once the "apex" disappeared—an aristocratic philosopher king—authority devolved to the next caste, the warrior aristocrats. Here, the monarchs were military leaders, lords of temporal justice, and in more contemporary times absolute rulers. In this sense, "regality of blood replaced regality of the spirit."[72] During this stage, the *fides* cementing the society no longer exhibited a religious character; instead a warrior mentality predominated embodied in the concepts of loyalty, faithfulness, and honor.

The second stage's collapse occurred as aristocracies fell into decay and revolutions replaced monarchies with constitutional democracies based on the will of the people. Perhaps, Evola had in mind the Restoration period in France where Louis XVIII, no longer an absolute ruler, adhered to the words of François Guizoit: "the king reigns but does not rule." The rise of parliamentary governments together with the formation of capitalist economic systems that placed great emphasis on the accumulation of wealth brought forth the shift from aristocracies to the third caste, the bourgeoisie. Here, capitalist titans of industry replaced the monarchs of blood and spirit. Unsurprisingly, the time of capitalist domination comes under harsh scrutiny for Evola. He believes the period was ruled by the social contract that assumed an economic and utilitarian character consisting of an agreement premised on personal convenience and material interest that could only benefit the merchant class. Gold became the standard of wealth and, consequently, a powerful tool to control not only political power but the means to shape opinion, all of this behind the veil of illusory, egalitarian democracy.

Although he does not mention Max Webber, his Protestant ethic surely lurks below the surface as an enabler of ostentatious wealth in the name of Christianity. Seen as a distillation of the Jewish spirit, Christianity sanctioned the promised land of Protestant puritanism, American exceptionalism, and certainly the capitalist spirit. Evola thinks that these congenial times opened the path for what he calls secularized Judaism to achieve world domination. In another conspiracy theory, Evola sees the modern banking system with its charge of interest on loans as purely Jewish in origin and as the foundation of the aberrant development of modern banking and capitalist economics.

The final crisis of bourgeois society brought on by class struggle, the proletarian revolution and the "socialist civilization of labor," initiated the third collapse where power transferred to the lowest of the traditional castes: the castes of the "beasts of burden and the standardized individual," what Evola refers to as subhuman forces.[73] This collapse resulted in the reduction of values to the level of matter, the machine, and every bit Guénon's reign of quantity. This shift, from human to subhuman, reveals a civilization beholden to a purely physical existence of gold and work. While Evola thinks the "regression of the castes" is visible in all aspects of human existence ranging from the arts, to family life, to war, and even to the aesthetic world, it is most pronounced in the realm of ethics.

The character of the first stage was represented by an ideal of spiritual vitality, initiation, and an ethics aimed at overcoming all human bonds. Similarly, the age of the warrior was noted for its ideals of heroism, victory, and lordship coupled with an aristocratic ethics of honor, faithfulness, and chivalry. During the period of the merchants, the overriding ideals were pure economics, profit, prosperity, and science as a mere instrument of industrial progress designed to propel a wanton consumer society. Lastly, the rise of the surfs corresponds to the slave's principle: work equated to the status of religion. This self-congratulating stupidity of the ideal of work contrasts with Evola's understanding of the ancient world's disdain for work as a material, impure means impregnated with purely human possibilities. The ideal of action regressed during this period to a form acceptable to the lowest classes as work or production.

Evola sees the present epoch in terms of nationalism and collectivism as opposed to traditionalism's universalism. Modern society's regression journeyed from the ideals of universalism to the decadence of collectivism where the individual losses all meaning other than as a function ensconced in a higher functioning machine. With regard to modern nationalism, Evola differentiates between nationality as a group of common elementary characteristics within a hierarchical society such as a warrior, a merchant, or an artisan, and nationalism as a form of centralizing and artificial unity. While nationality is described in terms of healthy and natural, nationalism stimulates the masses through propaganda and myths designed to awaken certain base elements projecting an air of superiority, exclusion, and power. As such, nationalism has a double face:

> it accentuates and elevated to the state of absolute value a particularistic principle; therefore, the possibilities of mutual understanding and cooperation between nations are reduced to a bare minimum, without even considering the forms of leveling guaranteed by modern civilization.[74]

Accordingly, what emerges in modern nationalism is an inversion. The homeland and the nation become the primary element of a self-subsisting entity that requires each individual belonging to it to pledge unconditional support—a stance that Sartre sees as a pivotal moment in the formulation of groups. Modern nationalism renounces the upward-oriented pursuit of unification through the supernatural and universal characteristic of Traditionalism. Evola argues that whenever the people become sovereign and the leader is no longer considered divine or ruling by the grace of god, but instead by the will of the nation, then at this point a schism develops that separates a political organism of a traditional type from communism with the end of the cycle closely at hand. Much as the ancient Greeks argued, liberalism and constitutionalism provided the impetus for democracy that eventually turns to socialism and then gives way to radicalism and ultimately to tyranny.

For Evola, the decadence of the West is not irretrievable; rather, it can be saved by a return to the traditional spirit in the context of a new consciousness that encompasses every aspect of human life such that a unitary spirit rules over every individual. But the real culprit for Evola is the loss of contact with the metaphysical realm. Modern materialism extinguishes every possibility of an authentic existence pursuant to traditional values. However, Evola sees only obstacles to a return to tradition in modern society's education system, its lifestyle of contingency, its collective mentality, and its idols and prejudices forming a feeling of false consciousness and false action based in human spirit.[75] What is really needed is a so-called complete housecleaning capable of liberating humans from this false identity. Even Guénon's reliance upon the Catholic Church as the only modern institution capable of leading the way back to Traditionalism comes under attack by Evola; the church as savior is a mere illusion.

The philosophical foundation of traditionalism found its voice in the work of Evola, who advocates a narrative based on perennial philosophy, but incorporates much of Guénon's thought as well. It is a philosophy rooted in a distant past, subsumed in the idealized myth of the heroic warrior, and premised on an elite social hierarchy of the superior white race. The issue that now arises is how this ideal takes hold within any given society; exactly what are the dynamics that allow individuals within a society to not only be intrigued by such political theories but to adopt them as one's own. For an answer, I want to turn to two theories of group formation. The first is social dominance theory, which sheds light on how this phenomenon takes hold. The second, Jean-Paul Sartre's analysis of group formation in his *Critique of Dialectical Reason*, engages the question why.

NOTES

1. Theosophy encompasses a wide array of positions within Christianity that focus on the attainment of direct, unmediated knowledge of the purpose and origin of the universe and the real nature of divinity. An American branch was established in the late nineteenth century by Russian émigré Helena Blavatsky (1831–1891) that emphasized an esoteric religious tradition.

2. Julius Evola, *Revolt against the Modern World*, trans. Guido Stucco (Rochester VT: Inner Traditions, 1995). Originally published as *Rivolta contro il mondo moderno* by Hoepli, Milan, 1934. See also Julius Evola, *Men among the Ruins: Postwar Reflections of a Radical Traditionalist*, ed. Michael Moynihan, trans. Guido Stucco (Rochester, VT: Inner Traditions, 2002), 124. Originally published as *Gli uomini e le rovine* by Edizioni dell'Ascia, Rome, 1953. Evola defines traditionalism as when a society or civilization "is ruled by principles that transcend what is merely human and individual, and when all its sectors are formed and ordered from above, and directed to what is above." Julius Evola, *Ride the Tiger*, trans. Joscelyn Godwin and Constance Fontana (Rochester VT: Inner Traditions, 2003), 2. Originally published as *Cavalcare la Tigre* by Edizioni Mediterranee, Rome, 1961.

3. Julius Evola, *The Path of Cinnabar*, ed. John Morgan, trans. Sergio Knipe (London: Arktos, 2010), 100. Originally published as *Il Cammino del Cinabro* by Vanni Scheiwiller, Milan, 1963. The Magna Mater (Great Mother) was the Ancient Roman name for Cybele, the Phrygian goddess associated with the fertility of the earth.

4. See, generally, H. T. Hansen, "A Short Introduction to Julius Evola," in *Revolt against the Modern World*, xvi.

5. John Morgan, "Introduction," in Julius Evola, *Metaphysics of War: Battle, Victory and Death in the World of Tradition* (London: Arktos, 2011), 8.

6. Julius Evola, *The Path of Cinnabar*, 106. Imperium was the power vested in the leaders of Rome and was thought to originate from divine sanction. See also Julius Evola, *Men among the Ruins*, 122–24; and Francis Parker Yockey, *Imperium* (Newport

Beach, CA: Noontide Press, 1962). Along with Oswald Spengler's *Decline of the West*, Yockey's book played an influential part in Evola's political philosophy.

7. Julius Evola, *Men among the Ruins*, 63. For a more complete discussion of Evola's relationship to Himmler's SS, see https://evolaasheis.wordpress.com/2016/04/14/report-to-himmler-on-julius-evola/.

8. From the first issue of the periodical, *La Torre*, published by Evola and quoted in Evola, *The Path of Cinnabar*, 107.

9. Evola, *Men among the Ruins*, 77; and Evola, *The Path of Cinnabar*, 170. The concept of *Volk* in German as the people or nation was expanded under National Socialism to refer to the Germanic people, of whom Germans were only a part, or the Indo-Germanic peoples as a whole. *Volksgemeinschaft* was a term also used by the National Socialists to designate the Germanic or European "people's community" they desired to establish. Evola, *Men among the Ruins*, 190.

10. Evola, *Metaphysics of War*, 59. Michael Bell lays out two forms of meta-biological forces. The first is similar to a collective consciousness, a sort of group-minded spirit that enters into a group member's body upon birth. The second form is limited to only a select, gifted few as an otherworldly force that is drawn into the blood through rites. As such, these select few are aware of immutable principles. Michael Bell, "Julius Evola's Concept of Race: A Racism of Three Degrees," *The Occidental Quarterly* 9, no. 2 (Spring, 2009): 101–12.

11. Evola, *Metaphysics of War*, 60.
12. Ibid., 66.
13. Ibid., 67.
14. Julius Evola, *The Elements of Racial Education*, 27, https://evolaasheis.wordpress.com/author/evolaasheis/.
15. Evola, *Metaphysics of War*, 77.
16. Ibid., 60.
17. Jon Stone, "Far-Right European Governments Launch Plan to Take over EU with Anti-Immigration 'Axis,'" *Independent*, January 10, 2019 (emphasis added), www.independent.co.uk/news/world/europe/far-right-europe-hungary-viktor-obran-italy-poland-immigration-axis-eu-a8720976.html.
18. Evola, *Metaphysics of War*, 60–62.
19. Evola, *The Elements of Racial Education*, 14.
20. Eli Watkins and James Gary, "Let Them Call You Racist," CNN, March 10, 2018, https://www.cnn.com/2018/03/10/politics/steve-bannon-national-front/index.html.
21. Evola, *Metaphysics of War*, 87.
22. Ibid., 90–91.
23. H. T. Hansen, "A Short Introduction to Julius Evola," in *Revolt against the Modern World*, xx–xxi.
24. Bhaktivedanta, *Bhagavad-Gītā*, §2.
25. Ibid., §§2.37–38.
26. Evola, *Revolt against the Modern World*, 3.
27. Ibid., 6.
28. Ibid., 7.
29. *Pontifex Maximus* (Greatest Priest) was the chief high priest of the College of Pontiffs (*Collegium Pontificum*) in ancient Rome. As the most important position in Roman religion, its occupant was chosen exclusively from the patrician class until 254 BCE.
30. Evola, *The Path of Cinnabar*, 189 (emphasis in original). See also Evola, *Men among the Ruins*, 116 and 124–26.
31. Evola, *Revolt against the Modern World*, 21.
32. Ibid., 24.
33. Ibid., 35.
34. Ibid., 41.
35. Ibid., 42.
36. Ibid., 43.

37. Ibid., 57.
38. Ibid., 59.
39. Evola, *Metaphysics of War*, 22–23.
40. Evola, *Revolt against the Modern World*, 94.
41. Ibid., 95.
42. Guénon, *Introduction to Hindu Doctrines*, 147.
43. Evola, *Revolt against the Modern World*, 107.
44. Plato, *The Republic of Plato*, trans. Allan Bloom (New York: Basic Books, 1991), line 434b–c. See also Bhaktivedanta, *Bhagavad-Gītā*, §18:41–47, for a discussion of the nature and function of the classes and the necessity to not disrupt the class orientation of the society.
45. Ibid., 111.
46. Ibid., 157. The Hindu impassible spirit is masculine; the active matrix of the very conditioned form is feminine.
47. Ibid., 159.
48. Evola, *Ride the Tiger*, 186.
49. Evola, *Revolt against the Modern World*, 167.
50. Ibid.
51. Steve King @SteveKingIA, March 12, 2017. King made his remarks in support of Geert Wilders, the far right Dutch politician, who was running for reelection at the time of the tweet. See also Tom Kludt and Brian Stelter, "White Anxiety Finds a Home at Fox News," *CNN*, August 9, 2018, https://www.cnn.com/2018/09/28/media/fox-news-laura-ingraham-tucker-carlson-white-nationalism/index.html. A website dedicated to the cause of the Great Replacement can be found at http://www.great-replacement.com/.
52. Evola, *Revolt against the Modern World*, 177. Evola expands upon his concept of the *Kali Yuga* by saying that the Dark Age's "essential quality is emphatically said to be a climate of dissolution, in which all the forces—individual and collective, material, psychic, and spiritual—that were previously held in check by a higher law and by influences of a superior order pass into a state of freedom and chaos." Evola, *Ride the Tiger*, 9.
53. Evola, *Revolt against the Modern World*, 184.
54. See, generally, René Guénon. *Le Roi du Monde* (Gallimard: Paris, 1927), chaps. 3 and 4.
55. Evola, *Revolt against the Modern World*, 189.
56. Ibid., 196.
57. Ibid., 213.
58. Ibid., 204.
59. Ibid., 209.
60. Ibid., 211.
61. Ibid., 230.
62. Ibid., 221.
63. It should be noted, and Paul Furlong points this out, Evola's historical method does not rest on the truth of his statements: "his history is an investigation of myth, for it is in the world of mythology both that the universal principles of history can be identified and the unending conflict of superior transcendent forces of good and evil can be most clearly seen. The frequent accusation that his version of history was a-historical left him unmoved." Paul Furlong, *Social and Political Thought of Julius Evola* (Milton Park: Routledge, 2011), 39.
64. Evola, *Revolt against the Modern World*, 278.
65. Ibid., 283.
66. Ibid., 303.
67. Ibid., 305.
68. Ibid., 306.
69. Ibid., 318.
70. Ibid., 321.

71. Ibid., 327.
72. Ibid., 327–28.
73. Ibid., 329.
74. Ibid., 339.
75. Ibid., 359.

Part II

Social Dominance Theory and Sartre

FOUR
General Outline of Social Dominance Theory

While many approaches to group-based oppression exist, no single method attempts to connect the realms of individual personality and attitudes with that of institutional and social behavior. Social dominance theory (SDT) is just such an effort to integrate multiple levels of analysis into a single coherent theoretical framework. This approach is particularly insightful because, from a philosophical perspective, Sartre also connects the psychological state of individual personality with not only the sociopolitical realities of organized groups but also the resulting *ressentiment* exhibited by those who view their hierarchical status as imperiled.

SDT's starting point is the basic observation that all human societies tend to be structured as systems of group-based social hierarchies.[1] At its core, this hierarchical structure consists of a small number of hegemonic groups at the top—usually one or two—and one or more subordinate groups at the bottom of the structure. The dominant group is generally characterized by a disproportionately greater share of *positive social value* consisting of all those material and symbolic things individuals usually desire or strive for. Here we are talking about such items as political power and authority, the "right" place to live and work, abundant nourishment, first-class health care, wealth, and high social status. On the other hand, and as one might expect, subordinate groups possess a disproportionately greater share of *negative social value* thought of in terms of such things as lack of political power and authority, low paying occupations, mediocre to nonexistent health care, poor living conditions, low social status, and severe negative sanctions including death associated with incarceration.[2]

SDT also emphasizes the distinction between group-based social hierarchies and their individual-based counterparts. In some instances, individual-based social hierarchies may see their particular members enjoying great power, wealth, and prestige as a result of their own highly valued individual abilities. Professional athletes come readily to mind as an example of individuals who excel at a particular sport and, thus, may form an individual-based social hierarchy within that particular athletic endeavor.

In contrast, group-based social hierarchies refer to the social power, privilege, and prestige an individual possesses by virtue of her membership in a particular socially constructed group determined by, among other things, race, religion, ethnicity, or social class. While one's individual characteristics cannot be totally severed from their group-based status, SDT argues that the power, prestige, and achievements of individuals is not completely independent of the power and prestige of the groups to which they belong. Obviously, while some individuals may possess great natural athletic ability, those skills will come to naught if there is no platform upon which to showcase their skills, and many of those platforms are team-oriented or group endeavors. As a result, within group-based social hierarchies, one's social status, influence, and power are a function of group membership and not necessarily a result of one's individual abilities. Obviously, individual and group-based characteristics will overlap to some extent, but the access to the means for individual achievement, such as high-quality education, will be differentially available to certain social groups.

Fundamental to SDT is the fact that human group-based social hierarchies entail distinctly different stratification systems.[3] In recognizing this observation, SDT articulates three such stratification systems: an *age system*, where adults have disproportionately greater social power over children and young adults; a *gender system*, where males have disproportionate social and political power over females; and an *arbitrary-set system*, which is filled with socially constructed and highly prominent groups based on ethnicity, nation, state, race, caste, social class, religion, or any other socially relevant group distinction conjured up through the human imagination. It is important to note that, and the authors point this out, the trimorphic system of group-based dominance is not interchangeable; rather, it constitutes three interlocking and mutually interdependent attributes of the social structure of society.[4]

In all these systems, one group dominates—either materially, or politically, or both—at the expense of another group. While the age and gender systems have an element of malleability in terms of who is considered young or old, male or female, the arbitrary-set system is characterized by its high degree of unpredictability, uncertainty, as well as flexibility as to situational and contextual sensitivity in determining the group distinctions that are socially relevant and the manner in which in-groups and out-groups are defined.[5] Thus, boundaries in arbitrary-set in-group/out-group characteristics are generally thought of in terms of membership in, for instance, a particular class, race, or nationality.

Moreover, it is commonly the case that arbitrary-set systems are associated with greater levels of violence, oppression, and cruelty than the other two systems. Not to discount the oftentimes brutal and oppressive forms of social control exhibited through the age and gender systems — the revelations of the #MeToo movement bear this out — the arbitrary-set system seems to exhibit greater degrees and intensity of violence. One need only look to the recent genocidal eradication of the Rohingyas from Myanmar to understand that genocidal arbitrary-set violence occurs in the twenty-first century at an alarming rate.

I want to highlight a particularly enlightening observation made by the developers of SDT with regard to the arbitrary-set systems. While age and gender systems are universally found in all societies, the authors argue that arbitrary-set stratifications are absent in small hunter–gatherer societies. The reason seems to lie in the fact that these societies lack sufficient economic surplus. It is thought that this lack of surplus combined with the nomadic lifestyle of such societies fails to spawn the development of highly specialized social roles. Thus, to the extent that political power exists, it is based on mutual agreement and not coercion.[6]

The reason societies producing substantial economic surpluses are also those that possess an arbitrary-set system of social hierarchy appears to be that when a society produces a stable economic surplus, certain individuals are free to specialize in intimidating actions, which allows the political elites to establish and enforce coercive economic and social relationships with the other members of the society. In addition, once the role of specialization results in expropriative relations among group members, hierarchical arbitrary-set systems emerge. Certainly, ancient Greece and Rome fall within this sphere, but more modern advanced industrial societies, such as the United States, Great Britain, Germany, and Japan, also have hierarchical arbitrary-set systems. One last point is of special importance with regard to arbitrary-set systems, and that is once established there is no evidence that they can be abolished. Neither revolutionary change nor small transformative social experiments within so-called utopian societies have succeeded in eradicating arbitrary-set systems.

BASIC ASSUMPTIONS OF SOCIAL DOMINANCE THEORY

Understanding the key observations surrounding SDT, I want to turn to two basic assumptions in addition to economies with excess surpluses underlying those preliminary observations. First, most forms of group-based conflict and oppression, such as racism, sexism, and nationalism, can be regarded as different forms of the same basic human predisposition to form group-based social hierarchies.[7] Inasmuch as SDT was originally designed as a model of social hierarchy, it focuses on the manner in which both social discourse in the form of ideologies, attitudes, and stereotypes, as well as individual and institutional behavior contribute to and are affected by the nature and severity of group-based social hierarchy. If, in fact, no social hierarchy exists, then SDT has, in principle, very little to offer. Consequently,

> the social dominance synthesis states not only that group-based social hierarchy will tend to be ubiquitous, especially within social systems producing economic surplus, but more importantly, that most if not all forms of group prejudices, stereotypes, ideologies of group superiority and inferiority, and forms of individual and institutional discrimination both help produce and are reflections of this group-based social hierarchy. *In other words, phenomena such as prejudice, racism, stereotypes, and discrimination simply cannot be understood outside the conceptual framework of group-based social hierarchy, especially within social systems of economic surplus.*[8]

This generalized statement cannot be emphasized enough; it is essential to not only an understanding of the foundation of SDT, but how it is that forms of oppression achieve a foothold within society, and equally important, why oppression is so difficult to eradicate. In a very fundamental sense, whenever social groups are formed a socially constructed hierarchy develops. When that hierarchy comes into existence, coercion and oppression will necessarily also come into existence. Sartre too ventures down this road as he analyzes the psychology of group based behavior that readily embraces oppression in its multifaceted forms as it organizes its praxis.

The second additional assumption acknowledges that human social systems are subject to two counterbalancing influences. The first such influence consists of *hierarchy-enhancing* forces (HE) that are responsible for producing and maintaining ever greater levels of group-based social inequality. Examples of HE forces are the police, the legal systems, and economic or social institutions. Counterbalancing the influence of HE forces are *hierarchy-attenuating* forces (HA), which are intended to produce higher levels of group-based social equality. Examples of these types of forces are civil rights and social welfare organizations, charities, and religious organizations. Each of these two forces operates within any given society and will act to "offset" each other in many instances. However, it should be noted that HE forces tend to be associated with institutions of power within or controlled by the dominant group, while HA forces are oftentimes associated with subordinate and out of power groups. As such, these forces not only counterbalance each other, they may well be in direct conflict with each other, oftentimes with violent consequences.

Given the basic assumptions of SDT, there are three proximal processes that drive group-based social hierarchies. The first such process is *aggregated individual discrimination*, such as everyday, sometimes clandestine, acts of discrimination perpetrated by one individual against another individual that taken in the aggregate and over time contribute to the clear and unmistakable differences in the power between social groups to which the individuals belong. While these individual actions can be insidious, as I have said they are oftentimes difficult to discern. One rather telling example of individual discrimination involves a group of three white women who called police on a black man for allegedly "gardening while black." Marc Peebles of Detroit was falsely accused of crimes, including pedophilia, as he built a community garden in a vacant lot, and worked to improve his neighborhood. The women involved desired the land the community garden occupied for their own use and wanted to see Mr. Peebles "incarcerated or seriously injured by law enforcement." After a period of time, and in furtherance of their plan, they erroneously told police that Peebles had made threats and had stolen property from nearby homes. When those allegations failed to achieve their desired objective, one of the women, upon observing Mr. Peebles teaching a group of homeschooled young people about gardening, called 911 and falsely reported that Peebles was a convicted pedophile and was not allowed near children. The call had its desired effect when the police arrested Peebles, not based on the allegations of pedophilia, but for stalking the women. An incredulous judge later dismissed all the charges.[9] Examples of this type of individual discrimination are plentiful, but I refer to this particular case because it illustrates the ease in which this type of discrimination is engaged in.

One of the primary means by which societies both promulgate and maintain group-based social hierarchy is through the second proximal process, or *aggregated institutional discrimination*. Such discrimination is utilized both as systematic terror in the form of violence disproportionately directed against subordinate groups as well as in the manner in which social institutions, such as schools, businesses, and governmental institutions, disproportionately allocate positive social values to dominant groups and, at the same time, disproportionately distribute negative social value to subordinate groups. In either instance, aggregated institutional discrimination functions to maintain expropriative relationships between members of dominant and subordinate groups.

While terror has taken on a somewhat ubiquitous meaning in today's seemingly horror laden world, SDT's reliance on the concept within aggregated institutional discrimination requires some further explanation. First, I should point out that Sartre also avails himself of the concept to describe interpersonal relations within the organized group as the means to ensure group unity through fealty to the hierarchical social structure. In much of Sartre's writings, violence is a common theme. Generally,

Sartre thinks all human relations are agonistic, and that violence, or what he terms terror, is indicative of those relations, especially once groups organize themselves around the pledge. In both SDT and in Sartre's work, actual violence and more importantly the threat of violence for any reason or no reason at all lends a pervasive feeling of terror in the minds of the subordinate group.

In its most pervasive usage, institutional discrimination as a form of systematic terror occurs when subordinate groups directly challenge and confront the hegemonic control of dominant groups. To refer to just one example among many, the nonviolent Civil Rights marches of the 1960s are a window into the role of systematic terror. Often what started out as peaceful demonstrations for human and civil rights angrily ended with violence not only by individual members of the dominant group directed at the marchers, but from the institutions controlled by that group, namely the police and the legal system.

While I shall discuss in more detail the following forms of violence and terror, suffice it to say at the present that, in its *official* (legally sanctioned violence by organs of the state), *semiofficial* (violence carried out by intimidation directed at subordinate groups by officials of the state, such as internal security forces or paramilitary organizations), and *unofficial* forms (violence perpetrated by private individuals from dominant groups against subordinate groups, such as the Ku Klux Klan and, more recently, the ultra-nationalist Proud Boys), systematic terror is often produced by the rules, procedures, and actions of social institutions resulting in a disproportionate allocation of positive and negative social value.[10]

Within the process of aggregated institutional discrimination, two distinctions are drawn. First, so-called *individual-mediated institutional discrimination* refers to those instances where individuals with biased or dominance-oriented attitudes, allow their beliefs to influence the decisions and actions they undertake on behalf of the institution they serve. The case of Kentucky County Clerk Kim Davis, who denied marriage licenses to same-sex couples in defiance of a Supreme Court ruling stating that she was acting "under God's authority," is an example of an institutional official allowing her own biases to influence official actions, even though those actions were entirely perfunctory.[11]

Along the same line, and perhaps more disturbing, is the recent confirmation of Allison Jones Rushing to the United States Fourth Circuit Court of Appeals. Ms. Rushing worked with the Alliance Defending Freedom (ADF), which the Southern Poverty Law Institute labels a hate group. The ADF "has supported the recriminalization of homosexuality in the US and criminalization abroad; has defended state-sanctioned sterilization of trans people abroad; has linked homosexuality to pedophilia and claims that a 'homosexual agenda' will destroy Christianity and society."[12] As a judge in the Court of Appeals she is in a position to influence the outcome of cases affecting many individuals, including those in the

LGBTQ community, based merely on her own prejudices and biases. While judges are human and carry with them personal points of view, they are expected to apply the law in an even-handed manner, free of those prejudices. However, associating oneself with a known hate group does not bode well for Ms. Rushing's judicial neutrality.

The second distinction involves *institutional discrimination in the guise of standards of practice*. Here institutional rules and regulations may be promulgated that are at an obvious disadvantage to one subordinate group or another. As part of the Jim Crow Laws enacted by several states after the ratification of the Fifteenth Amendment to the US Constitution (1870), poll taxes were assessed and literacy test administered as a requirement for registration to vote. Each was a method of choice of institutional standards of practice that disproportionately affected the poor and people of color from exercising their fundamental, constitutionally guaranteed right to vote, which had the effect of perpetuating the dominant group's power even though the dominant group may have constituted a minority of the population.

While many of the *overt* forms of institutional discrimination, such as racially or religiously motivated property deed restrictions, have been ruled unconstitutional or been legislated away, *covert* institutional discrimination is the method of choice of those societies espousing democratic or egalitarian ideals. In essence, covert discrimination allows differential allocation between dominants and subordinates while at the same time maintaining the false narrative of fairness. Like individual discrimination, covert discrimination is often very difficult to prove because many may not even be aware that they have been victimized. For instance the practice of redlining or the denying of services, either directly or through selectively raising prices, to residents of certain areas based on the racial or ethnic makeups of those areas, is an example of oftentimes difficult to prove profiling. In our saturated social media age, it should come as no surprise that social media giant Facebook recently was accused by the federal government's Department of Housing and Urban Development with violating the Fair Housing Act of 1968 by permitting advertisers to restrict access to housing advertisements based on user characteristics, such as race, religion, or ethnic origin—a far more contemporary form of redlining.[13] Such practices, while unknown to Facebook users, certainly have negative effects as part of a total environment of discrimination, or what the authors of SDT describe as the "circle of oppression."[14]

The third proximal process that drives group-based social hierarchy, *behavioral asymmetry*, recognizes the differences in behavioral repertoires of individuals belonging to groups at different levels of the social continuum, all of which are partially regulated by what are called *legitimizing myths (LM)*, such as "whites possess superior intellect." Importantly, these behavioral differences both contribute to and are reinforced by the group-based hierarchical relationships within the social structure.

One important point needs further examination. Most structural models of oppression, including classical Marxism, emphasize the manner in which individuals within the dominant group actively oppress and control those within the subordinate group. Even though SDT does not refute this notion, it importantly places emphasis on the manner in which the members of the subordinate group actively participate in and contribute to their own subordination. As a result, systems of group-based social hierarchy are not merely the result of the oppressive activities of the dominant group nor are they simply maintained through the passivity of the subordinate group, rather they tend to be coordinated and collaborative efforts of both dominant and subordinate groups. One need only look to Frantz Fanon's *Black Skin White Masks* to understand this phenomenon, where he relates the story of Jean Veneuse. A black man raised under the yoke of colonialism, Jean disavows his blackness to marry a woman who is white. While the woman's brother consents to the marriage, there is one stipulation: from then on, Jean is not black; he is merely "extremely brown."[15] Oppression for SDT is very much a joint effort.

Having generally outlined the parameters of behavior asymmetry, SDT further identifies four specific varieties of behavioral asymmetry: *asymmetrical in-group bias*; *out-group favoritism*, or *deference*; *self-debilitation*; and *ideological asymmetry*. Asymmetrical in-group bias holds across most cultures because people generally tend to be ethnocentric and favor their own in-group over out-groups.[16] Out-group favoritism or deference occurs when the degree of asymmetrical in-group favoritism is so strong that subordinates favor dominants over their own in-groups. Generally, when stereotypes and low expectations are shared among both dominant and subordinate groups, self-debilitation in the form of self-destructive behavior occurs within the subordinate group. All of these negative stereotypes serve to reinforce certain behaviors in subordinate groups so that the stereotypes become self-fulfilling prophecies.[17]

A much more subtle, and perhaps more prevalent, form of asymmetry occurs in ideological asymmetry. SDT assumes that HE, legitimizing ideologies are related to and driven by one's desire to endorse group-based social inequality and to advocate group-based social hierarchy dominance, or what Sidanius and Pratto refer to as social dominance orientation (SDO), a concept I shall discuss at length later.[18] Consequently, those holding HE social ideologies are more likely to champion social policies designed to increase the level of group-based social inequality while at the same time opposing group-based social policies thought to decrease social inequality. Yet the ideological asymmetry hypothesis argues that the degree to which HE and HA social ideologies and social policies are driven by group dominance systematically varies according to one's position within any group-based, hierarchical structure. In the end, however, "everything else being equal, the social attitudes and policy preferences of dominants are more strongly driven by social dominance values than is the case among subordinates."[19]

LEGITIMIZING MYTHS

While I have mentioned the role legitimizing myths or ideologies play in SDT, a more comprehensive analysis is in order. At the outset, one should not underestimate the important role these myths play in structuring group-based societies and in maintaining social hierarchies. Certainly, Guénon and Evola grasped the power of myth to not only guide society, but to propel it to action. Indeed, every civilization and society promotes its own stories and myths designed to unify the masses, emphasize acceptable moral behavior, lend a sense of identity to what may be otherwise diverse social, economic, and political inclinations, and to provide a point of origin to what many believe is the sacred, divinely inspired homeland. While myths and ideologies play an important role in traditional philosophy, modernity is certainly no different. The themes may have changed since humans first began telling stories around the communal campfire, but it is unmistakable that myths and legends, often associated with heroic actions and godlike demeanor, serve a unifying purpose within the group no matter when they arise. For this reason, it seems that every civilization needs a myth to hold onto.

For SDT specifically, legitimizing myths consist of "attitudes, values, beliefs, stereotypes, and ideologies that provide moral and intellectual justification for the social practices that distribute social value within the social system."[20] Such myths are distinguished by two independent characteristics: their functional type and their potency.

Functional type myths delineate whether a particular myth justifies group-based social *inequality*, and are thus termed *HE-legitimizing myths* (HE-LM) or whether they promote higher levels of social *equality* and are, therefore, referred to as *HE-legitimizing myths* (HE-LM). Examples of HE-LM cover a wide spectrum from those associated with the demeaning negative stereotypes of subordinate racial and religious groups to those justifying measures of inequality under, for example, the vindicating axiom of colonialism's "white-man's burden." While these are quite obvious, there are more subtle forms that oftentimes are more powerful:

> in contemporary U.S. and Western culture, among the most important HE-LMs are the notions of individual responsibility, the Protestant work ethic, internal attributions of misfortunes of the poor, and the set of ideas and assumptions collectively referred to as "political conservatism."[21]

Very similar to traditional philosophy, what is important to garner from HE-LM is the commonly held belief that each individual occupies a certain position, as well as function, along the social status continuum that she rightfully earned and deserves. In effect, this lends credence and a sense of fairness to hierarchical social systems as both legitimate and inevitable.

In contrast, beliefs, values, ideologies, and attitudes referred to as HA-legitimizing myths (HA-LM) directly confront HE-LM. These HA-LM serve to promote higher levels of group-based egalitarianism and are generally associated with various political theories, such as socialism, communism, multiculturalism, and feminism, as well as international legal declarations emphasizing human rights as, for example, the United Nations–sponsored Universal Declaration of Human Rights (1948).[22]

The second aspect of legitimizing myths, their potency, refers to the degree to which such myths promote, maintain, or overturn a particular group-based hierarchy. The potency of such legitimizing myths is a function of four factors: *consensuality, embeddedness, certainty,* and *mediational strength.*

In accord with arguments made by Antonia Gramsci, Emile Durkheim, and Serge Moscovici, consensuality refers to the degree to which social ideologies are broadly shared within the social structure.[23] In particular, SDT argues that consensuality is directed at the degree to which HE-LM and HA-LM are not only shared across the continuum of social power, but within both dominant and subordinate groups. Historically, classical racism promulgated the belief that blacks were inferior to whites. This particular belief was not only prevalent among whites but arguably shared by blacks, which suggests that "from the point of view of system stability, the largest and most important component of antiblack racism is not simply the beliefs held by whites, but rather the antiblack racism shared by blacks."[24] Consequently, SDT postulates that the greater extent to which dominants can convince subordinates to accept self-demeaning ideologies, such as antiblack racism, the less physical force or terror will be necessary to maintain the hierarchical group structure in place.

Embeddedness, the second potency factor of legitimizing myths, indicates whether the legitimizing myth is powerfully associated with and well attached to parts of the ideological, religious, or aesthetic components of culture. For example, the authors argue that antiblack racism is rather well embedded in American culture. As indications of such embeddedness, they point to the reactions individuals have toward the colors black and white. Often associated with concepts such as evil, bad, and fear, the color black stands in contrast to reactions to the color white, which is described in terms of good, truth, and purity.[25] These types of associations are, indeed, well embedded in the psyche of the culture. In the "Golden Age" of Hollywood, for example, it was not uncommon for the "good guys" to be portrayed in white hats while the "bad guys" invariably wore black. Obviously, the actions alone of the on-screen characters was inadequate to always allow the audience to discern good from bad so resort was made to reinforcing factors that were rather simplistic; the difference between black and white hats.

The third indicator of the potency of legitimizing myths, certainty, gives weight to whether any particular legitimizing myth enjoys a substantial degree of moral, religious, or scientific truth or certainty. During the nineteenth century, the belief in the inherent superiority of whites was substantiated through an emerging "scientific" literature, such as that associated with French aristocrat Joseph Gobineau, as well as evolutionary, social Darwinist theories.[26] As both Guénon and Evola make clear, this type of Darwinist "social racism" is still advocated by various individuals and groups and forms one of the foundational aspects of alt-right political beliefs.

Lastly, what is meant by mediational strength is the degree to which a given legitimizing myth serves as a connection between the establishment of group-based social hierarchies on the one hand, and the endorsement of HE or HA social policies on the other hand.

In summarizing the discussion concerning the observations and assumptions surrounding the development of SDT, it is reasonable to assume that human social systems predispose themselves toward a range of group-based inequality. Moreover, the level of group-based social hierarchy tends to stabilize around a given level of what is called the point of hierarchical equilibrium, or the fulcrum between HE and HA forces. Thus, the counterbalancing and mutually constraining HE and HA forces are among the primary factors maintaining hierarchical equilibrium in any given society over time. In fact, in relatively stable social societies, hierarchical equilibrium will be found at the point where the social system is organized in a hierarchical, trimorphic fashion so that the degree of group-based social hierarchy is neither morally offensive nor structurally destabilizing.

Hierarchical equilibrium does not mean, however, that group-based social hierarchies cease to exist. In fact, there are three additional common characteristics of group-based social hierarchies that tend to make them ubiquitous and stable: their increasing disproportionality, their hierarchical consensus, and their resiliency. SDT relies on the work of Robert Putnam to argue that the more political authority exercised by a given political position, the greater the probability that this position will be occupied by a member of the dominant group.[27] Putnam's law of "increasing disproportionality" plays out in all three forms of group-based stratifications: the age system, the gender system, and the arbitrary-set system. An example of what Putnam had in mind is his conclusion that the higher the position held by any given individual in the British government, the greater the likelihood that that individual will have graduated from one of Britain's two elite universities, Oxford or Cambridge. The same can be said, at least historically, for people in leadership roles in the United States. Generally, graduates from elite colleges and universities in the United States disproportionately occupy leadership roles in corporate, social, and political institutions.[28]

Group-based hierarchies are also characterized by their high degree of hierarchical consensus, that is, by the high degree of agreement within the social structure as to which groups are dominant and which are subordinate. Finally, while SDT recognizes that group-based social hierarchies tend to be stable over time, this cross-temporal stability is not absolute. There are times when group-based social hierarchies break down, especially with regard to arbitrary-set systems. Such was the case, for example, in the French Revolution when an attempt at an egalitarian based social transformation was undertaken. However, SDT also recognizes that these so-called social revolutions never succeed. Instead, some new arbitrary-set system emerges to replace the preceding one. Thus, even though one arbitrary-set system is overthrown, the phenomenon of arbitrary-set stratification lives on as extremely resilient. Sartre lends credence to this claim in his discussion of the aftermath of the French Revolution, as the revolutionary group-in-fusion topples the arbitrary-set system of the *Ancien Régime* and then pledges itself to group organization, and in the process inexorably establishes new arbitrary-set systems.

PSYCHOLOGY OF GROUP-BASED DOMINANCE AND SOCIAL DOMINANCE ORIENTATION

Fundamental to the psychology of group-based dominance is the understanding that the human mind both forms and is formed by society. This is true for both SDT and, as we shall see, for Sartre as well. Consequently, it is imperative to analyze the psychology of group dominance through SDO. Defined as "the degree to which individuals desire and support group-based hierarchy and the domination of 'inferior' groups by 'superior' groups," SDO is the most psychological element of SDT.[29] Broadly speaking, SDO concerns all group distinctions that are relevant within any given social structure and context. There are essentially an infinite number of potential distinctions between human groups, but examples usually involve sexual and gender differentiation, race, social class distinctions, religion, nationality, etc. As such, SDO has vast influence over the nature and extent of group-based social hierarchies through, for example, the implementation of HE and HA public policies.

SDO generally features an individual's preference for group hierarchies within the social structure and the domination of lesser-status groups. One can expect a predisposition toward anti-egalitarianism for those scoring high on SDO. Such people are typically characterized as dominant, tough minded, disagreeable, and unable to display empathy for others. Moreover, they usually report being motivated by self-interest and narcissistic self-indulgence.[30] As I have already shown, Traditionalism favors a strong, centralized authoritarian leader atop a socially constructed hierarchy who in all likelihood would score high on SDO.

Sidanius and Pratto articulate four factors that significantly affect SDO. It is argued that SDO is driven by one's identification with and membership in arbitrary, highly relevant, and hierarchically based arbitrary-set groups. It follows, therefore, that individuals who identify with or who are members of the dominant group will possess higher levels of SDO than those who identify with or are members of subordinate groups. Next, an individual's degree of SDO is affected by background and social factors, such as education and religion, as well as practical social experiences, such as military service. Third, there is adequate reason to believe that people are born with different "temperamental predispositions" and personalities, all of which affect one's level of SDO.[31] Finally, gender influences one's level of SDO. Known as the "invariance hypothesis," SDT argues that males have a significantly higher level of SDO than females.

While social class distinctions not only define the primary continuum for social stratification within Europe but also is the group distinction likely to propel social dominance drives, race is generally understood as the primary basis for social stratification and, thus, most likely to engage SDO in the United States.[32] SDT presents an empirical analysis of SDO, which I do not intend to replicate here. Rather, I shall concentrate on the ultimate findings of Sidanius and Pratto's discussion.

Before launching into a discussion of SDO, however, a few preliminary considerations must be undertaken. First, Sidanius and Pratto take pains to articulate SDO as separate from political conservatism. In their analysis, political conservatism, not unlike every political theory, is subject to numerous interpretations and definitions. However, they attempt to lay out a general and broad understanding of political conservatism as including the following factors:

> (a) resistance to change, (b) a political philosophy or attitude emphasizing respect for traditional institutions, (c) distrust of *any* government activism, (d) resistance to centralized government bureaucracy and the promotion of localized control . . . (f) cautiousness and the avoidance of risk taking, (g) the internationalization of parental prohibitions and conformity to socially acceptable beliefs and behaviors, (h) pessimism about the chances of improving people's behavior through social change, (i) opposition to universal suffrage, social and political equality, and popular democracy, (j) opposition to the "excesses" of personal freedom and emphasis on personal responsibility, (k) resistance to planned economies, the promotion of free-market, laissez-faire capital-

ism, and the sacrosanct status of private property rights, (l) support for lower taxes, and (m) the support of "true" religious belief.[33]

None of these definitions of conservative politics overlaps with SDO other than the broad opposition to sociopolitical equality and democracy. It should be noted, however, that many contemporary conservatives reject the argument against social equality of results and instead support equality of opportunity.

Second, contrary to what one might expect, SDO and authoritarianism are theoretically and conceptually distinct as well. Authoritarianism tends be characterized by several traits including, deference to authority, antipathy toward out-groups, rigidly construed hierarchical view of the social world, and resistance to new experiences. Moreover, the triggering point for authoritarianism is usually brought on by threats and fear, and authoritarians generally believe the world is a dangerous and threatening place.[34] Usually predominate in right-wing groups, authoritarianism can be found in left-leaning groups as well. Although SDO and authoritarianism are distinct, they share similarities in that those scoring high on SDO are not only assumed to be relatively racist, sexist, homophobic, ethnocentric, and politically conservative, but exhibit little empathy for those in lower-status groups. Substantiated by empirical research, the difference between authoritarianism and SDO concerns the former's submission to the authority *within* the in-group as opposed to the latter's attitudes toward hierarchical relationships *between* groups.[35]

Lastly, SDO is also distinct, both conceptually and empirically, from standard personality variables. Because SDO concerns one's attitude toward intergroup relations, it is distinct from the concern for one's personal status.[36]

Keeping these preliminary considerations in mind, SDT articulates at least three major influences on how people acquire varying degrees of SDO: *socialization experiences, situational contingencies,* and *temperament*.[37] With regard to socialization experiences, SDO expects that people from dominant groups will exhibit higher levels of SDO than people from subordinate groups. This general observation is supported by the belief that one's general desire for positive self-esteem is compatible with hierarchy-legitimizing myths for those in high-status, dominant groups, which make group superiority seem natural to them. In other words, because societies tend to adhere to social standards that benefit dominant groups, such groups then seem better to most people, which serves to justify the appropriateness of inequality in the minds of those in the dominant group. In support of the thesis that group status is related to SDO, studies have indicated that those in higher-status groups exhibit reliably higher levels of SDO than those in lower-status groups. For example, men, whites, and heterosexuals have higher levels of SDO than women, blacks, Hispanics, or homosexuals.[38] Moreover, it has been shown that SDO is linked to the relative status of groups when there are several stratified groups within a society. Accordingly, in the United States, racial groups ascend in the order Latino Americans, African Americans, Asian Americans, and Euro Americans.[39] Thus, each racial group's SDO level increases in accordance with increasing group status. In the end, not only do individuals possess consistent orientations toward group dominance but their levels of SDO are reliably related to their group status.[40]

SOCIAL IDEOLOGIES, LEGITIMIZING MYTHS, AND SOCIAL DOMINANCE ORIENTATION

The use of social ideologies is one of the most important habits associated with SDO. As I have already discussed with regard to Traditional Philosophy a well as SDT, ideologies are often used to guide actions, justify beliefs and behavior, and help decide the suitability of others' actions. In times of social stress brought on by change, social ideologies play an important role in guiding individuals' actions and behavior. As a result, it is expected that those scoring high on SDO prefer social ideologies that *enhance* group inequality while those who score low on SDO to prefer social ideologies that *attenuate* group inequality. Regardless, "it is the social implications for intergroup relations that ideologies have, rather than their specific contents, that ... orient people toward those ideologies in ways compatible with their SDO levels."[41] To substantiate this claim, Sidanius and Pratto examined several intergroup relations, such as ethnic prejudice, sexism, and political conservatism. In each case, SDO was found to highly correlate with those dominant group's attitudes and beliefs that demean subordinate groups. This correlation appears to be a psychological response to intergroup dominance in every form and not merely a construct based on one particular form, such as racism.

The kinds of beliefs one espouses are also important because they influence whether individuals accept or reject policies designed to impact intergroup relations. Again, the analysis led to two general predictions: First, those scoring highest on SDO exhibit the most opposition to social policies designed to aid lower-status groups or HA social policies. Likewise, they exhibit the most support for social policies that favor higher-status groups, or HE social policies. Second, in an implication for a more specific relationship between SDO and policy attitudes, there is a general expectation that rationales for policies that are HE should appeal most to those with high SDO scores, while rationales for policies that are HA should appeal most to those with low SDO scores. In both cases, ample evidence was shown to substantiate the predictions.[42]

The primary reason that SDO is considered the key to understanding individuals' influence on social hierarchy is that it explains who discriminates against which social groups. In other words, it was found that individuals with high SDO generally apply ideologies that justify their discrimination in favor of group inequality and seek social roles that implement those ideologies. On the other hand, individuals with low SDO generally apply ideologies that justify their discrimination to reduce group inequality and seek social roles that allow them to do so.[43] Affirmative action programs are a prime example. Designed to make up for past periods of discrimination by favoring members of minority outgroups for admission to academic programs, affirmative action has come under increasing scrutiny by whites who were otherwise denied admission. Their claims are based on a litany of alleged abuses including the denial of equal protection afforded by the Fourteenth Amendment to the US Constitution as a form of reverse discrimination that is, in effect, discriminatory or racist toward dominant group members. In fact, a 2015 poll released by the Public Religion Research Institute (PRRI) showed that 50 percent of white Americans believe discrimination against whites is as great a problem as discrimination against minority groups.[44]

In an important statement regarding SDO's use as an indicator of, for example, racism among political conservatives, the authors point out that while SDO is not merely another indicator of authoritarianism, social dominance, or even political conservatism, there is a "mutual commonality" with SDO that largely explains the persistent correlation among such variables. Moreover, even though theorists of what are referred to as "principled conservatism" deny any correlation, political conservatism has consistently been found to be related to racism, ethnocentrism, and nationalistic xenophobia.[45] The argument put forth by the authors of a robust empirical relationship between conservatism and ethnic prejudice is a result of the common psychological motive shared by both ideologies, that is, the desire for dominance of one group over another.

DOMINANT GROUP USE OF IDEOLOGIES TO MAINTAIN CONTROL OVER SUBORDINATE GROUPS

Pursuant to SDT, there are two primary methods in which dominant groups maintain their hegemonic control over subordinate groups: the first is the threat of or actual use of force and the second is control over ideology and legitimate social discourse, in other words, the control of the message. The use of force can prove problematic because excessive force often results in the delegitimizing of the dominant group's right to rule in the eyes of the subordinate group with the result that the subordinate group becomes hardened in its resistance and resentment. Moreover, the use of excessive force may result in unintended consequences, such as the erosion of usefulness of the subordinate group to the dominant group. Consequently, the resort to group-based social hegemony is often more efficiently and effectively maintained by the exercise of ideology and discourse.

Although there are different terms to discuss this phenomenon, they all share a common understanding that ideologies and social attitudes are generally used to convince both dominants and subordinates of the purported righteousness, justice, and fairness of hierarchically organized social relations. Deviating from more standardized traditional formulations of justifying ideologies, the authors suggest that the so-called truth or falsity of legitimizing beliefs is oftentimes difficult to discern, but more importantly have nothing to do with their power to legitimize inequality. In other words, ideologies can justify beliefs whether or not they are true. We witnessed this phenomenon when discussing Evola's use of history to justify the origins of the Aryan races. As I pointed out there, Evola was not terribly concerned with historical accuracy; he was, on the other hand, very interested in providing a heroic story in the form of myth that would attract the attention of like-minded believers.

An interesting example of false legitimizing myths includes the publication of the anti-Semitic *Protocols of the Elders of Zion*. Originally circulated as a secret manuscript depicting a Jewish conspiracy to take over the world by subverting Christian morals, it was subsequently found to have originated in Russia and authored by the Czar's secret police in 1903 with an enlarged edition published in 1905. Undaunted by its apparent fallaciousness, Henry Ford published 500,000 copies of the document in the 1920s. While acknowledging its shadowy origins, Evola wrote a preface to an Italian translation in 1938, which substantially legitimized the content of the *Protocols*. Regardless of the *Protocols'* veracity, what is significant is the degree to which these myths are accepted as true and therefore justified.[46]

The more firmly myths are associated with the basic values and points of view, such as religious, political, and economic as well as social beliefs and ideologies within the social system, the more powerfully they enhance social policy and the more difficult they are to dispel. Yet it is the degree to which these ideologies achieve a level of consensuality within a group that regulates how behaviors are coordinated among members of the group, if and how social practices within the group become meaningful, whether people within the group exhibit psychological security, and whether they provide a mechanism to evaluate people's behavior or the ability to alter course within a group.[47] Such consensual legitimizing myths operate in the following manner:

> while socially constructed groups (ethnic groups, races, genders, social classes, etc.) at different points along the social power continuum are naturally expected to differentially endorse legitimizing ideologies in relatively predictable ways, there remain a substantial portion of these legitimizing ideologies that these socially constructed groups qua groups will still share in common.[48]

While several conclusions regarding the power of legitimizing beliefs are offered by Sidanius and Pratto, only two need concern us here. First, legitimizing ideologies support public policy; that is, they are neither politically nor socially passive. Rather, they play an active, direct role in shaping and developing the type of social policies any society is likely to implement.

A prime example of legitimizing myths, reflecting public policy positions by taking on a life of their own, is President Trump's proposed wall on the southern border between the United States and Mexico. Originating in the 2016 campaign, Trump castigated immigrants from Mexico, saying, "when Mexico sends its people, they're not sending their best. . . . They're sending people that have lots of problems, and they're bringing those problems with us [sic]. They're bringing drugs. They're bringing crime. They're rapists."[49] Exacerbating the claim of criminality and general inferiority, this myth became something almost sacrosanct to Trump and his followers as it morphed from campaign rhetoric into a "national emergency." To support the need for a wall, the administration increased its negative rhetoric to allege that the United States was under "invasion" from caravans of innumerable undesirable migrants whose swelling ranks included terrorists and members of the notorious MS-13 (*Mara Salvatrucha*) gang—none of which was ever verified.

A wall—not unlike a container—Trump argued, was the only means to protect American citizens from the onslaught of the inferior people from the south. However, a major means of reducing intergroup prejudice is through optimal intergroup contact, which has been found to diminish prejudice by reducing intergroup fear and by promoting empathy. It is, therefore, significant that growing evidence points out that white Trump supporters experience less contact with minority groups than other Americans, which tends to confirm their biases toward those groups.[50]

A second important aspect of consensual legitimizing ideologies is their ability to serve as conduits, or mediators, between the desire to assert and maintain group-based social hierarchy and opposition to redistributive social policies.[51] The authors argue that beside direct influences, the desire for group dominance, or SDO, not only has a direct but also an indirect or mediated effect on the social policies as a result of single or multiple consensual legitimizing myths.

Before concluding the discussion on SDT, I want to briefly explore an area of particular concern, institutional terror and the legal system. While I have previously discussed aspects of this topic, I want to focus explicitly on what SDT has to offer.

INSTITUTIONAL TERROR AND THE LEGAL SYSTEM

The question has arisen as to why minorities are disproportionately imprisoned in the United States. SDT attempts to answer this question, based on which one of three models of the law one chooses: the *value consensus model*, the *pluralistic model*, or the *class conflict model*. The value consensus model views the law as impartial in its expression of the common will directed toward the common good.[52] Under this model, one accepts that the law in general and the criminal justice system in particular serves to maintain societal order and mediate between competing group interests in an impartial manner. This is the primary model for most Western democratic societies where the dominant group generally believes that all citizens are granted the equal protection of the law by the criminal justice system. Pursuant to this model, it is argued that the overrepresentation of minorities in prisons is simply because they commit more crimes.

The pluralist model, on the other hand, emphasizes that the promulgation and enforcement of laws in any society is a compromise between competing social and economic interests of rival elites, and are not for the benefit or promotion of the common good.[53]

Lastly, the Marxian class conflict model argues that the law is a reflection of the will of capitalist owners designed to protect their economic interests at the expense of the common good. It can be argued that in both the pluralist and the class conflict model, the law is seen as an instrument to protect and advance the power and prestige of the hegemonic group while at the same time restricting the power of subordinate groups. Much like Thrasymachus's definition of justice in the *Republic* as the advantage of the strongest, these two models can be thought of as a general dominance approach to law. Under these models, the overrepresentation of minority groups in prison is the result of the dominant group's desire to maintain its power in the social hierarchy.

Rather than adopting either one of these models, SDT argues that there is substantial truth in each. The law does function in the interest of the common good, but it also functions to maintain and protect the interests, status, and privileges of the dominant group in power. The use of the law and the judicial system to maintain dominant group hegemony at the expense of subordinate groups was recently illustrated by a shocking admission published in *Harper's Magazine* in April 2016. John Ehrlichman, President Richard Nixon's domestic policy advisor, declared that the administration's war on drugs was squarely aimed at two enemies,

> the antiwar left and black people. You understand what I'm saying? We knew we couldn't make it illegal to be either against the war or black, but by getting the public to associate the hippies with marijuana and blacks with heroin, and then criminalizing both heavily, we could

disrupt those communities. We could arrest their leaders, raid their homes, break up their meetings, and vilify them night after night on the evening news. Did we know we were lying about the drugs? Of course we did.[54]

Some may argue that the war on drugs originated as a random legal reform policy and is not indicative of a flawed legal system. However, SDT argues that the errors committed by the judicial system are not merely random in nature or unsystematic; rather, they are clearly systematic and inseparable from the exercise of power by the dominant group. Mr. Ehrlichman's statement poignantly bears this out. Thus, the law performs two simultaneous functions: it maintains *and* reproduces group-based social order.[55]

As I have already discussed, the authors argue that terror is the primary means by which the social hierarchy is maintained, a position Sartre also shares. While many think of terror as the use of abject violence by a small band of individuals intent on obtaining political goals, terror can also be state sponsored where it is usually directed toward the suppression of the activities of subordinate groups thought of as posing a threat to the continued power of the dominant group. SDT identifies three forms of terror: *official terror, semiofficial terror,* and *unofficial terror*.

The first form, official terror, is more prevalent than the other two in democratic forms of government, and is generally thought of in terms of the legally sanctioned and publicly displayed violence and threat of violence perpetrated by the state's security forces (generally the police) or the justice system.[56] While an active role is usually played by the police, the primary means of terror in its official form is through the criminal justice system. For various reasons, SDT was not able to demonstrate this type of discrimination through controlled field studies, but rather it utilized case records, archival data, as well as other methods to show institutionalized discrimination against subordinates as both powerful and compelling.[57] After sifting through the various data and records, SDT determined that societal institutional discrimination occurs pursuant to five so-called law of laws, each applicable across a multitude of systems.

The first such law, *the disproportionate prosecution principle*, says that, when society's laws are violated, regardless of the nature of the crime, the level of negative sanction (e.g., incarceration, harsh penalties including capital punishment) directed against subordinates will be greater than that against dominants, everything else being equal.[58] The second law of laws, *the out of place principle*, indicates that when subordinates are accused of violence against dominants, the perpetrator faces a particularly high risk of being found guilty and suffering severe punishment.[59] The reason for this law is twofold: hierarchical based organized social systems invariably consider the lives and well-being of dominant group members more valuable than subordinate group members. More importantly, the violent acts of subordinates against dominant group members are considered not just a breach of civil order but an attack on the established sociopolitical system.

The third law of laws, *the social dominance orientation/social role congruency principle*, argues that within the criminal justice system, the level of SDO among hierarchy enhancers will be relatively high, while the level of SDO among hierarchy attenuators will be relatively low. According to this law, one might expect that police officers, as hierarchy enhancers, would show a high level of SDO, while others in the criminal justice system, such as public defenders, might show just the opposite. This is, in fact, the case.[60]

The fourth law of laws is *the tolerance of abuse principle*, which states that "the degree of negative sanctions against security forces for abuse of power will tend to be exceedingly small, especially in cases of abuse against subordinates."[61] In the past several years, there have been numerous cases of force used by local police against members of subordinate minority groups. Some of this force has been excessive resulting, for instance, in the death of unarmed members of minority groups, yet relatively few individual police officers face sanctions for their behavior. As Phillip Stinson, a criminologist at Bowling Green University who studies arrests of police, says, "to charge an officer in a fatal shooting, it takes something so egregious, so over the top that it cannot be explained in any rational way."[62] In effect, police officers find themselves almost invulnerable to either dismissal or prosecution as a result of civilian complaints for excessive force or brutality.

Lastly, the fifth law of laws, *the hierarchy-terror principle*, argues that "the greater the degree of social hierarchy, the greater the use of formal and informal terror there will be."[63] Ideological consensus alone is not sufficient to assure that hierarchical social structures will remain in place. Ultimately, threats and the use of actual force are necessary to maintain the power structure. Subordinates may accept ideological consensus for a time, but that consensus eventually breaks down with subordinates resenting and eventually resisting their place in the social hierarchy. Therefore, the more hierarchical the social structure, the greater degree of terror will exist within the society.

Sidanius and Pratto offer these five laws of laws to substantiate the claim that criminal justice systems are more likely to be used as an instrument of terror against subordinates than dominants. If this hypothesis proves correct, then subordinates should experience the criminal justice system as more threatening than dominants do. It should come as no surprise that their evidence clearly supports this hypothesis.[64] Interestingly, however, the authors found that while there is ample evidence to show that subordinates are more likely to face harsh sanctions within the criminal justice system than dominants, the principle applies only to arbitrary-set systems and not to age or gender systems.

The evidence presented by SDT indicates that while many argue the law and the judicial system is value neutral, this is not the case. Consequently, the law must be seen as a mechanism through which the rights and privileges of the dominant group are sanctified and protected, and, at the same time, the manner in which those laws are brought to bear on the weaker subordinate groups.

NOTES

1. Jim Sidanius and Felicia Pratto, *Social Dominance: An Intergroup Theory of Social Hierarchy and Oppression* (Cambridge: Cambridge University Press, 2001), 31, hereinafter referred to as "SDT."
2. Ibid., 32.
3. See Pierre van den Berghe, *Man in Society: A Biosocial View* (New York: Elsevier, 1978).
4. SDT, 299.
5. Ibid., 33.
6. See, generally, Judith Brown, "Economic Organization and the Position of Women among the Iroquois," *Ethnohistory* 17, no. 3/4 (1970): 151–67.
7. SDT, 38.
8. Ibid. (emphasis added).
9. Muri Assunção, "Detroit Man Sues Three Women Who Allegedly Filed Reports against Him for 'Gardening While Black,'" *New York Daily News*, March 6, 2019, https://www.nydailynews.com/news/national/ny-news-detroit-gardening-while-black-20190306-story.html.
10. SDT, 127.
11. Alan Blinder and Richard Pérez-Pena, "Kentucky Clerk Denies Same-Sex Marriage Licenses, Defying Court," *New York Times*, September 1, 2015, https://www.nytimes.com/2015/09/02/us/same-sex-marriage-kentucky-kim-davis.html.
12. *Alliance for Justice (AFJ) Nominee Report: Allison Jones Rushing*, https://www.afj.org/wp-content/uploads/2018/10/Rushing-Full-Report.pdf. See also Southern Poverty Law Center, *Extremist Files: Alliance Defending Freedom*, https://www.splcenter.org/fighting-hate/extremist-files/group/alliance-defending-freedom.
13. Katie Benner, Glenn Thrush, and Mike Isaac, "Facebook Engages in Housing Discrimination with Its Ad Practices, U.S. Says," *New York Times*, March 28, 2019, https://www.nytimes.com/2019/03/28/us/politics/facebook-housing-discrimination.html.
14. SDT, 129.
15. For a further discussion of the relationship between Fanon and Sartre, see William L. Remley, "'Can You Justify Your Existence Then? Just a Little?': The Psychological Convergence of Sartre and Fanon," *Diogenes* 61, no. 1 (2016): 44–58.
16. See William G. Sumner, *Folkways: A Study of the Sociological Importance of Usages, Manners, Customs, and Morals* (Boston: Ginn and Co., 1906).
17. Robert Merton, "The Self-Fulfilling Prophecy," *The Antioch Review* 8, no. 2 (1948): 193–210.
18. SDT, 302.
19. Ibid., 45.
20. Ibid.
21. Ibid., 46.
22. The United Nations Office of the High Commissioner of Human Rights lists almost twenty conventions and declarations concerning issues of human rights promulgated and adopted by the United Nations General Assembly. The subject matter of these declarations and conventions extends to issues such as migration, rights of wom-

en, genocide, the rights of children, and human rights in the administration of justice. See www.ohchr.org.

23. Gramsci's idea of "ideological hegemony" in Antonio Gramsci, *Selections from the Prison Notebooks*, ed. and trans. Quintin Hoare and Geoffrey Smith (New York: International Publishers, 2018); Durkheim's concept of "collective representations" in Emile Durkheim, *The Division of Labor in Society*, trans. G. Simpson (New York: Macmillan, 1933); and Moscovici's notion of "social representations" in Serge Moscovici, "Notes toward a Description of Social Representations," *European Journal of Social Psychology* 18 (1988): 211–50.

24. SDT, 47.

25. Ibid.

26. Joseph Arthur de Gobineau (1816–1882) championed the scientific construction of racism as well as the superiority of the Aryan race. In his *Essay on the Inequality of the Human Races* (1853–1855), Gobineau argued that aristocrats were superior to the masses because they experienced less inbreeding with inferior populations, a theme echoed by advocates of traditionalism. Many of Gobineau's theories were adapted by the Nazis for their own racial theories.

27. Robert Putman, *The Comparative Study of Political Elites* (Englewood Cliffs, NJ: Prentice Hall, 1976), 31–35.

28. See, for example, Lauren A. Rivera, *Pedigree: How Elite Students Get Elite Jobs* (Princeton, NJ: Princeton University Press, 2015).

29. SDT, 48 and 61.

30. S. Levin, C. Frederico, J. Sidanius, and J. Rabinowitz, "Social Dominance Orientation and Intergroup Bias: The Legitimation of Favoritism for High-Status Groups," *Personality and Social Psychology Bulletin* 28, no. 2 (2002): 144–57.

31. SDT, 49.

32. For a discussion of class in America, see Nancy Isenberg, *White Trash: The 400-Year Untold History of Class in America* (New York: Penguin Books, 2016).

33. Ibid., 72–73 (emphasis in original).

34. Thomas Pettigrew, "Social Psychological Perspectives on Trump Supporters," *Journal of Social and Political Psychology* 5, no. 1 (2017), 108.

35. Ibid., 74.

36. Ibid., 76.

37. Ibid., 77.

38. Ibid.

39. Ibid., 78.

40. Ibid., 81.

41. Ibid., 84.

42. Ibid., 89–93.

43. Ibid., 95.

44. Robert Jones, Daniel Cox, Betsey Cooper, and Rachel Lienesch, "Anxiety, Nostalgia, and Mistrust: Findings from the 2015 American Values Survey," *PRRI*, published November 17, 2015, https://www.prri.org/research/survey-anxiety-nostalgia-and-mistrust-findings-from-the-2015-american-values-survey/.

45. Ibid., 97. See also Jim Sidanius, Felicia Pratto, and Lawrence Bobo, "Racism, Conservatism, Affirmative Action, and Intellectual Sophistication: A Matter of Principled Conservatism or Group Dominance?," *Journal of Personality and Social Psychology* 70, no. 3 (1996): 476–90.

46. Julius Evola, "Preface to 'The Protocols of the Elders of Zion,'"https://evolaasheis.wordpress.com/2016/04/14/preface-to-the-protocols-of-the-elders-of-zion/.

47. SDT, 106.

48. Ibid., 123.

49. Michelle Ye Hee Lee, "Donald Trump's False Comments Connecting Mexican Immigrants and Crime," *Washington Post*, July 8, 2015, https://www.washingtonpost.com/news/fact-checker/wp/2015/07/08/donald-trumps-false-comments-connecting-mexican-immigrants-and-crime/?utm_term=.597dca090d92.

50. See, generally, Thomas Pettigrew and L. Tropp, *When Groups Meet: The Dynamics of Intergroup Contact* (New York: Psychology Press, 2011).
51. SDT, 118.
52. Ibid., 204.
53. See Thorston Sellin, *Culture, Conflict, and Crime* (New York: Social Science Research Council, 1938).
54. Dan Baum, "Legalize It All: How to Win the War on Drugs," *Harper's Magazine*, April 2016, https://harpers.org/archive/2016/04/legalize-it-all/.
55. SDT, 205.
56. Ibid., 206.
57. Ibid., 207.
58. Ibid.
59. Ibid., 214.
60. Ibid., 217–18.
61. Ibid., 218.
62. See Kimberly Kindy and Kimbriell Kelly, "Thousands Dead, Few Prosecuted," *Washington Post*, April 1, 2015, https://www.washingtonpost.com/sf/investigative/2015/04/11/thousands-dead-few-prosecuted/?noredirect=on&utm_term=.0d098a97da93.
63. SDT, 219.
64. See, generally, Michelle Alexander, *The New Jim Crow* (New York: The New Press, 2012).

FIVE

Group Formation, Hierarchy, and Human Freedom in Sartre's *Critique of Dialectical Reason*

Sartre's *Critique of Dialectical Reason* is notoriously difficult. Written over a three year period and finally published in 1960, the *Critique* is thought to be Sartre's political manifesto, but more realistically it is a culmination of his political thought from a very early age that gained enormous traction in the post war period. The book engages in many subjects, but the area I want to concentrate on is Sartre's concern with group formation. In that process he takes us from what he calls the human collective, or living our lives in impotency where everyone is only tangentially aware of the other's existence. This fundamental human condition alters in the face of necessity or need and calls on humans to band together for a common purpose by forming groups not only for individual protection but ultimately for the survival of the group through unity. Along the way, Sartre details various stages of group development delineating both their positive, but more importantly, their adverse effects on intragroup dynamics.

While SDT concentrates on intergroup relations, Sartre expands our understanding of groups by pealing the veil from the question why groups act the way they do, what causes hierarchies to form once groups organize their praxis and eventually institutionalize themselves. And importantly, why those institutionalized groups accept a cult of personality so relevant to alt-right politics of today.

COLLECTIVES AND SERIALITY

The discussion of group formation starts with the immediate experience of individual human existence in what Sartre calls, the "collective." As the foundational basis upon which groups emerge within the social realm, collectives are comprised of passive individual participants with relations of *exteriority*. As I stand shoulder to shoulder on the narrow, crowded subway platform, the complete stranger next to me expresses his anger that the trains are once again delayed. Ever polite and not wishing to offend, I concede to his ire by expressing my solidarity before quickly turning away. Even though we have shared a momentary interval, our relationship is purely superficial residing on an abstract plane as passive isolated individuals with no specific personal relationship—once our brief conversation ends, I shall neither see nor talk to the stranger again.

Groups, on the other hand, are characterized by their *interior* relations of individual reciprocity and their pure praxis striving to eliminate all forms of inertia such as my encounter on the subway platform.[1] Accordingly, collectives are characterized by their *passiveness*, while groups are inherently *active*, and here, Sartre uses the word social in its broadest context, which means that social structures exist in either a collective or group form.

Sartre reminds us that in the abstract, the collective is not the aggregation of isolated individuals joined together by external circumstances. On the contrary, I am always in a social environment even if that situation is totally superficial such as my encounter on the subway platform. Yet the collective should not be thought of as united in common purpose because, at this stage, there simply is no common purpose. Other than getting on the next train, I have virtually no commonality with the aggrieved stranger on the subway platform. The collective, then, is what Sartre calls the "interpenetration" with the material environment in its passive and inert dimension. The passive inertia associated with collectives synthesizes all relations of reciprocity so that they are intrinsically altered to one of exteriority, or what Sartre refers to as a "pseudorelation of reciprocity." Consequently, the unity of the members of the collective does not depend on active human involvement, but exists outside of human thoughts and actions. The collective is thus understood by its *being*, which should be thought of in terms of a disposition or even habitual behavior, where the multiplicity of individuals is constituted in their passive synthesis. Every day I wait for the same train on the same subway platform alongside a multitude of other riders who will always remain anonymously the same, even if we are united by the tardiness of the next train.

COLLECTIVES AS SERIES

An initial aspect of the collective is that it structures individual existence as a member of a series where each member of the collective ensemble is determined in their alterity by the other. Similar to my waiting for the subway, Sartre illustrates his serial structure of human behavior through the mundane experience of waiting in line for a Parisian bus.[2] The concern here is with a multitude of isolations. The queue constitutes everyone in their interchangeability with everyone else, where the social ensemble produces each individual as united with his neighbor in an effort to get on the bus. In such an environment, the unity of the group lies outside of itself in a future object where everyone is determined by a common interest (the destination where the bus takes them), and where the only differentiation from others is through one's own materiality.

At this stage, human relations are neither one of conflict nor one of reciprocity; they are abstract moments of identity with a certain, albeit limited, common interests. Sartre argues that material objects (in his example, the bus) determine serial order as the social reason for the separation of individuals: simply stated, there is not enough room on the bus for everyone in the queue. The scarcity of space is a systemic problem and, unlike a Marxian understanding where there is generally just enough, for Sartre there is always too little.

To avoid conflict, although conflict may occur, practices arise whose sole purpose is to create a system of social order. A machine dispenses a ticket indicating my time of arrival at the bus stop, which concomitantly designates the order of my entry onto the bus. This means I remain in the terrain of common interest as passive activity, and implicitly accept the impossibility of deciding whether I should or should not get a seat on the bus in terms of my "intrinsic qualities."[3] After all, I may be elderly, disabled or pregnant; the system does not take those qualities into effect when I get on the bus. While the ticket imposes a serial unity as my common interest, its intent is to eliminate conflict. The seriality of the queue is, therefore, not a structured reality; it is a gathering with a contingent number of participants where everyone is other because there is merely a dispersion of separate bodies for everyone. No matter the ordering procedure used, seriality derives from what Sartre refers to as practico-inert matter as an ensemble of equivalent possibilities.[4] As a result, we are locked within the "Formula of the Series" that acts as:

> a dynamic scheme which determines each through all and all through each. *The Other*, as formula of the series and as a factor in every particular case of alterity, therefore becomes, beyond its structure of identity and its structure of alterity, a being common to all (as negated and preserved interchangeability) . . . finally, it is the passive Unity of the multiplicity in so far as it exists in itself; it is the reinteriorization of exteriority by the human ensemble, it is the being-one of the organisms in so far as it corresponds to the unity of their being-in-themselves in the object.[5]

Much like Sidinaus and Pratto argue for SDT, the Formula of the Series means everyone determines everyone else, but at the level of collective existence each is determined in his passive unity of the multitude through a process of interiorizing the exteriority of the human ensemble. Unity of the ensemble is, however, paramount. The system imposes upon the serialized collective a sense of order which, in turn, means those waiting in the queue experience a sense of unity in anticipation of the soon to be arriving bus.

At this stage, the glue that holds the series of bus riders together is a bond of impotence because it is the other who decides whether my action remains individual, or whether it becomes the action of the group. In a crowded elevator, for example, no one takes the first step to push the lighted button because to do so means reaching over and between hordes of unfamiliar protruding arms, legs, and backpacks to be the first to push the button. The other always decides who will go first, and the other determines whether my actions remain an individual initiative of abstract isolation or whether they become a common action of the group.

The alterity of the collective fashions, in Sartre's mind, its own laws: what everyone believes about the other is what the other conveys because they are other. Serial being, as a practico-inert reality, is then a process of development, caused by a force of exteriority, which results in actualizing the series as a temporalization of the masses in the fleeting unity of a violence of impotence.

An essential element to the collective is Sartre's notion of collective praxis. The common structure of collectives is objectified praxis where the practico-inert field negates that praxis and replaces it with passive activity that becomes the common structure of collectives. At this stage, there are two distinct praxes at work: individual praxis and the group as praxis. Individual praxis is collective praxis because it is part of a seriality of praxes interwoven with alterity and impotence. However, if seriality is rejected, then the unification into groups can occur through group praxis. In this field, everyone's actions disappear and are replaced by what Sartre terms a "monstrous force."[6] The practico-inert force tries to appropriate individual freedom by a transformation that it imposes on objects; in other words, by the transformation of free praxis into passive activity.

A bit more is necessary to understand the importance of the practico-inert. As a practical matter, it surrounds us and conditions us; we need only look out the window to see the hundreds of exigencies rising up to greet us: road signs, pedestrian walkways, notices, prohibitions, exact positions for buses to stop and lanes prohibiting taxicabs. While the commonplace experiences of the practico-inert are readily recognized, this field operates on a different level as well. Most importantly, the practico-inert includes both the seen and unseen apparatuses of the state and government as institutions, including the police and judicial systems. As I discussed with regard to SDT and the oppression associated with institutional terror and the legal system, upon entering the practico-inert environment, I become its thing. In fact, the constraints of need, the exigencies of the worked thing, the demands of the Other, and my own impotence are all revealed to me and interiorized by me by the practico-inert. As such, the practico-inert field envelops my activities in a weblike existence; one that is inherently difficult to escape.

This means that my free activity lived as my freedom, takes upon itself everything surrounding me including the oppression and exploitation of everyday life. In short, my freedom is the means chosen by the thing and by the Other to crush me and transform me into a worked thing. As a result, freedom does not engender the possibility of choice, but the necessity of living these constraints and exigencies through praxis. It would be wrong to interpret Sartre as saying that humans are free in all situations as he asserts in *Being and Nothingness*. In fact, he means quite the opposite: "all men are slaves in so far as their life unfolds in the practico-inert field."[7] Sartre understands that human reality everywhere encounters resistances and obstacles not of its own creation, but these forces have meaning only in and through the free choice which is human reality. The practico-inert field represents a real servitude to "natural" and "mechanical" powers and to "anti-social apparatuses," where everyone struggles against an order that literally and figuratively crushes them and which sustains itself by the very struggle against it.

For Sartre, seriality, characterized by its otherness, is the fundamental type of sociality. Naturally, any social group that forms will either embrace practico-inert reality or oppose it. Sartre points to two basic forms of seriality in the *Critique*, first the collective itself and later seriality returns in his discussion of the institution, but in a much different form. However, it is important to recognize that the collective is the paradigmatic construction of unity in exteriority because the collective object constitutes our exterior unity.

What Sartre is attempting to convey is the notion that in this situation relations between humans are not those of true, positive reciprocity as they are in groups; rather, they are essentially what Nietzsche terms the "mass" or the "herd" where the collective reacts like a thing mechanically producing and reproducing the environment it inhabits. Serialized individuals within the collective are just that: isolated and superficially connected. As we shall see, Sartre's second degree of sociality—the group—occurs when the mass of individuals unifies through their participation in a common project. The act of "fusion" marks the movement from seriality to group as the birth of social freedom, and here I want to make a key point: this movement grounds Sartre's claim that humans are freer in society than alone. In the group, everyone is what he calls sovereign, just as everyone is impotent in seriality.

Before entering into a discussion of groups, I want to move to one other example Sartre utilizes in his discussion of collectives and that is the world of public opinion, which he says is an important topic from the point of view of rulers. Sartre thinks that public opinion "tends to be seen as a collective consciousness arising from the synthetic unification of the citizens into a nation, and imposing its representations on everyone as an integral part of the whole, just as the totality is present in each of its parts."[8] What interests Sartre is not every day public opinion, but public opinion run amok. The Great Fear of 1789, which caused widespread chaos and destruction in the countryside of France in the immediate aftermath of the early phase of the French Revolution, is the example he points to. In the chaos and uncertainty of the revolutionary moment, peasants were seen by their fellow countrymen and those in authority as bandits and foreigners. Even though outlaws had always existed, at this precise time they, as well as many poor peasants, took on a particularly sinister persona, as dangerous criminals. Fearing that anybody one might encounter could be treacherous, survival became paramount, which ultimately resulted in violence.

This unchecked fear, however, should not be understood in terms of mass hysteria or merely actions perpetrated by one individual against another. Sartre argues that fear propagates itself in a serial fashion as a "material wave" with its own laws and temporality. In normal times, the future approaches me as made by others with the possibility of being remade by others as well. While I ordinarily do not recognize myself as alien, in the case of public opinion, where seriality is triggered, I encounter the future not only in the guise of an alien humanity, but as a dangerous alien humanity. I do this because I fail to reflect critically on my actions; rather, I willingly accept without challenge whatever comes my way, including the so-called alien other. I enter into the series accepting the fact that the alien other is evil and dangerous and that, to survive, I must become something other than what I customarily am. In essence, my worst fears are realized despite all evidence to the contrary; in fact, it is a self-fulfilling prophecy because I would not believe any evidence to the contrary presented to me. But Sartre also believes that the conditions of possibility for this wave of fear already exist within the practico-inert because it is part of the very fabric of alterity and seriality.

Oftentimes, in our more contemporary politics, those advocating certain positions utilize fear to engender support. The alt-right is no stranger to this tactic. The rhetoric surrounding the immigration issue plays upon people's concern not only for their personal well-being, but in a not so subtle manner for their very existence, including a desire for a type of idealized life they wish to live even if facts argue against such positions. I also discussed this phenomenon with regard to conspiracy theories. Here too, the one advocating or living out such theories sees the other as alien and acts without reflecting on their actions just as Edgar Welch did when he stormed the pizza parlor with an assault rifle in hand.

The question then arises as to why facts do not seem to change our minds. Humans are naturally social animals; in fact, solitary confinement is generally devastating to the human psyche. The answer lies, perhaps, in the human desire to avoid problems associated with living in socially formulated collaborative groups. And one way we attempt to succeed at that process is by embracing information that supports our beliefs and rejects any information to the contrary. Known as "confirmation bias," the process shows up most palpably in the current political divide where neither side is willing to admit that the other is correct about anything. The process unfolds through traditional media such as newspapers or television cable news programs, but more likely the vast amount of information we receive comes from a myriad of other sources such as the internet, like-minded friends, or social media. To substantiate our beliefs we may pick friends, who share our political beliefs and avoid those who do not, or we may become addicted to some extreme group's ideology found on the internet, or we may only watch particular news programs geared to our political beliefs. Fox News or CNN is the obvious dichotomy.

A downside of confirmation bias is the fact that we often believe we know more than we actually do. Within our own group of similarly believing people, our *milieu* is very homogeneous, which means that our trust is placed in like-minded people who do not challenge our most deeply held political beliefs. On the contrary, they reinforce whatever those beliefs happen to be, however superficial. And if my beliefs are superficial, but my friend agrees with me, then we both hold superficial beliefs. This "illusion of explanatory depth," becomes dangerous if, for instance, I am asked whether I support a particular social program such as the Affordable Care Act, more commonly known as Obama Care. I may adamantly oppose the program, but when asked to fully elaborate why I oppose it, or the effects my opposition will have on the more than twenty million people enrolled in the program, I may be at a loss to fully explain my attitude.[9]

The Great Fear with its theme of public opinion—the actions of the herd—is a fundamental starting point for Sartre's sociopolitical analysis of colonialism specifically and racism generally. It also plays a role in group behavior, especially in the institutional group where seriality again resurfaces.

GROUPS

From his more abstract discussion of collectives, Sartre begins to elaborate upon groups and their formation. Even though a group need not emerge, the collective gathering presents the conditions for the possibility of forming a group through its serial unity. We have seen how the collective gathering with a structure of seriality is the basic form of sociality, but when a common danger or need arises then groups invariably form. This leads, however, to a vicious circle because neither need nor some common objective defines a group unless it makes itself into a group by transforming individual need into common need, and by making those common objectives the common objectives of the group.

Although groups may become permanent, unlike collective structures groups come and go, they disintegrate and die, they ossify without dissolving into more generalized socialites. They are what Sartre refers to as metastable structures of ensembled groupings that are both praxis and practico-inert constituting and defining any social field.

When Sartre turns to groups, he defines them by their undertakings—their praxis—with their constant movement of integration that tends to turn them away from collective, practico-inert seriality and embrace pure activity. As Sartre delves into group formations within a society, he begins with a description of seriality as the contrast between the fundamental human relationship of reciprocity importantly viewed as a relation of interiority (groups) and the isolation of the individual as a relation of exteriority (seriality within a collective).

I should make it clear at the outset that the moments of Sartre's structuration of the social—collective, series, group-in-fusion, statutory group (pledged group), organized group, and institutionalized group—do not represent stages in a general linear, historical evolution or in the evolution of any particular type of society. They coexist as particular instances of a given existence. In any given social ensemble, there exists the practico-inert in either its serial, or collective form, or in the group. Likewise, the serial or collective exists in every similar ensemble and constitutes the initial substratum, the passive determination by socioeconomic facts of every form of sociality, with groups representing the "erosion of seriality."[10]

While praxis defines the group, absorption back into the practico-inert is a constant threat. For example, a social class has characteristics of both the serial and the collective as far as it is a passive mass of interest imposed as chance by the external realities of socioeconomic conditions. Similarly, it pertains to the group-in-fusion to the extent it establishes itself as unorganized action common to all (common action), to the statutory group as diffuse power of authority, to the organization in, for example, a political party, and in the institutionalized group to the extent it becomes the dominant class, with its own institutions. Consequently, the practico-inert is ever present, even if the group is also present.

THE GROUP-IN-FUSION

Storming the Bastille, the "beginning" of the French Revolution, provides an example of Sartre's thought. Before the act, the crowds live their lives in seriality where the superficial bond between them is one of alterity. They may inhabit the same space—the district of *Saint-Antoine*—but in their quasi-reciprocity they neither know each other in any concrete sense nor do they act as a "community." Everyone sees their own future and discovers their present action in the Other, but as inert movements. To overcome this inertia something more is required, and the act of taking up arms against a perceived attack by the King's troops galvanizes the gathering and transforms the passive reactions of seriality into an Apocalyptic, revolutionary praxis.[11] Freedom, so important to Sartre's work, manifests itself in the dissolving of inert passivity of the series by the "simple positive determination of *praxis* organized on the basis of its real objectives (defense against the troops of the Prince de Lambesc)."[12] After all, the Bastille is where the guns are and the urgency to confront the enemy, who may arrive at any moment, is the new necessity.

This transformation from series to group-in-fusion is, however, still amorphous, still unstructured. In fact, because it is a work in progress as "fusion," it remains a series negating itself in reinteriorizing exterior negations. The group-in-fusion emanates from the collective because its structure is developed over time where the exact circumstances of the situation determines the speed in which it is formed and how long it will last. The impact is quite clear, however, at the moment of Apocalyptic "fusion," there is no distinction between the group-in-formation and the series-in-dissolution, yet this event completely transforms social relationships and inaugurates social freedom.[13]

There is a key element to this fundamental stage of group development. While the district of *Saint-Antoine* is still a practico-inert structure, within the group-in-fusion it is now differentiated because it possesses a general awareness of an impending emergency formed by the common objective of getting to the Bastille ahead of the King's troops. The practico-inert structure not only makes the group-in-fusion, through everyone, the unity of all, it also makes it a structured unity through its suggestion of an initial differentiation of function and division of labor. In other words, the group-in-fusion is quite capable of eventually organizing itself into a hierarchical structure. Likewise, just as the nascent group is about to coalesce, albeit in its metastable form, the conditions necessary for preventing the group-in-fusion from falling back into an impotent collective are also emerging. Sartre's example of the group coming into existence by the liquidation of an inert seriality under pressure from external circumstances does not, however, ensure that the process actually ends in a group. Before the attack, the people of Paris inhabited the same space, but afterwards the residents of *Saint-Antoine*, who may just as likely live their lives as collective, are now an "alter ego" for each other by the external action of an organized group, the soldiers of the king.

It is not enough, however, that groups emerge from gatherings due to some apocalyptic event. Again, Sartre's analysis requires much more because the possibility for unity is only one aspect, it is also necessary that the instruments for snatching it from recurrence should be present. The concept Sartre inaugurates seems quite modest and clear: everyone is a third party for everyone else. In its application, however, this seemingly simple concept asserts an enormous impact. For Sartre, the third party is structured *a priori* as the Other, and through the third party practical unity, as the negation of the threatening organized danger, reveals itself by what he calls the "constellations of reciprocities."[14]

THE THIRD

If a group is to emerge from the former collective structure of seriality, then the question becomes if completely isolated individuals—whether as a result of institutions, social conditions, or as purely inadvertent acts—seem to possess relations of absolute exteriority, why is it then that in their very separation their concrete and historical bond is one of interiority? Simply stated, how does individual praxis become group praxis? Sartre argues that the answer lies in the operation of the "third" as the party of mediation, with all of its complex ramifications.

If the example is seemingly straight forward, the consequences are anything but: Sartre is standing at a window overlooking a walled-in garden adjacent to a road. Peering out the window, he notices a gardener busy tending her flowers, and, separated by the wall, a road mender equally at work repairing the highway. As the *mise en scène* unfolds, the wall is adequate in its height and bulk so the two workers are completely unaware of the other's existence just as they are unaware of Sartre's voyeuristic gaze.

Because we inhabit the same world, the universe unites everyone as a whole. The simple fact of seeing what the other does not see establishes, in Sartre's perceptual field, a relation of reciprocity transcending his perception. The mutual ignorance of the gardener and the road mender only come into being with Sartre's (as the third) mediation. Standing in his window, he constitutes them as a reciprocity of ignorance, which is not a subjective impression. The two workers are not ignorant of each other *because* of Sartre, they are ignorant of one another *through* Sartre to the same extent he is ignorant of them *through* them; each is for the other an implicit reality. In Sartre's abstract analysis, each of the workers, through their work, produce themselves as a certain exposure of the world that objectively makes them the product of their own product. They each affirm the unity of the world by inscribing in it through their work and through the particular unification this work brings about. In effect, each "discovers" the other as an object actually present in the universe within one's own situation because ignorance becomes reciprocal through the third.[15]

Sartre's example highlights his notion that the organization of the practical field in the world determines a real relation for everyone. This means unification only comes about through praxis, which is itself unified within this field by the unification of the other, or as Sartre puts it, in accordance with the *"plurality of unifications."*[16] This new moment of the contradiction between the unifying unity of praxis and the exteriorizing plurality of human organisms Sartre labels the reciprocity of relations. In the *Critique's* more sociological discussion of organized groups, we shall see how the organization unifies reciprocal relations through function. At this level, however, each of the three parties in Sartre's example stands as a center in relation to the other as a point of escape, and as unified by the other. Importantly, while this is also a negation of interiority, it is not a totalizing unification. As it is for SDT, the emphasis here is the assertion that the foundation for all human relations is the immediate and perpetual determination of everyone by the other, and by all.

Regardless of what the third party does or does not do, each of the two strangers produces their being in the presence of the other, but always within a human social world. Therefore, reciprocity takes on a permanent structure of every object defined by collective praxis, which allows the integration *of* everyone *by* everyone to the extent of their integration into the other's project. Reciprocal ternary relations are, consequently, the basis for all relations between humans whatever form they may subsequently take. Essentially, this means that the fundamental and structural human relationship is a relation of interiority. At this stage, relations of reciprocity as well as ternary relations are not totalizing; rather, they are multiple adhesions between humans that, as Sartre says, keep society in a "colloid" or gluttonous state.

Returning to the Bastille once again, the residents of *Saint-Antoine* made themselves into a group, but at the same time, their real membership in the district is serial, manifested in the inertia of alterity. They still have not undertaken the one thing that is able to transcend this contradiction: action.[17] But at a particular moment, whether out of political zeal or mundane curiosity, the residents begin to venture into the streets and gather about, still in a mode of seriality but now with a quasi-intentionality.

At this point, the concept of the third party becomes essential because the third is praxis, yet the third is also sovereignty as "nothing but freedom positing itself for itself."[18] It is the third who no longer embraces the pseudo-action of the serial structure—escaping the impending danger by blending back into the practico-inert. Rather, the two contradictory aspects of other and the third party are now directly opposed in an indissoluble unity of praxis. The third becomes sovereign through praxis, but more importantly, the third is the organizer of the actions of the group turning individual praxis into common praxis. Most likely, one does not wish this eventuality; it just happens; the situation designates the outcome. In other words, the real possibility of attack by the King's soldiers spontaneously motivates me, as well as all others, to act. At that very instant, the third party unifies the gathering multiplicity and makes it a group. There is one cautionary note, however. Through the group, "I indicate myself as a *necessary culmination* of the totalizing action; but this operational indication never actually has its effect."[19] I am neither fully integrated into the group that has been realized through praxis, nor am I totally outside the group. What Sartre has in mind is the situation where I see my immediate neighboring protestors as we march along the street, but I cannot see every one of the thousands of protestors marching along with me. However, through my very act of protesting I synthesize, or bring together, the actions of protesting of everyone wherever they may be.

The group has transformed, no longer a binary relation of individual to community, it is now a ternary relationship. Indeed, my group of protestors possesses a common reality, and, at the same time, it is a mediation between myself and every third party. Even though relations of simple reciprocity exist because of the common action of my group, these relations, though transfigured by their being-in-a-group, are not constitutive. The reason lies in the fact that all members of my group are third parties, and, as such, each individual member totalizes the reciprocities of all the others.

This is what Sartre terms mediated reciprocity, which is both the mediation of the group between third parties and the mediation of each third party between the group and third parties outside the group. Consequently, when I join the group, my bond is, as every other third party, one of interiority. This internal, synthetic constitution of me by the group is really totalization returning to me to give me my first glimpse of the collapse of seriality, and it confers this quality upon me as power.

By now it should be clear that mediated praxis is never solipsistic; it is always regulated by the third. Within the group, I am not alone in carrying out the operations that form the group; in integrating the ensemble of individuals into the group and in revealing by my action the unity of group praxis, I produce every third party as a mediation between the group and any other third party. Accordingly, I am integrated into the common action of the group when the common praxis of the third party posits itself as regulatory. However, the group does not constitute itself-for-itself; rather, Sartre sees the motivational force behind the group as what he calls terror. Those in *Saint-Antoine* would not depart from their otherwise mundane but relatively safe collective structure and embrace the unknowns of the group, if the threat of terror or terror itself had not surrounded them. The freedom of protest reconstitutes itself as common violence against the practico-inert character of the established regime, and its future objectification is, as Sartre says, "the free violence of men against misery and the impossibility of living."[20]

For Sartre freedom is, as the sovereignty of individual praxis, not violence but the reorganization of the environment. When alienation is unmasked, freedom assumes the structure of its own impossibility in the form of necessity. Here, in the group-in-fusion, a sliding scale of freedom and alienation emerges. At the level of the group-in-fusion lies a type of freedom, which in Sartre's analysis is the least alienating. A key element is that the group-in-fusion emerges from serial impotency, or our lives lived in anonymity. Once the Apocalyptic event occurs and the fusion of the group commences, Sartre says the task is at hand such as storming the Bastille. If the goal is achieved, the participants may return to their seriality. But they do not necessarily have to do so.

In fact, a return to the serial is of no interest to Sartre. His enquiry focuses on the case where the individual members of the group do not disband but stay together. The consequences of those actions absorb Sartre's thoughts as the group asks itself a key question: should the group survive, how would it act? As we shall see, at this exact moment, the scale of human freedom begins to tilt in another direction toward alienation and oppression at the expense of freedom, a movement that appears to be unstoppable and ultimately proves the downfall of freedom.

THE PLEDGE (THE PLEDGED OR STATUTORY GROUP)

The victory of the protestors brings with it a new reality: what shall we do now? How can the group survive? As with the Bastille, the conquering of the fortress, the taking of its guns—however few in number—represents a victory for the district of *Saint-Antoine*, but the moment it passes it signifies merely a preservation of the past glory of the group. At this moment, with the dangers that precipitated the liquidation of seriality temporarily vanquished, the regulatory third party has little to regulate. The urgency that once helped fuse the group together now dissipates, with a concomitant breakdown in group behavior. To stem the apparent dissolution, the group begins to envision itself in its past glory; it takes itself as its own end, first implicitly and then explicitly. The focus shifts as the group itself becomes the common objective for everyone, and not the Bastille. The permanence of the group is now imperative, and unity takes precedence over all other considerations. Sartre gives voice to the structure of the unity of sociological group formations, but, more importantly, the consequences they invoke.

Sartre sees the actual conditions of survival of the group driving it back into a contradiction: the common objective achieved through common *praxis* manifests itself as freedom in the form of violence leading to the destruction of that common objective. The very cause that brought the people out of the safety of their homes and into the uncertainty of the street has now disappeared. If the group is to continue, it must comprehend that:

> *praxis* is the only real unity of the fused group: it is *praxis* which creates the group, and which maintains it and introduces its first internal changes into it. In the moment of the *praxis* of organization and anticipation, it is the group which guarantees that every separate action is a common action or, to put it differently, it is the group as a reality which produces the unity of the common *praxis*.[21]

The fear of dispersal of the group, fueled by distrust and suspicion, is internalized as the danger of seriality, which means the ontological statute of the surviving group is initially the practical contrivance of free, inert permanence of common unity in everyone. When freedom emerges as common praxis, it provides the foundation for the group's permanence by producing its own inertia through itself as well as through its mediated reciprocity in a new statute, or what Sartre refers to as the pledge (*le serment*).[22]

While it can take many shapes, the pledge is still mediated reciprocity; however, unlike Hobbes it is neither a social contract, nor is Sartre describing the basis for particular societies; rather, he is explaining the necessary transition from the immediate form of the group in danger of dissolution to another form, which is reflexive as well as permanent. The pledge is an inert determination of the future, not as a possibility, but a practical device. In effect, when I swear an oath it results in my assertion that the dispersal of the group in the future is an impossibility. Furthermore, through its creation of a fictitious inertia—the pledge is behavior as immediate praxis, and is mediated praxis whether spoken or silent—the group freely turns itself into a tool to guard against a return to seriality that would threaten its very existence.

The curious part about the pledge is that I give it freely out of fear, both of the third party and of myself. At this stage, my fear is isolation from the group as well as from everyone else. Thus, the pledge brings with it a sense of community and comradery as the still nascent group transforms itself from an unorganized, rudimentary praxis of the group-in-fusion into what Sartre calls a statutory group. And, at the moment it is given, the pledge assumes a critical role as a diffuse power of jurisdiction or control of all over all that manifests itself in reciprocal rights and duties, and, as we shall see, it continually reaffirms itself whenever group unity tries to break down. "The *common* characteristic of the individual (or one's being-in-the-group) becomes everyone's juridical power over individuality in himself in every third party."[23] Sartre explain that:

> the framework of the pledge provides the multitude of rights and duties of third parties: now, all these abstract moments of concrete exigency are given together in my way of acting, of realizing my function through my action and of basing my action on my powers: the right which the group has through me over all, and the duty towards the group as defined by all, the reciprocity of right (I have the right that you should assert your rights), that of duty (my duty is to remind you of yours), that of right and duty(I have the right that you should allow me to do my duty), that of duty and right (I have the duty to respect your rights) — the infinite complication of these reciprocities . . . these lines of force may appear, as a form, against the synthetic background of all the others; but if they are not all present, the group will break up.[24]

For Sartre, law is the mechanism of cohesion of the social group organized for its permanence through the pledge, which demands a level of predictability of practices on the part of its members, and necessitates a differentiation of tasks to achieve a common goal. At the same time, and seen from a different point of view, Sartre recognizes that:

> the law is a response to certain social disturbances or to a strike that has just taken place. It shows, at this precise moment, the given (and singular) relationship between the various forces. . . . Moreover, it singularizes and realizes on a specific point the conception of the State that the sovereign formulates: i.e., in the last resort its political praxis; and this in turn reflects in depth the historical conjuncture (i.e., once again the relationship of forces, but envisaged in the light of economic and social "whole" and the direction of socio-economic changes), which is — at its own level — equally singular. Thus the decree or law has this dual character of determined indetermination.[25]

Much like SDT theorized, as a relationship of forces, law fashions apparatuses of state and sovereign authority in a determined and, at the same time, undetermined manner designed merely to enforce the sovereign will, which in most instances represents the dominant group. The pledge within the statutory group provides the foundation upon which the group begins the process of establishing a sense of order, a structure based on an ever expanding concept of law and rules. The nascent seeds of institutionalism are sown the moment I take the pledge.

Through my regulatory actions, the pledge becomes a modification of the group. When I swear an oath, through my mediated reciprocity, I guarantee the others will also swear and thus not abandon the group. But I also swear to protect myself. As such, my pledge is not a mere free act describing my future behavior. Rather, it acts as an enforcement mechanism negating any possibility that I may change my mind regardless of the circumstances.

While the twofold structure of fear is the origin of the pledge, in reality the problem no longer emanates from the original danger that brought the group together in the first place. The present danger is the gradual disappearance of common unity because of a number of special interest subgroups participating in the main group. The pledge itself provides the answer to the dilemma facing the group: by pledging one to all and all to one, the group recreates its project by substituting "a real fear, produced by the group itself, for the retreating external fear, whose very distance is deceptive."[26] Yet a different fear could arise again should subgroups come into conflict. Should this possibility arise, and Sartre thinks it will, within the institutional group one subgroup will seek to dominate the other through a process of eradication.

The portrayal of group formation takes a dark turn at this point. The regulatory third party reveals that the diminishing fear of external danger is the real threat to the group's existence; the only remedy is an increasing anxiety of destroying the group itself. Regardless, the ultimate goal is to protect the unity of the group, but at present, there is no external pressure requiring concerted action.

The only course left for the group is to produce itself as a material pressure on its members. Here again, violence as terror comes into play. The very act of pledging is itself the common production of violence through mediated reciprocity: once I pledge myself, the group must guarantee my freedom against attack even at the cost of the life of another member. Sartre elaborates by saying "everyone's freedom demands the violence of all against it and against that of any third party as its defense against itself (as free power of secession and alienation);" in short, to swear is to say as a common individual: "you must kill me if I secede."[27] The aim of the pledge is, therefore, to instill terror within myself as a free defense against the fear of the enemy. The pledge serves to remind me that in actuality violence is the diffuse structure of my group. In the end, my death is a certainty should I decide to betray the limitations of being-in-the-group.

Sartre justifies this violence by saying transcendence is present in the pledged group as an absolute right of all over every individual. The free attempt to substitute the fear of all for the fear of oneself and of the Other in and through all the members of the group further justifies the need for violence within the pledge, but only in so far as the pledge suddenly reactualizes violence as the intelligible transcendence of individual alienation by common freedom. This does not imply, however, that the structures of freedom and reciprocity disappear. Quite the contrary, they take on their full meaning once they appear in the material movement of terror. My pledge is still a guarantee for the third party, but it is a guarantee whose meaning is violence. In a word, the fundamental statute of the pledged group is terror.

Does this mean a terror so thick that death at the hands of the group's members of those who transcend the group is not problematical but certain? Well, not exactly. Sartre maintains terror is situationally determined. That is, if circumstances are not "especially restrictive" I remain at the level of exigency and untranscendability. I perceive the exigency as my committed freedom in the other. However, if the pressure increases, either from external or even internal sources, I still freely consent to my own "liquidation" as free constituent praxis. I freely consent, therefore, to the right of the group over my actions.[28]

Only the group itself can arguably decide if one of its members transcends its boundaries, but as we progress this factor alone becomes murky, especially as the group seeks to institutionalize itself. It is worth noting, what constitutes an act of betrayal—a transcendence of the group's praxis—is by no means explicit.

The statute of the pledged group is crucial to an understanding of the *Critique*. In a fundamental way, the pledge elucidates "the original *practical, and created* (and constantly re-created) relation between active men within an active community."[29] The permanence of the group-in-fusion, constructed in concrete circumstances, is never reduced to natural occurrences, spontaneous acts, or immediate relations. The permanent group only arises when external circumstances occasion a reflexive praxis within the surviving group. As a result, and to keep it in line, the members of the group establish themselves as a community acting on itself, but this also means that violence as terror is at all times and in all places the initial common statute. Uniquely, however, terror unites instead of separates:

> indeed, in so far as these men have constituted themselves by their pledges as *common individuals,* they find their own Terror, in one another, as *the same; here and everywhere* they live their *grounded* (that is to say limited) freedom as their being-in-the-group, and their being-in-the-group as *the being* of their freedom. In this sense, Terror is their primary unity in so far as it is the power of freedom over necessity in everyone.[30]

Being-in-the-group is, therefore, the intermediary step between free common praxis and seriality. In effect, it is the statutory guarantee that I will not relapse into the practico-inert field, and that my individual action escapes alienation to the extent it becomes common. As Sartre reminds us, as a reflexive construction, this guarantee is everyone's solicitude for everyone, even if this solicitude is a bearer of death.

While it may be difficult to believe, there is a positive aspect here and it is highly significant: through this solicitude and as a common individual I am created as a new entity. We all unite in a bond of brotherhood where our group-being is lived as a nature of freedom within a fraternity, which establishes itself as the real bond between common individuals in the form of untranscendable reciprocal obligations. The relationship is one of:

> fraternity, that is to say the fundamental, practical structure of all the reciprocal relations between the members of the group. What is later

> called comradeship, friendship, love—and even fraternity, using the term in a vaguely affective sense—arises on the basis of particular circumstances and within a particular perspective, for a given reciprocity as a dialectical, practical enrichment, as a free specification of this original structure, that is to say, of the practical, living statute of the sworn members. This constituted group is produced in and by everyone as his own birth as a common individual and, at the same time, everyone can grasp, in fraternity, *his own birth as a common individual* as having been produced in and by the group.[31]

Sartre is pointing out that when I join a group, I probably do so to socialize with like-minded individuals. In the process of assimilation, the comradery of fraternity emerges as a driving force. While I undergo that process, I seek not only to accept but positively espouse the group's convictions and norms in order for me to further entrench myself into the group. Oftentimes, groups require uniforms as a way to set the members apart in the eyes of nongroup members, but they also distinguish the hierarchical structure of the group within its members—my uniform may have more medals than yours. Although Sartre couches his notion of fraternity in agreeable terms, such as friendship and love, one should not be misled. Fraternity is very much the right of all through everyone and over everyone. We should not lose sight of the fact that the origin of fraternity is violence, and it is unmistakably violence reaffirming itself as a bond of immanence through positive reciprocities; it is what Sartre labels, "Fraternity-Terror."

For Sartre, this allows us to comprehend the intensity of the group's action arising from the equally powerful external threats to the group's existence. If the perceived real danger no longer exists, then the passion shared by the members of the group dissipates. In such a case, the group resorts to the artificial substitute of Terror. But Fraternity-Terror also plays a role not only in my desire to be a member of the group but to adhere to the beliefs and convictions of the group as a bond of brotherhood.

THE ORGANIZATION OF THE GROUP

The pledged group, with its ontological structure of Fraternity-Terror, gives rise to the organization. In Sartre's lexicon, the word organization refers both to the internal action by which the group defines its structures and to the group itself as structured activity. Simply put, an organization is a distribution of tasks among individuals, and through which the group defines, controls, and constantly corrects its actions. What interests Sartre is the relation between the action of the group on itself, and the action of its members on the objective of the group. This undertaking leads Sartre to a new definition of the common individual within the organized group, which allows him to examine the "logistics" of organized systems and further describe their structures. The result is an articulation of a new human, social product he calls *passive-activity*.

As I previously pointed out, at the level of the group-in-fusion, the common individual interiorizes the multiplicity of third parties and unifies that multiplicity through praxis. Moreover, the common characteristic of the individual's being-in-the-group is everyone's juridical power over that individuality in himself and in every third party. This is still an abstract power, however. Only at the level of organization does this abstract and essentially negative power become concretized and act as a positive force as it defines itself for everyone in the context of the distribution of tasks. In a word, it is *function*.[32]

As function, it is still an inert limit of the freedom of the third party and remains Terror. In organized activity, however, either the entire group assigns function to the individual or some organ of the group makes that determination. Regardless, the person assigned a particular function carries out a certain task and only that task. In one sense, function retains its negative purpose: I have a certain role in the organization, but that does not mean I can perform any role within the organization. Thus, the meaning of any particular undertaking lies in the use made of it elsewhere in the undertakings of other members of the organization.

In Sartre's analysis, as an integrated member of the group, the common individual is dependent entirely on the mediating moment of praxis. Thus, the process of organizing the group itself is an operation the group performs on itself as it distributes tasks among its members as functions. Played out in the form of action on its members, the group's main purpose is to perpetually organize and reorganize itself. As a result, function determines the right-duty tension established by the pledge because "function defines itself both as a task to be carried out (an operation defined in terms of the transcendent object), and as *a relation* between each common individual and all the Others."[33]

Because this right-duty tension exists strictly as a human relation of interiority, the group passes from one sustained by fluid homogeneity to one of regulated heterogeneity. Within the community, alterity reappears once again, and within the organized group, the alterity of its members is both created and induced by them. Even though a flexible and reciprocal group may maintain order, the concentrated authority of a definite office or fixed function curtails individual freedom. While it was only beginning to emerge in the pledged group, the organized group invariably needs leaders, and as we have seen in SDT, once this occurs, a hierarchical social structure takes over the group. Predictably, some will be at the top while others will occupy the bottom rung of the socially constructed ladder.

The pledged group produces a bond of sociality as freedom in the guise of common praxis, which, in turn, creates concrete forms of human relationships. Every function has both a negatively defined reciprocal relationship that limits competences, and a positively defined relationship of necessary and possible action. The implication is a transformation from function as common individual, defined as everyone's being-in-the-group, to a new level of the organization where being-in-the-group is no longer an abstract, multifaceted determination of human relations; but the organized relation uniting me to everyone else.

The "cost" of this human relation, Sartre observes, may be quite high: a rigidity based on inertia emerges within the group. The members adopt limits with the aim of leaving nothing undetermined. Hierarchy now defines relations within the group, but more importantly the group determines competences, which means, as a functional individual the relationship I enjoyed with all those in the group-in-fusion is forever changed. For instance, if I am member of a certain out-group who joined the struggle in the group-in-fusion's siege of the Bastille and stayed in the group to take the pledge, I may find myself, when group functions are determined, at the bottom of the social hierarchy. As a result, I will never have the same type of relationship I experienced in the group-in-fusion with those who now occupy the top of the hierarchy. Because the unity of the organized group is always defined by its concrete objective, the relations I have as a common individual within an organization and the one who leads the organization, must be constantly created within the limits dictated by the tangible tasks ahead of us, and solely with a view to the success of our efforts.

A concomitant feature of the hierarchy is the establishment of roles for each of the group's players. The role I assume locates me in a hierarchy that is both concrete as well as representational, and in this sense—regardless of whether I reside at the top, in the middle, or occupy the bottom like most of my fellow group members—I will never be outside the hierarchy. The role I play initiates me into the group, it imposes the group's mechanization upon me as structure, it requires sacrifice of me, but fundamentally my role seeks to construct a behavioral unity within the group as I, along with all others, seek to identify myself with the role I now play. Even if my role is mundane and commonplace and decidedly not at the top of the hierarchy, I should not forget that to live without a role is to not live at all.

The organized group is, as we have seen, a complex circularity of mediated reciprocities. In comparison to the group-in-fusion's mediated reciprocity that emerged from praxis itself in the spawning movement of the group, at this point in the organized group a new level of reciprocity emerges. The pledge itself assumes the position of reciprocity, but this reciprocity produces in me a limitation of my freedom.[34]

This is what Sartre terms *worked* reciprocity because it allows inertia to affect practical freedom. Each pledged member of the group uses mediation by the group to transform the otherwise free spontaneous relation that appeared earlier. Once the pledge is given, however, reciprocity becomes centrifugal. Instead of being a lived bond between two individuals, it is now the bond of their absence. Whether in my isolation or as a member of a subgroup, I derive my guarantees and imperatives from the inertia affecting common individuals whom I no longer interact with or even see. As a result, reciprocity is not the living creation of bonds, but a reciprocal inertia. At the level of the pledge, I may rebel against the separating power of inert materiality, but I also interiorize it. My reciprocity, as an inert limit on my freedom, comes to me from the outside and exists in me as worked matter.

Up until this point, Sartre has examined the *conditions* of common action but not common action *itself*. That is, action is not only singular as individual action; it is singular with regard to the objective as well as in relation to its temporality. But, are individual praxis and common praxis homogeneous? Sartre argues they are because it would not be possible for the individual to understand either his own common action in terms of group praxis if the structures of common praxis were of a different order than those of individual praxis.[35] The common aim of the group is always doubly common: there is an interest defining the group as valid only for this particular group and is, accordingly, only accessible through it.

This section of the *Critique* shows Sartre working his way through the question of how and importantly why individuals come together to form groups characterized by reciprocal social structures. Just as critical are the consequences of those organizing activities. Sartre thinks humans are naturally social, but he also sees sociality capable of bringing about the alienation of its members through successive and ever increasing modalities of oppression. These "monstrous forces" curtail human freedom and require adherence to the group, its goals, and ultimately its leaders. Sartre is anxious to expose this troubling side of group formations, complete with pledged and organized structures. Yet, as we shall see, should the organized group evolve into an institutionalized group, that group would exemplify the fears and inherent dangers posed to individual freedom in any group where functions are institutionalized.

We must now ask where the process leads, or does our group merely remain in the realm of organized functionality. While this is possible, in Sartre's scheme it is equally the case that the group disintegrates and returns to the impotency of the practico-inert, but I have already shown this is unlikely. More realistically, the organized group continues to develop, and Sartre now enters into the structured environment where alienation overtakes freedom as the organization strives to unify itself by institutionalizing itself.

THE INSTITUTIONALIZED GROUP

As Sartre moves from the organized praxis of the group and enters the realm of group institutionalization, we witness the disintegration of common, individual freedom. The group must survive, and Sartre continues our journey back to the impotency of the practico-inert, as the sovereignty of the group comes to reside in a single individual who alone takes on the role of the untranscendable third. The road back to the impotency of seriality within the institutionalized group is, however, not exactly the same as it was when standing in the queue waiting for the bus, or when I encountered the angry stranger on the subway platform.

Within the institutionalized group, the term "atomization" does not convey the correct situation of individuals dispersed and alienated by institutions. As an individual, I cannot be reduced to the absolute solitude of the atom even though institutions attempt to replace concrete relations between people with at best tangential and at worst disconnected associations. Even within a group structure, such as the institution, a collective can still emerge. Simply put, it is not possible to exclude me from all forms of social life at this stage of social development. Like everyone I ride the subway, I buy groceries, and I work and interact with other people. Even so, the collective structure, represented by the institution, addresses me as a member of a series—the series of subway riders, the series of grocery shoppers, the series of workers. Individuals, then, become identical with all the other members, differing only by the serial number assigned to each in whatever form.

At this stage, the being-in-the-group undergoes another transformation or, as Sartre describes it, we again discover a new statute of intelligibility as the organization, whose foundation is the pledge and whose structure is the heterogeneity of function, moves toward institutionalization. Those of us who are now members of the organized group have a reciprocal relation to all others within the group. At this level, the group is already organized and functional because we have ostensibly come together to produce a given result through our organized group praxis. Consequently, but unlike my membership in the group-in-fusion, the others' regulatory act or their common individual behavior does not arise in me.

I am formed, trained, and equipped in such a way as to foresee my future action in the action others undertake. All of us are situated in a common field, based on a common objective and, in fact, under common conditions, making each of our individual actions regulatory for the other. Under these conditions, the structure of our regulatory acts, while complex in nature, provides a limited affirmation of our freedom however transitory it may be.

This does not mean that the exercise of sovereignty is complete. Sartre posits the limit of sovereign synthesis as the reciprocal bond existing between the other and myself because my situation is the same as the other and, in effect, it constitutes both of our situations. The limits of sovereignty prove to be its very reciprocity, but Sartre does not think that no one is sovereign. In fact, each of us is sovereign over the sovereignty of all the others in the group, and at the same time, we are the organized object of all the other's practical synthesis because we are both quasi-sovereign and quasi-object. As a result, the group itself is in a state of perpetual disorganization or disunity. In this situation, the relation between the other and me is a simple modality of intersubjectivity because it is the other who integrates me into the group as I reciprocally integrate the other. We are, again, each other's alter ego. At this point, everyone is determined in their inessentiality in relation to the group by integrating the sovereignty of the other. In order for this to occur by means of the alter ego, everyone posits themselves in their irreducible essentiality as the guarantor of the other's membership in the group by means of the pledge.

When I take the pledge, through my regulatory action I am the object of a mediated integration by the other. Through my obedience to the group, I produce all others as quasi-sovereign as well as quasi-excluded from the group. At the very moment I ground this quasi-sovereignty through mediated recognition of my powers and the other's functions, I produce myself as regulatory and I also realize myself as quasi-exile or quasi-sovereign, just like all the others. As members of the group, we are all beings-in-the-group manifested through a double failure: each of us is as unable to depart the group, as we are equally unable to completely integrate ourselves into the group. However, our being-in-the-group does actually exist because the group unites us through our "pledged inertia." My freedom is other through the mediation of everyone else.

Sartre thinks the untranscendable conflict between the individual and the common naturally establishes new contradictions within the organized group. Where the previous pledge gave rise to the institution, new contradictions help to transform the institutionalized group into a steadfast hierarchy. As I have pointed out, however, within every organization a certain malaise surfaces, which carries with it an uneasiness that tends to strengthen the integration of the group. This leads to the common individual who is, as a group individual, defined by the practices of all the members of the group in terms of a determinate function, power, and competence. Sartre is essentially indicating that the common individual assumes a juridical and ceremonial status just as the group devolves into a system of rights and duties (in the form of a legal system) in its quest to become more unified through institutionalization. Associated with this juridical status are, among others, class or ethnic distinctions. As the group solidifies its hierarchical structure and, in fact, legally sanctions it, ingroups and outgroups naturally emerge.

At this level, the group operates quite differently than it did as an organization. In fact, each function performed by the common individual is now inessential or merely "relatively essential." Sartre explains that:

> no individual is essential to a group which is coherent, well integrated, and smoothly organized; but when anyone realizes the mediation between the common individual (who has no real existence except through the organic life of the agent) and the object, he reaffirms his essentiality *in opposition to the group*.[36]

For example, if I deem my function and thus myself to be essential to the group, I remove myself from it. On the other hand, if I remain inessential as the common individual I neither betray the pledge nor transcend the group, I merely perform my function. There is a slight "catch," however. Even when I remain inessential, a new fear arises within me as a common individual because in a way I transform myself through my powers and responsibilities into a new isolation.

The fear Sartre speaks of this time is not the fear encountered in the group-in-fusion that initiates the pledge out of concern the group may dissolve by default; rather, the fear is now dissolution through excess—I may be in the group today, but I might be outside the group tomorrow. In this situation, the pledge is powerless to ameliorate the fear as it did before for the simple reason the fear arises from pledged fidelity itself. This means the group maintains itself through ritual recognition of others within the group, which leads to a way of living one's own being-in-the-group as a constant but disguised separation. Accordingly, as subgroups form within the group, there may be an element of recognition by the dominant group of the inferior group, but it will most likely be of a deferential, superficial quality. Even though they may not overtly wish the destruction of those they dominate, the dominant group will not wish to mingle, and to avoid the possibility of such contact they will resort to all kinds of protective devices including an impenetrable barrier. While Sartre does not address this problem, walls, or other protective barriers not only keep people out, but they prevent intergroup contact essential to ameliorating oppression.

The group seeks, therefore, the protection of a space or a barrier, a protective wall that identifies its being as what Sartre describes as a "container." This container creates in the common individual an interiority as a spatial bond between the container and its contents—between myself and all the others in the group—as a mystification. "If the group is protected by a wall, for example, then I may see myself as *being really in it*, but this only means that I identify its being with that of its container."[37] But what is actually realized by "everyone is interiority as a spatial bond between the container and its contents *in its inadequacy* and as an anonymous mystification."[38] Once again, I may be inside the container now, but I am afraid I may be outside at any moment. In grasping the full extent of my quasi-sovereignty, I am fearful the social organization, whether it is large or small, may expel me for whatever reason or no reason at all.

It is true that the container establishes a social bond between those within its confines, but it also produces two quite different but allied outcomes. On the one hand, the container keeps those deemed undesirable away from those in the container. Fearful of a physical invasion, those within the container seek refuge where their beliefs, convictions, and style of life are unaffected by those of a supposed lesser quality. Gated communities, exclusive clubs and other socially restricted endeavors tend to lessen intergroup as well as intragroup contacts that only exacerbate feelings of privilege and bias. On the other hand, and even though Sartre often talks about an actual death the pledge implies, the death I subsequently suffer is more like a death of exclusion from the group, which in many ways is more insidious than actual death itself. Simply put, physical death presents a finality lacking in mere exclusion from any group. In Sartre's analysis, we are all fundamentally social beings who yearn for nothing more than to interact with other social beings. Carried to its extreme, our fear of exclusion is as much a real fear as it is a psychological trauma. However misanthropic I may be, in the Sartrean world, isolation is not a condition I readily accept.

Sartre emphasizes this development as a key to understanding his notion of sovereignty because once freedom, and here Sartre is denoting freedom as the dissolution of inertia found in everyone in the serialized collectivity, becomes afraid of itself,

> and discovers in anguish its individual dimension, the dangers of impotency and the certainty of alienation which characterize it, and the regulatory third party has become a regulated, integrated, third party, integration by the Other will be revealed to it by dislocated reciprocity both as a danger to sovereignty (through the reification of the group within the practical field of a single individual) and the danger of exile (which means a danger of being killed—for the third party seen in his implicit secession—as well as a danger of betrayal).[39]

At this moment, freedom gives way to the fear of alienation and removal. My being-one of the group depends on my individual freedom, which constitutes itself now as the movement of exclusion, physical liquidation, and betrayal as real possibilities for me. As suffered inertia, my separation from the group only reinforces pledged inertia as it increases the tension between sovereign exile and impotent dependence. The organized group, through its own freedom, develops a circular form of seriality. As it does so, the "group creates itself in order to create, and destroys itself by creating itself."[40]

The fear of separation-secession causes the group to react with new practices as it transforms itself into the form of an institutionalized group whose very organs and functions become institutions. The group seeks a new type of unity by institutionalizing sovereignty so that the common individual once again transforms himself into an institutional individual. For Sartre, we have reached a decisive point: the community becomes "degraded" because the origin of the group, founded on the effort of individuals to gather together to dissolve seriality in themselves, now produces *alterity* in itself as it freezes into a lifeless form. In a startling turn of events, Sartre describes a journey that has traveled full circle: we have retreated toward the practico-inert from which Freedom-Terror of the pledge removed us.

CONFLICT WITHIN THE PLEDGED GROUP: SUBGROUPS

Sartre now turns his attention to the details of institutionalized group dynamics. As I have pointed out, within the organization the distribution of tasks falls on individuals, but within any pledged group, including the institutionalized group, the distribution of tasks is eventually assigned to specific subgroups. Such a structure oftentimes gives rise to disagreements.

Sartre initially notes, "every internal conflict takes place between pledged individuals and against the synthetic background of fraternity-terror."[41] Moreover, the conflict itself arises in the name of group unity each opposed party claims to represent exclusively. As a result, the conflict pits common individuals, transformed by the pledge, against each other. Even though the opposed subgroups may exist harmoniously except for the dispute itself, Sartre sees conflict as the only real form a group-in-activity embarks upon, but the underlying cause of the dispute may be as simple or banal as over competency within the group.

As we saw in the discussion of the organized group and its initiation of functions, each subgroup is defined by the task assigned to it to be carried out, which imposes a right-duty obligation wherein one subgroup has both the right to perform their function as well as the duty to carry out their function. Should one subgroup claim authority over the function thought to be the domain of another subgroup, conflict arises. The cause of the conflict either results from a lack of specificity as to whose function is responsible for the object of the dispute, or an indeterminacy of competencies within the group.[42] But a conflict could arise should a deemed inferior subgroup seek to invade the function of a dominant subgroup. Even though functions may be indeterminate, contradiction will not necessarily always appear. After all, neither subgroup may pursue its claim against the other, especially if institutional systems are in place to impede conflict. Only at the exact moment, "when *the same matter* is claimed by each subgroup *against the other*" will the conflict ignite.[43]

The conflict over function produces the contradiction between the subgroups, and, as a result, individuals themselves decide if they can coexist with other individuals. Yet, at this stage, and for as long as the struggle continues, there will be within the subgroups an illusory notion that the conflict is resolvable. As a result, the struggle between the two competing subgroups takes on a dual character: first, it freely realizes conflict and, at the same time, it mediates between the two contradictory terms of nontranscendable inertia. Second, and as a direct result of the first characteristic, the common determinations derived from the group's external actions and internal consequences are now lodged within the common individual. In other words, the conflict has hardened within the minds of the members of the group.

The key to understanding the issue between the two subgroups revolves around the group's unity: each group sees its action as ensuring the unity of the group while at the same time each subgroup sees the action of the other subgroup as detrimental to the very same unity. It is important to remember that the institutionalized group is a hierarchical social structure based on organized function. However, if each subgroup claims to produce the same unity, a rupture of the internal structure of the group invariably occurs. While members of the opposed subgroups may at one time have been compatible within the group, the contradictions and conflicts transform the relationship of identity and turn it into a threat:

> the identical *is the Other*, in a milieu *where there are no Others*. But it is a particularly hateful and dangerous Other: each sub-group, inasmuch as it is identical to another, discovers the other as its own reality become alien praxis. And the practical existence of that other is a danger *not just for the identical and opposed sub-group*, inasmuch as identity contests the uniqueness of its relation to the totality in the course of totalization, *but also for the totalization-of-envelopment*—i.e. for the whole group, its efficacy and its aims.[44]

Even though each subgroup seeks the destruction of the other based in part on need, emotion, and self-interest, the unity of the group ultimately validates the action of the subgroups: "it is unity that engenders the duality of the epicenters; it is unity that—in them and in all—is produced as the absolute exigency of transcending the duality; it is unity, finally, that is incarnated in each epicenter as liquidatory violence."[45] While mediation of the conflict may take place, it does not necessarily have to. When the subgroups confront each other, more likely one group eliminates the other, and in that event, it is critical to know what the group will look like once the conflict is resolved.

Sartre answers this question in the following manner. As he often does, very descriptive language is used to portray exactly what the victorious party does to the loser; and here the victor "liquidates" the other.

As is usual for Sartre, there is no middle ground. He takes this path because he sees the unity of the group as paramount, and to leave a remnant behind invites a recurrence of the conflict.[46] Next, the new unity assimilates the tasks and functions of the defeated subgroup. Lastly, Sartre considers the liquidation of one of the parties who caused the disunity in the first place as a transcendence only if the action of the whole group is transcended toward a moment of tighter integration and greater effectiveness toward its ultimate objective.

The victory by one subgroup results in a general reorganization of perspectives by the ensemble of individuals reappearing as unity. From this point of view, the victory by liquidation is intelligible because it produces the reunification of an otherwise disassociated unity. This does not mean, however, that resistances are not evident. In every twist and turn, there exist passive resistances related to the practico-inert, but the impotence of the institutionalized group directly corresponds to the apparatuses of coercion controlled by the sovereign to prevent such resistance. The victory is a transcendence by a diffuse mediation of the entire group; in fact, the entire group—not as a group, but as individuals within the group—decides.

While victory comes about through the mediation of the entire group, this does not necessarily mean it realizes a progress toward its ultimate goal. Only the circumstances of the praxis and its material conditions can tell us if progress is achieved. As Sartre rightly points out, the deep conflict does not have to be over one's function or valid perspective, it can occur over "myths and absurd 'opinions,' or over articles of dogma."[47]

The mythologizing of the conflict's object expresses itself on an abstract level through the clash of fetishized symbols, which are highly important to the nature of the conflict. These symbols produce themselves "by producing the prison which encloses it."[48] Accordingly, the operations of either of the subgroups is intelligible based solely on the profound movements that engender them, but, at the same time, those operations become bogged down and eventually the entire conflict is led astray. Fetishes, then, not only lead to alienation, but struggle and victory are necessarily alienated through these various fetishes.

The comprehension of the struggle lies in its understanding as mediated opposition where sought after unity itself not only produces conflict but maintains it as well.

THE PURGE

The conflict between the subgroups means the victorious group is the only one left at the top of the hierarchy, but not all conflict ceases. As an institutionalized group, any disagreement among its members—either real or imagined—gives rise to suspicion that is ultimately deemed a threat to an otherwise maniacally sought unity. To further its own view of uniformity, the group undergoes a purge; it is the only course of action open to the group if it is to reestablish internal homogeneity. In reality, however, the purge manages only to replace a quasi-structured heterogeneity with a diffuse one. Once the purge occurs the survivors are comrades or, in Sartre's words, the *same again*, but they are also simultaneously and secretly Others.[49]

As the purge commences, my bond with my fellow brothers in the group is terror. The regulatory action by which the other unites me to all gives me a reprieve for myself because the group constitutes me, but the other also determines my bond as residing at the limit of interiority. As a result, the other's regulatory action highlights the infinitesimal gap between the regulatory movement of my quasi-sovereignty in the common praxis and the true sovereignty of the absolute Other. We are, Sartre says, united but threatened. As an arbitrary member of a group:

> I perceive, in the two forms of my praxis (regulated and regulatory), freedom, the *non-being of the future* which has to be made, as an indication of the *group non-being*. And my individual terror behavior consists in consolidating inertia within myself in so far as this reciprocal practice of consolidation is also realized in the other third party through the mediation of all others.[50]

Here, the pledge is a necessary but insufficient basis for common unity, but this inert unity Sartre describes is different from the serial inertia I talked about previously because it is the struggle of freedom against an internal revival of seriality.

While the common individual in the group-in-fusion is not inessential, the degraded group displays the common individual, in his negation of his own freedom, as inessential with regard to his function. At this stage, function is the very concrete determination of the common individual. Freedom, therefore, conceived as a common transcendent subject denies individual freedom and expels the *individual* from function; thus, function posits itself for itself and produces individuals who perpetuate function in the form of an institution.

THE INERTIA OF INSTITUTIONALIZATION
(FIRST TRANSFORMATION)

At this point, Sartre thinks two transformations of the organized group operate simultaneously. One is abstract, the other a concrete act of differentiation. Initially, the institution possesses contradictory characteristics of both praxis and thing. With regard to its praxis, its objective end is now obscure either because the institution is a mere skeleton, or because those who are institutionalized are incapable of articulating the real aim of the group. The teleological characteristics of the group are a paralyzed dialectic of alienated ends. Coupled with these alienated ends, the institution possesses a considerable force of inertia as it posits itself as essential, while, at the same time, casting its individual members as the inessential means to its perpetuation.

Inessentiality does not arise, however, from the individual to the institution or vice versa; it takes place because of new human relationships based on serial impotence. As a member of the institutionalized group, I regard the institution as sacrosanct; it is not alterable because my actions, or in this case lack of actions, are incapable of changing it; my impotency derives from my relation to everyone in the institutionalized group as circular alterity. Once more, terror descends on all who dissent, and everyone lives mistrust as reciprocity of impotence. I am suspect in the other's eyes when I seek to modify some structure, practice, or power and ask the others to join with me in some certain endeavor. Behind closed doors and in hushed tones, the others remind me, for my own well-being (to say nothing of theirs), I should be quite leery of making any proposals or taking any initiative. Neither the others nor I know how any such proposals will be taken; they may be misconstrued and turned against not only me but the others to destroy us all. The others repeatedly tell me it is better to remain silent.

Once the group assumes a degraded status, every proposal is divisive and threatening, and its proposer suspect. Sartre also argues that if I am suspect, it is because I am offering a very glimpse of my own freedom that at best is a fleeting occurrence. The group tells me it is too bad if I disagree, I have to come to terms with it; after all, because nothing can change it, I might just as well go along. This attitude, lived in a concrete mode of impotence, alters the group giving rise to the institution by the mere fact that alterity erodes the long sought after unity, which becomes powerless to change it without a complete disruption of itself. As an institution, its real strength comes to it from "emptiness, from separation, from inertia, and from serial alterity; it is therefore *the praxis as other*."[51]

Sartre considers the institution a "declining group" transforming from the *active-passivity* of pledged inertia to the *passive-activity* experienced in the practico-inert. Produced as a bond between its members, the being-of-the-institution is the nonbeing of the group where the unity of the institution, as the unity of alterity, replaces the absent unity of the group. A new statue of power emerges. I have a duty to do my best in order for me to have my duty recognized. In short, what is required is the creation of the "institutional man" who receives recognition by means of two opposed practices. In the first instance, he rids himself of all "otherness" so as to liquidate it in the others. In the second instance, and at the very moment institutional man exercises his power, he immediately constitutes himself as the absolute Other. In his style and manner, he bases the firmness of his power on institutional-being, which is, in realty, inertia.

At this point, mystification sets in with the institution remaining a practice within an undissolved group.[52]

Eventually, what Sartre refers to as the "power-man" reveals himself as institutional-being through which the organized individual comes to believe himself integrated into the group through the institutional ensemble. The power-man's freedom is, at least for the individual who acknowledges his power, a pure mediation between the inertia of the institution and the inertia of the particular order. At this moment, freedom is completely hidden or inessential and becomes an "ephemeral slave of necessity."[53] In effect, what happens is the systematic self-domestication of man by man:

> the aim is, in effect, to create men who (as common individuals) will define themselves, in their own eyes and amongst themselves, by their fundamental relation (mediated reciprocity) with institutions. More than half of this task is carried out by circular seriality: everyone systematically acting on himself and on everyone else through all, resulting in the creation of the strict correlate of the man-institution, that is to say, the institutionalized man.[54]

Sartre refers to this behavior as the ossification of ossified praxis, which in the institution is the result of impotence that constitutes for everyone reification. The result is a common degradation where everyone seeks to expel freedom from themselves to realize the endangered unity of the declining group as a thing.

THE RISE OF THE LEADER: CULT OF PERSONALITY, AUTHORITY AND SOVEREIGNTY (SECOND TRANSFORMATION)

If Sartre's first transformation of the institutionalized group concerns itself with institutional inertia, his second transformation is more concrete and even more destructive of freedom: the institutional system, based in exterior inertia, necessarily reinteriorizes inertia as authority. Authority, by its very nature and as a guarantee of institutions, incarnates power as power over all powers, and over all third parties through these powers. However, sovereignty (as the quasi-sovereignty of the regulatory third party after the stage of the group-in-fusion) grounds authority, and Sartre further explains that the leader emerges at the same time as the group itself and produces the group that produces him.

In the movement toward an understanding of the basis for authority, Sartre thinks from the moment the regulatory third party becomes the pledged holder of the power of regulation as function, and when the regulatory third party concentrates the internal violence of the group in the form of a power to impose his particular regulation on the group, everyone's quasi-sovereignty is "immobilized." In a sense, it is suspended or bracketed. This immobilized quasi-sovereignty becomes authority as a specific relation of one particular individual to all the rest. While this relation appears at the level of the organized group, it does not come to full fruition until we reach the institutionalized group. What is necessary for authority to blossom is the rebirth of seriality and impotence allowing the establishment of power where the institution, through its permanent mystification, presents itself as the only real unity of the group in decline.

Clearly, Sartre thinks authority comes into full existence only within an institutionalized group. However, he does not think once authority is constituted, individual freedom is eliminated forever. He distinctly says it is merely immobilized, which means it could arise again should the individuals within the group shed their serial impotence, and reformulate their actions as a group-in-fusion. As I have said, while Sartre could have taken us in the direction where praxis reformulates the group-in-fusion, he does quite the opposite and for a simple reason. Sartre wants to show exactly what happens when praxis fails to materialize and serial impotency reigns supreme. In this situation, my immobilized quasi-sovereignty becomes incarnated in the body of a particular individual as sovereign.

Sartre concludes that it is not sovereignty that must concern us or even be explained. On the contrary, what deserves our attention now is why and on what basis does the circular reciprocity of quasi-sovereignty suddenly grind to a halt, and why is the common individual, at the material point at which circular reciprocity is blocked, defined as sovereign.

The problem is often obscured by assuming the sovereign's power is always already there from the outset, and by ascribing some positive force that arises or reflects a collective sovereignty. To do this requires us to overlook the fact that quasi-sovereignty is, much like mediated reciprocity, characterized by its ubiquity and not by some synthetic virtue combining all the powers of the group. Quasi-sovereignty is not, and can never be, a totalized power of the group over its members. While quasi-sovereignty reveals itself in every third party as the synthetic power of reorganizing the practical field, it also manifests itself as a membership of the rearranged group, and as the same in everyone. Thus, common praxis is realized everywhere at the same time, and is both means and ends. In contrast, a particular statute the reality of which is negation defines the sovereign. No one can claim to be outside the group, and thus no longer a third party. As institution, sovereignty designates the common individual who assumes the function of the sovereign as a nontranscendable third party, as other than everyone. Eventually a common individual who, while still a member of the group, is other than all because he can no longer become a regulatory third party constitutes the group. This untranscendability means the existence of the sovereign is founded negatively on the impossibility of every third party becoming directly regulatory again.

Sartre is clear, this does not mean every reorganization or every initiative of the group emanates from the sovereign; it does mean mediation is no longer the free mediation of all by all. Now, it passes through a single mediator—the sovereign—so as to be reinteriorized by him, and, through him, appear to the group as a new orientation. In an effort to preserve the group's unity, the sovereign becomes the insurmountable mediator in the external relations of seriality grounding the relations of all the group's members. Because of the pledge, every third party obeys the new orientation with the consequent result that this basic structure of obedience, realized in the *milieu* of Fraternity-Terror, is always set against the background of violence.

Sartre points to the impossibility of refusal because that would dissolve the group. Action here is the interiorization of an "other will" that introduces an induced passivity carrying with it an untranscendable sovereignty without reciprocity. This means the refusal to dissolve the group legitimates common violence in the form of repressive terror that means the pledge is now an act of submission to the individual decisions of the untranscendable third party, and to his quasi-sovereignty as violence without reciprocity. At this level, freedom "becomes alienated and hidden form its own eyes,"[55]

Sartre thinks two additional transformations take place, one at the level of the group and the other at the individual level. With regard to the first, the common individual is still within a reciprocal organization, but that organization takes the form of univocal rearrangements without reciprocity. In the second transformation, at the level of my own individual activity, freedom is "stolen from me."[56]

Here, the true function of sovereignty emerges: the institutional reinteriorization of the exteriority of institutions, or the institution of one person—and the birth of the *cult of personality*—as mediator between institutions. This is, indeed, a stunning concept Sartre has been gravitating toward in his discussion. Most theorists, for example Hobbes, see the sovereign as a mediator between individuals, and not between the institution and authority that the group becomes. The impact of Sartre's analysis reveals, as institution, the sovereign is in no need of group consensus simply because the members of the group freely abandon their freedom and are impotent to respond. The centralization of authority in the form of one sovereign directly negates reciprocal relations between individuals, and renders them impotent. Because of my impotence, it is impossible for me to enter into a social contract with my fellow individuals to appoint a sovereign representative and abandon the war of all against all at the expense of my freedom.

The rise of authoritarian governance throughout the world is hardly a revelation. Leaders such as Viktor Orbán in Hungary, Andrzej Duda's

Law and Justice Party in Poland, Recep Erdogan in Turkey, Russia's Vladimir Putin, and Jair Bolsonaro of Brazil are just a few of the elected leaders, and in most cases from supposedly democratic regimes, who have sought to consolidate political power through a populist, nationalist agenda knotted to an aura of personality. While some of these leaders push for an "ill-liberal" agenda, historically populist-autocratic politics, associated with such figures as Hitler, Mussolini, and Stalin, adopted policies of ingroup/outgroup dynamics as a means to solidify their followers' identity as members of the beleaguered collective. In America, President Trump has followed this typical pattern of personality by, among other things, presenting immigrants as a lower form of out-group, nonhumans ready to invade and take over the prevailing hegemonic social hierarchy. In his populist and nationalist rhetoric, Trump plays upon the fears of his supporters, many of which seem to be locked within a type of practico-inert collective thinking.

In commenting on the present political situation, then Senator Bob Corker chided his fellow Republicans for being "cultish" and "fearful" under President Trump.[57] In a subsequent interview, Janja Lalich, a noted sociologist specializing in cults, found similarities between Corker's comments and Trump's activities. Lalich identifies four salient characteristics of "totalistic" cults, or those that consider their ideology sacrosanct: an all-encompassing belief system, extreme devotion to the leader, reluctance to acknowledge criticism of the group or of its leader, and a disdain for those not members of the group.[58] Moreover, cult leaders commonly follow a pattern of behaving in such ways that reinforce the group as a relevant social entity by walling themselves off from conflicting information or ideas. Part of that container attitude involves the demonization of the "enemy," either real or imagined. But the enemy need not be limited to immigrants.

In the United States, Trump has consistently vilified the press, asserting that news coverage of his actions is merely "fake news;" such news does not even have to be unfavorable, it may just report the actual events in a factual matter, but if those events happen to be embarrassing then the news is deemed fake. A more serious similar allegation is Trump's assertion that the press is the "enemy of the people," which is a particularly ugly ploy wielded by dictators and tyrants who seek to stifle public information. While news sources are not always accurate, generally, the news Trump denigrates as fake has, more often than not, turned out to be correct. Yet, by repeatedly calling particular news sources he personally dislikes as fake, he undermines the truth and instills in the minds of his followers a sense of doubt as to the legitimacy of news that in any way differs from their beliefs. Again, such news does not have to be unfavorable, but if those events happen to be embarrassing then the news is deemed fake and its messenger considered an enemy of the people. Famously, Senior Counsel to the President Kellyanne Conway, when asked why then Press Secretary Sean Spicer would lie about a provable number such as the crowd at the President's inauguration, said that Spicer was utilizing "alternative fact." This "through the looking glass" strategy adopted by the White House was, in effect, saying the real facts are fake, but the "alternative facts," however inaccurate, should be believed. The desire to control and manipulate the news is another indication of an authoritarian leader.

Trump seems to qualify on all grounds as a cult personality. But there are other well-known attributes to such behavior. One of those is the desire for self-adulation and crowd approval. As a charismatic populist leader, Trump needs to constantly keep the collective in a state of enchantment, telling them he is the only one who can solve their problems, which means that only he cares about them. While not necessarily a religion, his endless rallies oftentimes resemble revival meetings by revving up the crowd for an extraordinary length of time, and exacting a "pledge" of loyalty from the faithful. But the pledge, it seems, applies to more than just the ordinary faithful. Trump has pursued a twofold strategy of praising those who have remained loyal to him even though they face considerable legal obstacles. Perhaps the most well-known loyalist is Paul Manafort who refused to cooperate fully with government prosecutors investigating Russian interference in the 2016 election, and now faces considerable time in jail. In the opposite camp are those who have broken the pledge of loyalty and acted against Trump's personal interest. Michael Cohen is the obvious poster boy for this position, but there are many who have occupied high level positions within the administration that have suffered a similar fate. Just ask former Attorney General Jeff Sessions, an early Trump supporter when no one else among the GOP establishment supported his nomination, who steadfastly promoted the Trump agenda but committed heresy by recusing himself from an obvious conflict of interest. I might note, and as Sartre acknowledges, for Trump the pledge is not reciprocal.

One further point with regard to the cult of personality: An almost religious atmosphere descends upon the beliefs and rhetoric of the collective. In an effort to mythologize the leader as anointed by God, the cultish group resorts to the heavens as a means to justify and, indeed, sanctify the leader's actions. Mike Pompeo, the US Secretary of State, agreed with suggestions that God meant for Trump to be president to be the modern-day protector of Israel from Iran. Pompeo was not, however, the first to suggest a divine intervention on behalf of Trump. Earlier, White House Press Secretary Sarah Sanders declared that God wanted Trump to be president. Exactly how this was revealed to her remains unknown. The reverence accorded the cult of personality requires the leader to be divinely inspired to justify his actions and cement the faithful to his cause.

The consequences of anointing Trump, or anyone else, a cult leader are obvious for Sartre. He starts his analysis by observing that every action reinteriorizes the institutional system such that only the sovereign is free. The sovereign alone produces his actions as moments of free development, so for any member of the group there exists only one freedom that, nevertheless, can only rise to an ambiguous freedom because it is both the common freedom and the sovereign's individual freedom in the service of the collective. As organizational freedom, it rearranges the group by issuing orders having the effect of detaching everyone's free praxis and submerging it beneath institutionality. While the ambiguity of the now obedient third party indicates the function of the sovereign, it also points out the failure of sovereignty to act as a point of unity for the institutionalized group.

In essence, embodiment emerges as a fact of sovereignty. The group produces itself in the form of a particular body with certain characteristics and particular qualities, and in so doing a particular style is adopted; naturally, it is the style of the sovereign. For instance, Trump's oftentimes "tough talk" has incited various white nationalist hate groups to more violent acts. For the collective faithful, the sovereign is the living *one*, the universal mediation who reveals common unity in the "half-dead" group as a synthesis of the human body in his body. Analogized to the situation of a machine, the sovereign's praxis exerted upon the group is expressed in two forms.[59] First, some type of mechanical unity, set in motion by the sovereign, articulates the goal of the group. Alternatively, the group defines itself as an extension of the sovereign. Either way the group witnesses the institutionalization of the freedom of a single individual as an institution.

When the organized group views its own survival as paramount, Sartre brings us face to face with the reality of institutionalized praxis and its nefarious attributes. As the freedom of quasi-sovereignty becomes afraid of itself, the sovereignty of one person emerges. Along with the rise of the leader, we experience the presence of authority designed to assure the permanence of the institutions mediated by the sovereign. Throughout this discussion, Sartre points out how human need for group unity solidifies the institutional powers of the ruling class, which results in the degradation of individual freedom. What Sartre shows us is the power of individual freedom within groups to negate itself in the perverse desire to protect itself.

NOTES

1. Joseph Catalano defines interior and exterior in the following manner: "'interior' refers not to an intimate awareness, but to both our prereflective awareness of our relations to our environment and our ability to thematize those relations. Reciprocally, 'exterior' refers to the environment as unified by both our [human] spontaneous and our reflective behavior." Joseph Catalano, *A Commentary on Jean-Paul Sartre's Critique of Dialectical Reason* (Chicago: University of Chicago Press, 1986), 94. When Sartre uses

the term *individual* he does not mean that society is composed of atomized, entirely free individuals mutually agreeing to live together. But neither is society an organized whole where individual meaning can be derived merely by examining that whole. The term *immanence* is humankind's material being as it joins our otherwise seemingly disparate parts into a unified whole. Transcendence also refers to humankind's unity as it unfolds in an outward manner into the environment. Ibid.; see also Jean-Paul Sartre, *Critique of Dialectical Reason*, vol. I, trans. Alan Sheridan-Smith, ed. Jonathan Rée (London: Verso, 2004), 827–30, hereinafter referred to as *CDR I*. Originally published as *Critique de la Raison Dialectique* by Éditions Gallimard, Paris, 1960.

2. Sartre defines series as "*a mode of being for individuals both in relation to one another and in relation to their common being* and this mode of being transforms all their structures. In this way it is useful to distinguish serial *praxis* (as the *praxis* of the individual in so far as he is a member of the series and as the *praxis* of the whole series, or of the series totalized through individuals) both from common praxis (group action) and from individual, constituent praxis. Conversely, in every nonserial *praxis*, a serial praxis will be found, as the practico-inert structure of the *praxis* in so far as it is social." Ibid., 266 (emphasis in original).

3. Ibid., 261.

4. The practico-inert is the basic mode of sociality. As such it is a collective composed of effectively separated, albeit ostensibly united, individuals forming the practico-inert field. In its operation, the practico-inert acts as antipraxis, but at the same time it makes an overriding master or leader impossible. The group, on the other hand, arises on the basis of the negation of the practico-inert, but it is at the practico-inert level that seriality is produced in humans by things as a bond of materiality that transcends and alters individual human relations. The bond of materiality as the practical ensemble is the collective.

5. Ibid., 266–67 (emphasis in original).

6. Ibid., 320. Sartre defines monstrous forces as the necessities and counter finalities (generally, unintended consequences) of the various systems or apparatuses of collectives to which individuals subject themselves or find themselves subject to.

7. Ibid., 332.

8. Ibid., 293. A totality is a being that is distinct from the sum of its parts, yet, at the same time, it is wholly present in all of its myriad forms. Unlike a totality, a totalization is an open-ended process that is continually being shaped by current activity. In other words, it is a process of becoming. See Catalano, *Commentary*, 72.

9. See, generally, Amos Tversky and Daniel Kahneman, "Judgment under Uncertainty: Heuristics and Biases," *Science, New Series* 185, no. 4157 (September 27, 1974): 1124–31. For more recent discussions of confirmation bias and illusory knowledge, see Hugo Mercier and Dan Sperber, *The Enigma of Reason* (Cambridge: Harvard University Press, 2017); and Steven Sloman and Philip Fernbach, *The Knowledge Illusion: Why We Never Think Alone* (New York: Riverhead Books, 2017).

10. *CDR I*, 564.

11. The notion of Apocalypse Sartre is referring to originates in André Malraux's *Days of Hope*, trans. Stuart Gilbert and Alastair MacDonald (London: George Routledge & Sons, Ltd., 1938). In the novel, the revolutionary crowd in the Spanish Civil War (meaning the Republican side of the conflict) is defined as the "Apocalypse of fraternity," which works on one's emotions. Malraux thinks they are one of the most moving things on earth, and one of the rarest. He also says "that fervor spells certain defeat, after a relatively short period, and for a very simple reason: it's in the very nature of an Apocalypse to have no future. . . . Even when it professes to have one." Ibid., 117. Sartre first elaborates his own idea of the apocalyptic moment in his *Notebooks for an Ethics*. There he asserts human freedom constantly bursts apart ideology and rituals as it realizes liberation through new ideas and behavior. This is, he says, the moment of the Apocalypse, but as it projects itself from itself into the element of the Other, it gives way to order. Moreover, the ethical moment is that of the Apocalypse as the liberation of oneself and all others in reciprocal recognition. Paradoxically,

Sartre adds, it is also the moment of violence. Jean-Paul Sartre, *Notebooks for an Ethics*, trans. David Pellauer (Chicago: University of Chicago Press, 1992), 413–14.

12. *CDR I*, 357.

13. Ibid., 358. Howard Burkle outlines what he calls six essential "marks" of fusion: (1) The first is *action*, which is essential to the unity of the group as coming together to achieve a common aim. (2) The fusion brought about by action must also result in a fusion of *consciousness*. In other words, the unity of the group-in-fusion arises from everyone seeing themselves as united in a group. Unity is, therefore, the mutual consciousness (active and not merely contemplative) of seeing everyone together. (3) The third element is that of *polarity*. Freedom here is achieved through opposition much like Sartre espoused in *Being and Nothingness* for individuals. This is the contingent freedom Sartre spends so much time developing in the *Critique*. (4) A fourth element of fusion is *interiorized multiplicity*, where individuals identify themselves with the acts of others, if only for the moment. Each member of the group-in-fusion interiorizes the others through their shared goals in the face of the common enemy. This form of unity preserves and enhances the pluralistic base. Importantly, Burkle adds it is this element whereby the free person voluntarily uses the free decision of others to regulate his own choices. (5) The next element of the group-in-fusion is the coalescence of *ubiquity* and *singularity*. Here, Sartre argues that the genuinely individual choice, which agrees with the genuinely individual choices of others, is simultaneously here and everywhere. In other words, space is overcome, competition ceases to exist, and opposition is curtailed. (6) Lastly, the group-in-fusion is characterized by its *novelty and spontaneity*. For Sartre, the unity of fusion emerges spontaneously form seriality. Burkle also points out that the unity of the group-in-fusion endures only so long as the process continues. Otherwise, it fades away and solidifies as unfreedom and the alienation of the condition of competitive opposition from which it came. Howard Burkle, "Jean-Paul Sartre: Social Freedom in *Critique of Dialectical Reason*," *The Review of Metaphysics* 19, no. 4 (June 1966): 747–49. I think these six elements indicate adequately all that is involved in the movement of fusion of the group. However, one should not think this is necessarily a linear progression and that a group-in-fusion may not at any point in time fall back into the practico-inert, regroup only to fall prey to the practico-inert once more.

14. *CDR I*, 367.

15. Sartre makes clear that once this relationship of reciprocity comes into being, it closes in upon itself. As a result, if the triad is necessary for relations "stranded" in the universe, and actually linking two individuals who are ignorant of each other, it is, at the same time "broken up" by the exclusion of the third party as soon as people or groups either help one another or fight with one another. The human mediator transforms the elementary relations whose essence is to be lived with no mediation other than matter into "something else." What this something else is becomes clear as Sartre progresses through his analysis of collectives and groups. Even in the event individuals are face to face with each other, the reciprocity of their relation is actualized through the mediation of the third, and is immediately closed off from itself. Ibid., 106.

16. Ibid., 104 (emphasis in original).
17. Ibid., 369.
18. Ibid., 187.
19. Ibid., 373.
20. Ibid., 405.
21. Ibid., 418 (emphasis in original).
22. At one point, Sartre says pledges are "A free attempt to substitute the fear of all for the fear of oneself and actualizes violence as the intelligible transcendence of individual alienation by common freedom." Ibid., 433.
23. Ibid., 449 (emphasis in original).
24. Ibid., 451–52.
25. Ibid., 191–92.
26. Ibid., 430.

27. Ibid., 431.

28. Sartre is explicit here in asserting that the pledge carries with it the right of the group to eliminate me physically, by which he means not merely exiling me from the group, but eliminating me altogether. Moreover, it does not matter if the right of death arises out of a duty to the group, or whether it is conceived as a power of the group to which I have freely consented to the taking my life if I do not act in accordance with a given directive. Furthermore, for Sartre, this is not a moral issue. As he says, "the important point is that within itself, and implicitly, the concrete duty contains death as a possible destiny for me; or, conversely, that the right of the group determines me, in so far as it is *agreed*." Ibid., 434 (emphasis in original).

29. Ibid. (emphasis in original).

30. Ibid. (emphasis in original).

31. Ibid., 438 (emphasis in original).

32. Sartre thinks our functions are one of the thousand ways in which the for-itself tries to wrench itself away from its original contingency: "we insist on our individual rights only within the compass of a vast project which would tend to confer existence on us in terms of the function we fulfill." Jean-Paul Sartre, *Being and Nothingness*, trans. Hazel Barnes (New York: Washington Square Press, 1956), 624. But, adds Sartre, our efforts to escape our contingency by relishing our function—"I am the Chief Judge of the Court of Appeals," for instance—succeed only in further entrenching this original contingency.

33. *CDR I*, 463 (emphasis in original).

34. Ibid., 470.

35. Ibid., 509.

36. Ibid., 584 (emphasis in original).

37. Ibid., 585.

38. Ibid., 586.

39. Ibid.

40. Ibid., 590.

41. Jean-Paul Sartre, *Critique of Dialectical Reason, Volume II*, trans. Quintin Hoare, ed. Arlette Elkaim-Sartre (London: Verso, 2006), 52, hereinafter referred to as *CDR II*. Originally published as *Critique de la reason dialectique, tomb II* by Éditions Gallimard, Paris, 1985.

42. Sartre wants to make it clear that the indetermination of function does not arise from the structural basis of the group, although historians may subsequently determine it did. Rather, the indetermination concretely and initially manifests itself as behavior. Ibid., 55. Moreover, Sartre's analysis accommodates the concept that the dispute may arise out of class or ethnic distinctions. In other words, a lower class group may decide to assert itself within the hierarchical social structure and thus precipitate conflict. Certainly, this was the case with the civil rights movement, especially in the 1960s.

43. Ibid., 56 (emphasis in original).

44. Ibid., 64 (emphasis in original).

45. Ibid., 68.

46. Ibid., 73.

47. Ibid., 86–87.

48. Ibid., 87.

49. *CDR I*, 593. Sartre defines the Other as, "simply a particular relation which manifests itself in precisely those circumstances which engender the attempt to destroy it; besides everyone is Other in the Other." Later on, he indicates that the world of the Other is the world of government. Ibid., 656.

50. Ibid., 598 (emphasis in original).

51. Ibid., 603 (emphasis in original).

52. The question of mystification and myth is important for Sartre and has certain connections with other writers on the subject such as Hans Blumenberg who focused on the element of fear in his theory of the "absolutism of reality." In his theory of

myth, humanity exchanges the fear of an unordered and chaotic nature for the fear of something of their own making because it is more certain and identifiable. Hans Blumenberg, *Work on Myth*, trans. Robert Wallace (Cambridge: MIT Press, 1985). Although it is arguable that Sartre reverses the Hobbesian notion of the state of nature as an atomized environment of the war of all against all because the serial impotence of the bus queue does not seem to involve its inhabitants in the behavior that so concerned Hobbes. In fact, to initiate violence one would have to break out of serial impotence and resort to praxis. Sartre says that within the institutionalized group, individuals exchange their unordered fear for something of their own making through the mystification of one individual. Ultimately, as Hobbes came to realize in his book *Behemoth*, political authority is more akin to captivity of the mind than bodily coercion. Thomas Hobbes, *Behemoth*, ed. Ferdinand Tönnies (Chicago: University of Chicago Press, 1990).

53. *CDR I*, 606.
54. Ibid.
55. Ibid., 615.
56. Ibid., 616.
57. Dartunorro Clark and Garrett Haake, "Corker Calls GOP 'Cultish' and 'Fearful' under Trump, *NBC News*, January 13, 2018, https://www.nbcnews.com/politics/congress/republican-sen-bob-corker-calls-gop-cultish-fearful-under-trump-n882791.
58. Tom Jacobs, "A Cult Expert Finds Familiar Patterns of Behavior in Trump's GOP," *Pacific Standard*, June 21, 2018, https://psmag.com/news/a-sociologist-explains-the-similarities-between-cults-and-trumps-gop.
59. *CDR II*, 347.

Part III

Ressentiment

SIX
Alt-Right, *Ressentiment*

The discussion of alt-right politics started with its philosophical foundation to better understand the underlying beliefs and convictions one might expect from its adherents. The analysis then moved to answer the question of *how* that particular political philosophy is implemented into society. Even though most have never heard of Julius Evola, or any other traditionalist philosopher for that matter, and even less have read anything they wrote, many are attracted to traditionalist positions, which is to say populist beliefs including white supremacy, nationalism, and racism. The answer, I argue, lies in the human desire to form groups within any society that invariably structures itself around an ingroup/outgroup hierarchical dichotomy.

In the United States this dichotomy has historically centered on race with whites at the top of the spectrum and blacks at the bottom. Since the civil rights movement of the 1950s and 1960s, this dichotomy started to break down, and while gains made by blacks toward equality have been substantial since that time, equality is far from being achieved. The election of the first African American President of the United States, Barack Obama, gave hope to some that racial inequality was nearing an end. However, it appears that the electoral results of 2008 only galvanized an otherwise quiescent, but underlying *ressentiment* on the part of a segment of the population, namely less educated, white, and middle to lower class mostly rural voters. Much has fueled the current feelings of *ressentiment*, but the primary concern is a loss of social hegemony—either real or imagined—at the top of the historical hierarchical structure. With the rise of the black middle class, a new group of outgroup participants has formed as the target of ingroup members, namely immigrants coming to the United States.

This view of racial status threat occurring after the Obama administration should, perhaps, not be surprising, but as indicative of a type of racism not focused on minorities as either morally or intellectually inferior, but one that regards minority groups as sufficiently numerous and gaining in power to pose a threat to the present white dominated hierarchical power structure. When dominant group members experience a perceived threat to their group's sociopolitical position, either in the world at large or their status as white in an increasingly multiethnic society, a sense of insecurity ensues resulting in a revision of how they understand their relative position within the social structure.

For support, I looked to social dominance theory as well as Sartre's discussion of group formulation in his *Critique of Dialectical Reason*. In each instance—one from a strictly sociological perspective analyzing intergroup actions, the other intertwined with primarily sociology, psychology, and philosophy exploring intragroup dynamics—groups form as necessary elements of human development. And, again, in the formulation process, those groups invariably cultivate a hierarchical social structure where some occupy the top of the social scale while others reside at the lower end of the social spectrum. As both SDT and Sartre point out, oppression of outgroup members by the power structure of society, including its institutions and those in positions of power, is the social outcome of this hierarchical structure. Taken a step further, Sartre sees the ultimate effect of this situation as pointing toward, in his words a sovereign, who becomes an authoritarian leader of a cult of personality.

The question that remains is not how support for alt-right political beliefs comes about, but *why*; why is it that some embrace this type of authoritarian politics with its desire to promote ingroup hegemony almost at any cost. For the answer to this troubling question, I want to focus on Friedrich Nietzsche and, again, Sartre. Each relies on a theory of *ressentiment* to address this crucial concern.

Before starting the discussion, however, a preliminary note is in order. While both Nietzsche and Sartre occupy well-deserved positions within the philosophical world, they come from an earlier time. Each wrote about ant-Semitism, but their views should be seen as applicable to all forms of racism and oppression at the hands of one group directed at another, and most importantly an attempt to answer why these positions come about in the first place. While Sartre engaged in many social and political topics after World War II, colonialism and its inherent racism accounted for a considerable amount of his attention. But Sartre was also ahead of his time in addressing an issue in the immediate aftermath of the war that most French people chose to ignore, "why were the Jews not returning to France?"[1]

To discuss Sartre's critique of anti-Semitism, and therefore all forms of racism, it is necessary to start with Nietzsche because it is his concept of *ressentiment* that provides a structural framework of why racism takes hold within the human psyche. Despite attempts to expropriate Nietzsche's work to lend credence to racist claims, most notably by the Nazi philosophy Alfred Bäumler (1887–1968), his dislike of anti-Semitism is well known and well documented.[2] Likewise, Sartre's discussion of the topic in *Anti-Semite and Jew* is a classic philosophical/psychological critique that can be applied to all forms of racism.[3] Just as Sartre does, Nietzsche grounds his point of view in psychological terminology; all three essays in *On the Genealogy of Morals* are "studies by a psychologist for the revaluation of all values."[4] In fact, as Robert Solomon points out, the genealogy of morals is a thesis about the motivation of morality, which is, by its very nature, psychological. But, to understand Nietzsche's direction, we must first understand why his position is different from more normative critiques of morals and morality.

Nietzsche's central theme is that moral values are born out of or originate from a condition he terms *ressentiment*. In fact, Nietzsche sees the three central phenomena that constitute modern morality — the distinction between good and evil, the feeling of moral guilt or "bad conscience," and the ascetic ideal — as having their origin in *ressentiment*.[5] As is well known, Nietzsche offers a two-pronged attack on our customarily held moral beliefs: on the one hand, he challenges our most deeply held views as to what we consider valuable, and, on the other hand, he opposes our widespread views concerning the universality and, indeed, the very validity of our moral judgments. In Nietzsche's opinion, our traditional views of morality are not universal in nature and can make no claim to such status. However, the view that morality is objectionable because it originates in *ressentiment* does not seem to fit nicely into either of his criticism. The reason lies, perhaps, in the difficulty in utilizing a psychological critique of morality in the first place; such a critique cast severe doubt on our ability to infer the veracity of the claim much less the validity of its content. Undoubtedly, even if psychology could establish that some belief originates in *ressentiment*, this fails to say whether that particular belief holds any value whatsoever let alone whether it can claim universality.

If Nietzsche's psychological critique does not operate on either of the levels mentioned previously, the question then becomes where does it belong? In answering this question, I shall turn to Bernard Reginster who argues quite convincingly that ultimately Nietzsche's psychological critique does not concern value judgments *qua* value judgments; rather, such a critique is concerned with the psychological state of the individual whose value judgments are born out of *ressentiment*.[6] Yet, even if moral judgments are nothing more than the expression of psychological attitudes that constitute their origin, then merely exposing what attitude a given judgment expresses will not amount to a critique of that judgment. But, as Nietzsche points out, a drive, in itself . . . has, *like every drive,* neither this moral character nor any moral character at all, nor even a definite attendant sensation of pleasure or displeasure; it acquires all this, as its second nature, only when it enters into relations with drives already baptized good or evil or is noted as a quality of beings the people has already evaluated and determined in a moral sense.[7]

It is incumbent, then, to not only show *what* is wrong with the "man of *ressentiment's*" individual psyche, but also to illuminate *why* such an attitude is mistaken, and this is precisely what Nietzsche has in mind, and it is essentially what Sartre portrays in the character of the anti-Semite. *Ressentiment* is, above all, an emotion based on individual power or the dearth of it, but with Nietzsche power or its lack does not cause *ressentiment*; rather, it comprises the content of *ressentiment*.

Sartre, on the other hand, sees anti-Semitism as an emotional passion and a predisposition toward hatred that is constitutive as well as primordial, and in this regard it is the culmination of psychic drives. Sartre's anti-Semitic subjective position is, as we shall see, a psychological state much like Nietzsche's *ressentiment*. Furthermore, Nietzsche's *ressentiment* eventually leads to bad conscience; Sartre's passion, in turn, results in the bad faith of inauthenticity. At first glance, much for these two thinkers appears to be aligned not only in their shared existentialist desire for human freedom, but also in their similar attitudes toward racism as an insidious negation of that very freedom. To pursue this enquiry further, it is necessary to first examine what Nietzsche has in mind by his psychological notion of *ressentiment*, which will then allow us to delve deeper not only into Sartre's notion of the anti-Semite, but, more importantly, how Nietzsche's *ressentiment* can be seen to form a basis for Sartre's polemic.

NIETZSCHE'S *RESSENTIMENT*

Nietzsche begins his analysis of *ressentiment* by metaphorically distinguishing between the master and slave moralities, and an equally famous theory that "bad conscience," or moral guilt feeling, originates from an internalization of the will to power.[8] To illustrate his position, Nietzsche has in mind two distinct human types: the noble master and the slave. Not to be taken literally, each is representative of a certain kind of disposition or psychological character indicative of the social and political behavior of those represented. Master morality belongs to a dominant, warrior-like life. The "good" is whatever they believe belongs to them and to their conquering instincts. Because the essence of master-morality is constituted by affirmation, its negatives such as "bad," "unhappy," and "base," are only offshoots, and are always designating the opposite of its affirmation. The noble believes himself to be of a superior or higher rank, and thus the good life for the noble includes political superiority as well.[9] Yet Nietzsche is quick to point out that what concerns him most is nobility as a type of character, which, as original and therefore good, is an expression of a strong character.

As one might expect, the slave morality is seen as a reaction, an inversion, a corruption; it is dominated by the negative. The overpowered slave, who revolts ideologically against his condition does so by *inventing* a series of distinctions by which to condemn his master as "evil" and to affirm himself, not directly and spontaneously, but indirectly and "reactively." It is clear that an ethics of *ressentiment* is merely an expression of bad character regardless of its principles and rationalizations. Nietzsche reminds us that:

> while the noble man lives in trust and openness with himself (*gennaios* "of noble descent" underlines the nuance "upright" and probably also "naïve"), the man of *ressentiment* is neither upright nor naïve nor honest and straightforward with himself. His soul *squints*; his spirit loves hiding places, secret paths and back doors, everything covert entices him as his world, his security, his refreshment; he understands how to keep silent, how not to forget, how to be provisionally self-deprecating and humble.[10]

Nietzsche's *ressentiment* entails the act of deception, the clandestine, and the opaque. Moreover, *ressentiment* relies on at least a dyadic relationship, ordinarily one cannot have *ressentiment* directed at oneself; rather, the slave believes himself to be worse off than others and takes revenge regardless of whether those others are imagined as a single, specific person, or some group to which that person belongs. *Ressentiment* aims at other individuals, other groups, or other institutions; its very essence requires one's view to be directed outward instead of back onto oneself. To exist, slave morality insists upon a hostile external world, which provides the necessary external stimuli to act at all, yet that action is fundamentally reaction. In language that foretells Sartre's later argument, Nietzsche explains that "man seeks a principle through which he can despise men—he invents a world so as to be able to slander and bespatter this world: in reality he reaches every time for nothingness."[11] The reverse is true for the character of the noble whose acts are spontaneous and who affirms life though passion. *Ressentiment* is, on the other hand, a nonreflecting, bitter emotional state oftentimes linked to either a real or imagined slight or injury. Just as often it is premised on fantasies and frustrations of revenge that further exacerbates the *ressentiment*.

It should be kept in mind and, in fact, Nietzsche tells us that a race of men of *ressentiment* is eventually bound to become more clever than such members of any noble race; it will also honor cleverness to a far greater degree: namely as a condition of the existence of the first *ressentiment* as the evil enemy, or "*the Evil One*." And it is this description that, in turn, allows the man of *ressentiment* to view himself and his attitudes as righteous and himself as the "good one." This evil one arouses fear in the slave because it is the slave's belief that "power and dangerousness are assumed to reside in this evil, a certain dreadfulness, subtlety, and strength, which do not admit of being despised."[12] For Nietzsche, it is clear that the man of *ressentiment* must divide the world in two; to affirm his very existence, he must portray that existence in Manichean terms.

Even though there is no direct correlate in the German language, there is a purpose for Nietzsche's use of the French term *ressentiment*. Frustration is an emotional feeling and *ressentiment*, which derives from the Latin *"resentire"* and means to feel, denotes a strong and often harsh emotional response balanced between vulnerability and imagined vengeance on the one hand, and an aristocratic sense of honor on the other.[13] In short, the resentful person has ingrained feelings, while the noble self overcomes those feelings and acts. No matter what language one utilizes, *ressentiment* harbors a feeling of vulnerability and implies reaction to an offense that includes schemes of revenge. As has been pointed out, however, more often than not these slights are imagined and the schemes are nothing more than fantasies of the imagination.

Such acts of revenge can take on many forms including, for instance, the Trump administration's active consideration to transport thousands of migrants seeking asylum in the United Sates to so-called sanctuary cities, mostly represented by opposition party Democrats. These sanctuary cities and their elected leaders refuse to cooperate with federal immigration enforcement agencies regarding the treatment of asylum seekers, who by law must be taken into custody until their claims are adjudicated. There are some obvious issues with this idea, including the fact that many sanctuary cities are thousands of miles from the southern border area where most migrants are housed. But foremost among the troubling issues is the use of human beings, mostly families including young children, as pawns in a political game of vindictiveness designed to ratchet up the pressure on a particular group. In this instance a city, its people, and its duly elected representatives.

But what is it that brings *ressentiment*, this emotional, psychological state of vengeance and vulnerability to fruition? For Nietzsche, *ressentiment* is primarily concerned with power, but not just as a feeling of self-pity for one's own plight in the word; rather, it is a personal vindictiveness or blame for a perceived and, perhaps, preconceived injustice. Moreover, *ressentiment* is typified by its obsessive nature, but it is not generally expressed as a specific desire other than as an amorphous yearning for revenge. This type of revenge seems to manifest itself in an abstract desire for the utter humiliation of its target followed by its total annihilation. One should not believe, however, that *ressentiment* is self-destructive. On the contrary, it is the ultimate emotion of both self-preservation and self-affirmation at any cost.

Ressentiment is a psychological form of repressed vengeance arising out of several key factors. Initially, the man of *ressentiment* desires to lead a certain kind of life that he deems of importance, and is generally thought of as a life of supremacy. Nevertheless, his weakness creates a feeling of inferiority or impotence. Next, this feeling of impotency assumes the essential role of a feature of one's own psyche. The result is the man of *ressentiment* sees himself as permanently and ineluctably weak. Of even greater concern is the fact that his loss of power is seen not as some aberration, but as evidence of his constitutional impotency. In the end, the man of *ressentiment* believes himself powerless, yet he retains his arrogance and his false sense of superiority. Thus, his will to power remains intact.[14] Finally, the man of *ressentiment* refuses to resign himself to this ignominious impotency; his sickliness or impotence does not eliminate his desire for control, it only makes those feelings more acute. Nietzsche argues that the man of *ressentiment's* hatred toward his rivals only "grows to monstrous and uncanny proportions."[15] It is this third definitional characteristic that sets *ressentiment* apart from other attitudes. The man of *ressentiment* maintains his commitment to his original goals and aspirations, and refuses to accept his inability to realize them. From a psychological point of view, the man of *ressentiment* is torn or alienated by the tremendous tension between the desire to live the life he values and the belief that he is powerless to attain it.

The entire notion of strength and weakness assumes special importance with regard to the man of *ressentiment*. What Nietzsche despises about *ressentiment* is not only its emotional impact and lack of energy or robustness, but above all its inability to affirm its own selfhood—and, therefore, its own self-worth—without first negating someone else. The strength or power Nietzsche refers to is neither physical nor military; rather, it is the spontaneous, personal confidence that remains free form self-doubt that he praises. Again, Nietzsche refers to his two moral types, the master and the slave, to illustrate his point. There are various interpretations of Nietzsche's master and slave morality including the description alluded to previously that attributes to the master such appellations as healthy, self-assertive, self-confident, and creative and, by contrast, portrays the slave as unhealthy, miserable, threatened, impoverished, unhealthy, and cowardly. In his description, Nietzsche utilizes a powerful metaphorical image of the bird of prey and the little lamb to illuminate this contrast:

> That lambs dislike great birds of prey does not seem strange: only it gives no ground for reproaching these birds of prey for bearing off little lambs. And if the lambs say among themselves: "these birds of prey are evil; and whoever is least like a bird of prey, but rather its opposite, a lamb—would he not be good?" there is no reason to find fault with this institution of an ideal, except perhaps that the birds of prey might view it a little ironically and say: *"we* don't dislike them at all, these good

little lambs; we even love them: nothing is more tasty than a tender lamb."[16]

While this metaphor is descriptively pertinent, other approaches, while not straying too far from the above interpretation, have added a different nuance to this standard interpretation.[17] In short, these interpretations see the master morality as represented by those who have the good fortune to be born well and raised with modern advantages—excellent education, superior cultural gifts, and a supportive social structure, all of which presupposes a certain social and economic status. This, in turn, breeds bold achievement born out of an attitude of superiority with its attendant lack of inhibitions and prohibitions. Such an interpretation should not be misconstrued, however. The characteristics of the noble can apply to anyone who overcomes the prejudices and biases rampant within a society. Consequently, the noble "spirit" is meant to embrace a certain enlightened nature, open to varying and divergent points of view and the people who espouse those views.

Slaves, on the other hand, are herd oriented and mutually dependent. While not necessarily lacking ambition, they see their goals and desires thwarted by obstacles not of their own design. The slave possesses an ideal image of the world that is made in his own image. In other words, his personal narcissism is, unlike the master's, more general in character and informs his outer world view. The slave, unable to accept this state of affairs, displays envy, becomes resentful, and adopts a rebellious attitude. The adopted mode of action is reaction against the situation the slave has been thrown into, and not action itself. As we shall see, Sartre's portrait of the racist can be seen to include these narcissistic character traits as well.

The confrontation between the master and the slave provides the starting point upon which *ressentiment* not only constitutes the psychology of the slave, but also bad conscience.[18] While the master draws strength from the spontaneous manifestations of power, the slave harbors a sense of hatred toward all powerful affirmers in life. The slave is the very paradigm of suppressed feelings of hatred that fails to connect to their desired outward object and, instead, manifest themselves in an intensely internalized destructive tendency. As Nietzsche points out, the origin of bad conscience is tantamount to an ever increasing inner world that is inhibited from any outward discharge. For Nietzsche, this tension seeks an escape, and eventually it turns back upon itself—man against man: "hostility, cruelty, joy in persecuting, in attacking, in change, and in destruction," this is how bad conscience manifests itself in the man of *ressentiment*.[19]

When Nietzsche directly addresses the particular issue of anti-Semitism, he argues that what underlies and makes it possible is, in fact, *ressentiment*. As he explains, *ressentiment* "blooms" among "anti-

Semites—where it has always bloomed, in hidden places, like the violet, though with different colors."[20] To affirm his own existence, the anti-Semite must negate the Jew who he sees as an absolute other. It is only through negation that the anti-Semite is able to recognize himself within a community, and become ensconced as a member of the "club."

SARTRE AND RACISM

Sartre structures his book, *Anti-Semite and Jew*, much like a play; there are active "characters" introduced to us in a rather lineal fashion. His main characters are the anti-Semite and the Jew, but for our purposes we will concern ourselves with Sartre's "man of *ressentiment*," namely the anti-Semite who is representative of all forms of racism. The anti-Semite chapter begins with an attempt to define what constitutes the psyche of the anti-Semite. Whatever an anti-Semite is, however, Sartre believes they do not merely possess *opinions* concerning Jews. In essence, Sartre refuses "to characterize as opinions a doctrine that is aimed directly at particular persons and that seeks to suppress their rights or to exterminate them."[21] How then does Sartre conceive of the anti-Semite? First of all, he believes that anti-Semitism is a psychological passion, and this is essential to his analysis because the act of being an anti-Semite, or a racist, cannot be based on experience if it resides in the passions. In psychoanalytic terms, neurosis occurs when drives within the ego are incapable of connecting with their object and seek another avenue of expression. In this sense, Nietzsche and Sartre are talking about similar phenomena. In Sartre's description of "passions," ordinary hate is associated with provocation— I hit you, you hit me—but the anti-Semite experiences no such outward insult. Rather, the anti-Semite's hate "precedes the facts that are supposed to call it forth."[22] A predisposition toward hatred, most likely a self-fulfilling prophecy, is not only fundamental to the very being of the anti-Semite, it is primordial. The anti-Semite's passions and psychic drives necessarily manifest themselves in a subjective position that preconceives an "idea" of the Jew as to the latter's nature as well as to their societal role. Anti-Semitism, then, must be seen as the total free choice of oneself; it is not the outgrowth of some external force.

To understand what Sartre his in mind by his use of the term passion we must look to his earlier work, *The Emotions: Outline of a Theory*.[23] Sartre's phenomenological explication of emotions begins with the premise that emotional consciousness is first and foremost unreflective. Emotional consciousness is consciousness of the world such that the person who is afraid, is afraid of *something*. That is, the subject affected by something and the affected object are inseparably bound in a symbiotic relationship. Each of us perceives the world through our acts, and emotions are merely a certain manner of apprehending the world in which we live.

What Sartre is developing is not a notion of unreflective action constantly engaged in a metastable relationship with reflective action, or from the world to the individual. On the contrary, he believes that an operation on the universe is carried out without the subject ever leaving the unreflected mode. Thus, action is spontaneous, unreflective consciousness that constitutes a certain existential level in the world. It is, therefore, not necessary to be conscious of the self acting in the world. Rather, unreflected behavior or action is not conscious behavior at all; it is conscious of itself only nonthetically, and its way of being thetically conscious of itself is to transcend itself and to seize upon the world as a quality of things. This quality of things is not, however, "furrowed with strict and narrow paths which lead to one or the other determined end, that is, to the appearance of a created object."[24]

In Sartre's thinking the path of life is littered with difficulties, which means that emotions are transformative mechanisms allowing one to cope with the difficulty. Accordingly, when the difficulty in the world becomes overpowering, life itself becomes too difficult. Even though we must act, all pathways seem barred to us. As a result, we endeavor to alter the world and live "as if the connection between things and their potentialities were not ruled by deterministic processes, but by *magic*."[25] The process that Sartre calls magic is neither a reflective attitude nor is it conscious of itself. By changing our behavior, in phenomenological terms our intention, we apprehend an old object in a different way such that it becomes a new object for us. This is not to say that the end the emotional behavior seeks is to act upon the object through the agency of a particular means; rather, "it seeks by itself to confer upon the object, and without modifying it in its actual structure, another quality, a lesser existence, or a lesser presence."[26] The emotionally driven body directed by consciousness seeks to change its relation with the world that the world may change for it. While this is a modified, transformed world, at the same time the emotion does not turn inward, but keeps feeding on the emotive object. This "degraded" consciousness only deceives itself and eventually becomes its own prisoner.

This brief but important discussion of Sartre's concept of emotions or passions is essential because the act of being an anti-Semite cannot be based on experience if it resides in the passions. A predisposition toward hatred is not only fundamental to the very being of the anti-Semite, it is primordial. In his passion the anti-Semite adopts a subjective position that necessarily preconceives an "idea" of the Jew as to the latter's nature as well as to his role in society.

An example of a predisposition toward a particular group can be seen when then candidate for President Donald Trump argued for a complete ban on any Muslim coming into the United States regardless of the circumstances. Once elected, he tried to implement his political position by banning entry to the United Sates by citizens of five mostly Muslim countries. In effect, Trump sought to condemn an entire religion of over 1.8 billion followers comprising about 24 percent of the world's population for the terrible acts of a relative few, a determination that George W. Bush refused to do after the events of 9/11. Similar to the anti-Semite, the wholesale condemnation of a particular religious group relies on a preconceived notion of all members of that religion as homogeneous when, in fact, they are not.

President Trump's position that all Muslims are alien reflects the world view adopted by his administration, which is driven by the principles of Traditional Philosophy. Sartre recognizes this behavior because he believes that the anti-Semite also exists on a universal level. By this he means not only is the anti-Semite controlled by passions, but those passions also control his world view. The anti-Semite, driven by psychologically generated drives, projects those passions onto the world and all those who inhabit it. The anti-Semite, reminiscent of Nietzsche's slave, perceives a hostile external world and reacts to that environment with hate, or in the case of the Trump administration with a blanket ban on one religious group. Consequently, the anti-Semite adopts, in Sartre's view, a "syncretic" outlook that is always already present in all circumstances. In other words, the racist expects to encounter what he hates, whether it is a preconceived notion of immigrants crossing the border or the actions of those from a despised religion; no matter the circumstances the racist will experience a self-fulfilling prophecy. In much of the language offered by the alt-right, no group other than whites seems to have contributed to humankind's progress; in fact, they have been a hindrance. This form of racist selectivity is motivated by preconceived notions of the relative worth of whites versus everyone else.

By syncretic Sartre means behavior that is, for the most part, submerged into the content of behavior itself rather than behavior that imposes its own demands on the elements of the situation. In probing this type of behavior, Sartre finds that the anti-Semite possesses a basic fear not only of himself but for the truth as well. This fear emanates from the form of truth itself with what Sartre describes as its ever elastic character of indefinite approximation. The anti-Semite, his certainty founded on passion alone, rules out reason and rationality in his search for impenetrability. No matter the compelling nature of evidence put forth to prove his beliefs wrong, the racist refuses to alter his ingrained views. Hate is freely chosen for the anti-Semite because hate is a faith.[27] The anti-Semite feels no compulsion to look within himself for his personality; his being lies entirely outside of himself, and, as a result, the anti-Semite runs away—he "flees himself"—from the very awareness of himself as a person.

Sartre's view is very similar to that of Nietzsche whose man of *ressentiment* also directs his view outward instead of reflecting on to himself. For Nietzsche, as well as for Sartre, this is the essence of slave morality and it is the essence of the anti-Semite or any form of oppression or racism. Sartre vividly displays this concerted effort of nonreflection in his short story, "the Childhood of a Leader," which should be read as a fictionalized account of the anti-Semite chapter of *Anti-Semite, and Jew*.[28]

In an extremely revealing passage, Lucien, the youthful, burgeoning anti-Semite, tells his fellow travelers that the "First maxim . . . [is] not to try and see inside yourself; there is no mistake more dangerous."[29] This grounding is, Sartre believes, nothing less than irrationalism. As I mentioned previously in the discussion with Nietzsche, even though the man of *ressentiment* is obsessive in nature he possesses only an amorphous yearning for revenge manifested in an abstract desire for the utter humiliation of his target. This is poignantly illustrated by Sartre when at an early age Lucien, in the midst of an identity crisis is afraid that he will never amount to anything significant, describes his existence in such evocative terms as small, sad, and vague; he even goes so far as to think that he does not exist. It is not until he encounters the rabidly anti-Semitic Lemordant that he sees a man who has found his place in the world, a place Lucien will soon covet.

At Lemordant's urging, Lucien signs some nebulous petition protesting Jewish students at the *École Normale Supérieure*, and the next day is elated to see his name printed in the right wing, ultranationalist *Action Française*. Lucien subsequently joins Lemordant's group, the *Camelots*, and is captivated by the camaraderie of his fellow anti-Semites. This camaraderie is, Lucien decides, based on strength; it is the power that Lucien feels he never before possessed. What Lucien desires is reliance or a mutual dependency upon a group of likeminded people—what Nietzsche would view as a herd mentality—and not unlike Nietzsche's description of the man of *ressentiment's* revenge that seeks to humiliate and destroy, the *Camelots'* adolescent pranks directed at various Jews and their establishments escalates over time into the verbal humiliation and severe beating of a helpless Jew. Lucien finds the violence to be an affirmation of a right and of a conviction so deep as to be "religious;" that right, that conviction is little more than the trite and prosaic slogan: "France for the French." In Lucien's narcissistically, obsessional, and irrational world, being born a Jew in France somehow does not render one French. Lucien's religious mystic played out in the comments of alt-right leaders, such as Jason Kessler and Richard Spencer, after the events of the Unite the Right march in Charlottesville, Virginia. Kessler called the march an "incredible moment for white people," while Spencer describing the demonstration as "religious," thought there was "nothing more beautiful than a torch-light march."

As Nietzsche probed the origin of the man of *ressentiment* and found him in the masses or the herd, Sartre sees the anti-Semite inhabiting a similar position in society. They move, Sartre says, among the anonymous crowd, they are the poor man's snob, and they belong to the lower middle classes of the towns and rural districts. They work in anonymous jobs as bureaucrats, obscure office workers, and ordinary businessmen. In short, they are every bit of Nietzsche's masses and the herd. These people who lack all power can only gain power through their perverse treatment of the Jews who are viewed as taking over, or as having everything. In our more contemporary context, racist views are directed at those seeking to cross the southern border who are viewed as alien human beings, dangerous usurpers intent on infiltrating a way of life and turning it into an unfamiliar culture. What Sartre is describing is our natural tendency toward exclusivity, and by excluding others from one group we affirm our superiority over those we have expunged. The anti-Semite, ensconced within a container, joins the exclusive "gated community" by treating the Jew as inferior.

In one crucial aspect, however, Sartre recognizes the paradoxical dependence the anti-Semite has for the Jew to sustain the life he has chosen. Without the Jew or some other targeted group, the anti-Semite would be forced to look to another cause or another hatred rather than be compelled to look within himself. In other words, those who seek to ostracize particular groups are quite capable of finding new groups to disparage should the need arise. The anti-Semite creates the Jew and as Sartre explains: "Far from the experience producing his idea of the Jew, it was the latter which explained his experience. If the Jew did not exist, the anti-Semite would have invented him."[30] In a similar vein, Nietzsche recognizes the other's effect when he asks: "have you ever seen your friend asleep—and found how he looks? What is the face of your friend anyway? It is your own in a rough and imperfect mirror?"[31] While Nietzsche is not as direct as Sartre in indicating that the other always determines human subjectivity, he poses the pertinent enquiry: "In short, the question is always who *he is*, and who *the other* is."[32] In this sense, Nietzsche is certainly aware of the "other" and its profound effect on human subjectivity in general, and for the man of *ressentiment* in particular who can affirm his own existence only through the negation of the other.

After all, the man of *ressentiment*, just like Sartre's anti-Semite, is reacting to something or more likely to someone, and that reaction, so essential to both Nietzsche and Sartre, is not a reaction to something ethereal. Accordingly, the psychological drives compelling the man of *ressentiment* are, in his hate and vengeance and in his desire for power, directed to the other, and that other for the racist are Jews, blacks, Muslims, and immigrants. In this sense, it is crucial for Sartre to formulate the "person" or identity of the anti-Semite, which includes character traits, social status, thoughts, and habits. As a result, anti-Semitism forms a web of intricate entanglements that envelops an entire personality, the effect of which is one is either an anti-Semite or one is not; there is no middle ground.

No middle ground can exist for the simple reason that the anti-Semite views the Jew as evil. To sustain his world view, the anti-Semite renounces all expectations that the Jew (or any targeted group) will reform himself and conduct his affairs in a so-called reasonable manner (reasonable, that is, to the anti-Semite). This impossible goal gives way to a metaphysical principle that there is an inherent drive within the Jew to do evil. But in case one asks, if the Jew can do evil surely he can just as easily do good? The anti-Semite, Sartre declares, declines our entreaty by indicating: "The Jew is free *to do evil*, not good; he has only so much free will as is necessary for him to take full responsibility for his crimes which he is the author; he does not have enough to be able to achieve a reformation."[33] As the master fought the slave in a duel to the death, so the anti-Semite sees the Jew as one to be annihilated. Good, for the anti-Semite, can only come through the destruction of the Jew. The anti-Semite's Manichaeism is essential to an understanding of his psychological makeup. At the same time, it plays a crucial role in Nietzsche's development of the man of *ressentiment* and his concomitant notion of *the Evil One*. The man of *ressentiment* views his attitude as righteous and himself as good; he views the evil man, and in this case it is the Jew, with fear and trepidation. Nietzsche's Manichaeism rests secure in the anti-Semite's psyche.

As we have seen, Sartre paints a portrait of the anti-Semite whose character is defined by his passion and not his reason. Emotion alone rules this character's individual as well as world view. His fear is, Sartre says, of himself, but inherent within that fear resides a fear of the other, and for the anti-Semite the other is the Jew. This fear of the other emerges for the anti-Semite in his Manichean attitude of good and evil. Our anti-Semite is, Sartre informs us, the ordinary member of the masses; he occupies the herd. The picture we gain of the anti-Semite is of a man who is afraid, not only of the Jew, but of himself, of his own bad faith, and his own limitations. For this character, the Jew is a device, a means to ensure one's own existence; an existence as implacable as stone.

While Sartre rarely mentions Nietzsche in his writings on anti-Semitism, there are parallels between their views. Nietzsche's prescient portrayal of the man of *ressentiment* plays out in the anti-Semite chapter of Sartre's book as well as in his fictionalized account of the burgeoning anti-Semite Lucien. Each delves into the psychological makeup of the character to understand, in Nietzsche's case, not only what is wrong with the psyche of the man of *ressentiment* but why it is wrong when compared to that of the character of the noble. No less than Nietzsche, Sartre also delves into the psychologically based motivation of the behavior of the anti-Semite, and seeks to expose that character as weak, impotent, unhealthy, and reactive—all words that Nietzsche would approve of.[34]

I have argued that it was not the economic "left behind" theory that primarily shaped the American political landscape in 2016 nor did that theory propel the alt-right political movement to prominence in the Trump administration. Rather, the argument I put forth is that to understand public acceptance of derogatory, demeaning, and racist public statements concerning minorities, immigrants, women, and foreigners, one must see it in terms of preexisting racist and sexist attitudes. However, to fully comprehend this dynamic, one must also understand the threat to dominant group status perceived by certain members of the white social hierarchy. Certainly when members of a dominant group sense their social position in jeopardy, several well-constructed reactions take place to allow these groups to regain their threatened wellbeing and dominance. If one's social position status quo is threatened, then hierarchical social and political arrangements become more attractive and hardened in the eyes of those who feel threatened. The idea of regaining an always "better" past, with its stable social structure, where everyone had a function and only performed that function becomes a prevalent sentiment. But the threat also triggers a defensive mode by the dominant group with stricter reliance on group norms and conventions—a desire for deeper group unity—and increased negative attitudes toward outgroups. In fact, the dominant group often looks to authoritarian leaders who promise to rectify the inequity and return the society to a past glory, but at the very least the current status quo.

These threat attitudes of intragroup and intergroup relations should also be viewed in a broader context. The Great Replacement concern represents a deeply held belief among some Americans that in a very short period of time, whites will be a minority race with so-called inferior nonwhite races taking over. Even if such an outcome occurs, it will probably not alter the social status of white Americans as the most economically well-off racial group. There is, however, a substantial symbolic fear that a way of life is drawing to a close, and what that world would look like presents an unknown—something humans dislike—that results in psychological factors confirming already existing racist feelings of replacement by inferior races or religions.

The broader context also includes a quite different fear. The fear associated with increasing interdependence of the United States on other countries. Globalization, it is argued, is the boogeyman causing the loss of American hegemony in the world. Part of the appeal of Trump's presidential campaign was the allegation that seemingly all trade agreements such as the North American Free Trade Agreement (NAFTA) or trade pacts with other nations, most notably China, were "rigged" against American interest and only conducive to foreign economic interests. Such arguments blamed these agreements for the loss of jobs and the erosion of American influence throughout the world. Moreover, the Trump administration viewed nontrade global agreements like the 2016 Paris Accord on Climate Change as furtherance of a globalist agenda, and decidedly against American interests. Trump argued that every prior President was inept at negotiating such treaties and that only he could set the world right by implementing an "America First" agenda and either removing the United States from such agreements or renegotiating them altogether. To date, the administration has met with limited success.

While social status threat and global eminence are distinct occurrences, in practical terms they are difficult to distinguish. They must be seen as overall apprehensions driving the move to embrace an alt-right political philosophy. In a widely discussed article, political scientist Diana Mutz, argued that status threat and not economic disadvantage explains the 2016 presidential outcome.[35] Ultimately, she concluded that Trump voters were not lured by anger over the past, but fear as to what the future may hold. White, Christian, and male voters turned to Trump because they felt their social hierarchical status was at risk. In her research, Mutz posed two questions: is there evidence to support the economic left behind theory, and did the fear of lost social dominance cause some to vote for Trump? With regard to the first question, Mutz found that losing a job between 2012 and 2016 did not translate into votes for Trump. Moreover, one's mere perception of financial instability did not turn into votes for Trump.

While economic anxiety did not explain Trump's appeal, Mutz found a correlation between the perceived threat of globalization and unfair trade agreements and those who voted for Trump. Americans feared their global dominance was in danger, a concern that benefitted the Trump campaign. Equally important was the finding that people who exhibited a growing belief in group dominance as measured by social dominance orientation were more likely to vote for Trump hoping that the social status quo would be protected. These two outcomes indicate that personal economic issues had less to do with the presidential outcome than fear of global entanglements and a perceived loss of social status within the social hierarchy. This, in turn, helped to advance the alt-right political agenda by playing on these fears.

While the study was concerned with voting habits in the 2016 election, the results of Mutz's research has relevance to the present discussion. From an empirical point of view, the study reinforces the present underlying thesis that social status is the spark that ignites the alt-right political objectives. Moreover, those objectives are directly related to a traditional philosophic view that not only informs a domestic policy based on fear of the other as an alien human force ready to alter and disrupt the hegemonic hierarchical order of American life, but a world view that is antiglobal, antimulticultural, and antithetical to traditional liberal democratic ideals.

NOTES

1. A very good discussion of this issue can be found in Jonathan Judaken, *Jean-Paul Sartre and the Jewish Question* (Lincoln: University of Nebraska Press, 2006), 126.

2. See, for example, Yirmiyahu Yovel, *Dark Riddle: Hegel, Nietzsche, and the Jews* (Cambridge: Polity Press, 1998); John Andrew Bernstein, *Nietzsche's Moral Philosophy*

(Rutherford, NJ: Fairleigh Dickinson University Press, 1987), 134–38; Yirmiyahu Yovel, "Nietzsche, the Jews, and *Ressentiment*," in *Nietzsche, Genealogy, Morality*, ed. Richard Schacht (Berkeley: University of California Press, 1994), 214–36; Jacqueline Scott, "On the Use and Abuse of Race in Philosophy," in *Race and Racism in Continental Philosophy*, ed. Robert Bernasconi and Sybol Cook (Bloomington: Indiana University Press, 2003), 53–73; Michael F. Duffy and Willard Mittelman, "Nietzsche's Attitude toward the Jews," *Journal of the History of Ideas* 49, no. 2 (April–June 1988): 301–17.

3. Jean-Paul Sartre, *Anti-Semite and Jew*, trans. George J. Becker (New York: Schoken Books, 1948), hereinafter referred to as ASJ. The first chapter of *Anti-Semite and Jew* appeared in an early edition of *Les Temps Modernes* as "Portrait de l'anti-Semite," *Les Temps Modernes* (December 1, 1945).

4. Friedrich Nietzsche, *Ecce Homo*, trans. Walter Kaufman (New York: Vintage Books, 1989), III "Genealogy of Morals."

5. Friedrich Nietzsche, *On the Genealogy of Morals*, trans. Walter Kaufman and R. J. Hollingdale (New York: Vintage Books, 1989), I §7; II §11; III §11; hereinafter referred to as GM. Max Scheler, while not always agreeing with Nietzsche's moral assessments, nevertheless describes *ressentiment* as follows: "among the scanty discoveries which have been made in recent times about the origin of moral judgments, Friedrich Nietzsche's discovery that *ressentiment* can be the source of such value judgments is the most profound. This remains true even if his specific characterization of Christian love as the most delicate 'flower of *ressentiment*' should turn out to be mistaken." Max Scheler, "Ressentiment," in *Nietzsche: A Collection of Critical Essays*, ed. Robert C. Solomon (Garden City, NY: Anchor Books, 1973), 242–57.

6. Bernard Reginster, "Nietzsche on Ressentiment and Valuation," *Philosophy and Phenomenological Research* 57, no. 2 (June 1997): 282–83.

7. Fredrich Nietzsche, *Daybreak: Thoughts on the Prejudices of Morality*, ed. Maudmarie Clark and Brian Leiter, trans. R. J. Hollingdale (Cambridge: Cambridge University Press, 1997), I §38 (emphasis in original).

8. GM, II §6; §§14–19. See also Friedrich Nietzsche, *Human, All Too Human*, trans. R. J. Hollingdale (Cambridge: Cambridge University Press, 1986), II §39; and Friedrich Nietzsche, *Beyond Good and Evil*, trans. Helen Zimmern (Amherst, NY: Prometheus Books, 1989), § 260, hereinafter referred to as BGE.

9. GM, I §§5–6; BGE, §§257–58.

10. Ibid., I §10 (emphasis in original).

11. Friedrich Nietzsche, *The Will to Power*, trans. Walter Kaufman and R. J. Hollingdale (New York: Penguin Books, 1968), II §461.

12. BGE, §260.

13. Arthur C. Danto, *Nietzsche as Philosopher* (New York: Macmillan, 1965), 164–67.

14. GM, I §6; III §15; see also Friedrich Nietzsche, *The Gay Science*, trans. Walter Kaufman (New York: Vintage Books, 1974), §359.

15. GM, I §7.

16. Ibid., I §13 (emphasis in original).

17. See, for example, Robert C. Solomon, "One Hundred Years of *Ressentiment*: Nietzsche's Genealogy of Morals," in *Nietzsche, Genealogy, Morality*, ed. Richard Schacht (Berkeley: University of California Press, 1994), 95–126.

18. Nietzsche's paradigm for bad conscience is the broken contractual relationship between the debtor and the creditor. While the creditor is in the stronger position and has the right to punish and cause suffering, the creditor is weighed down by his plight of impotency. The ineluctable result of this situation is the emergence of a tortuous *ressentiment*, followed by an inner nurturing of feelings of vengeance and hatred. The culminating instant of this suffering is the violent repression of the instinct of freedom, which invariably leads to bad conscience. GM, II §§7–8.

19. Ibid., II §16.
20. Ibid., II §11.
21. ASJ, 9.
22. Ibid., 17.

23. Jean-Paul Sartre, *Emotions: Outline of a Theory*, trans. Bernard Frechtman (New York: The Wisdom Library, 1948).
24. Ibid., 57.
25. Ibid., 59 (emphasis added).
26. Ibid., 60–61.
27. As Sartre will later say, "as regards feelings . . . they reduce to undertakings; hate and love are *oaths*." Sartre, *Notebooks for an Ethics*, 476 (emphasis added).
28. John-Paul Sartre, "The Childhood of a Leader," in *The Wall and Other Stories*, trans. Lloyd Alexander (New York: New Directions Publishing Corporation, 1948), 84–144.
29. Ibid., 142.
30. ASJ, 13.
31. Friedrich Nietzsche, *Thus Spoke Zarathustra*, trans. Walter Kaufman (New York: Penguin Books, 1978), I, "On the Friend."
32. BGE, §221 (emphasis in original).
33. ASJ, 39 (emphasis in original).
34. It is interesting to note that, in "Childhood of a Leader," Lucien is "seduced" into a sexual encounter with an older man in a hotel room. Sartre portrays Lucien's actions as somewhat comical and pathetic, and, in this manner, he can be said to be showing the weakness and "unhealthy" character of the anti-Semite.
35. Diana Mutz, "Status Threat, Not Economic Hardship, Explains the 2016 Presidential Vote," *PNAS* 115, no. 19 (April 2018): 1–10.

Bibliography

Alexander, Michelle. *The New Jim Crow*. New York: The New Press, 2012.
Alliance for Justice (AFJ) Nominee Report: Allison Jones Rushing. https://www.afj.org/wp-content/uploads/2018/10/Rushing-Full-Report.pdf.
Assunção, Muri. "Detroit Man Sues Three Women Who Allegedly Filed Reports against Him for 'Gardening While Black.'" *New York Daily News*, March 6, 2019. https://www.nydailynews.com/news/national/ny-news-detroit-gardening-while-black-20190306-story.html.
Baum, Dan. "Legalize It All: How to Win the War on Drugs." *Harper's Magazine*, April 2016. https://harpers.org/archive/2016/04/legalize-it-all/.
Bell, Michael. "Julius Evola's Concept of Race: A Racism in Three Degrees." *The Occidental Quarterly* 9, no. 2 (Spring 2009): 101–12.
Benner, Katie, Glen Thrush, and Mike Isaac. "Facebook Engages in Housing Discrimination with Its Ad Practices, U.S. Says." *New York Times*, March 28, 2019. https://www.nytimes.com/2019/03/28/us/politics/facebook-housing-discrimination.html.
Bernstein, John Andrew. *Nietzsche's Moral Philosophy*. Rutherford, NJ: Fairleigh Dickinson University Press, 1987.
Bhaktivedanta Swami Prabhupada, A. C. *Bhagavad-Gītā As It Is*. Los Angeles: The Bhaktivedanta Book Trust, 2013.
Blinder, Alan, and Richard Pérez-Pena. "Kentucky Clerk Denies Same-Sex Marriage Licenses, Defying Court." *New York Times*, September 1, 2015. https://www.nytimes.com/2015/09/02/us/same-sex-marriage-kentucky-kim-davis.html.
Blumenberg, Hans. *Work on Myth*. Translated by Robert Wallace. Cambridge, MA: MIT Press, 1985.
Brown, Judith. "Economic Organization and the Position of Women among the Iroquois." *Ethnohistory* 17, no. 3/4 (1970): 151–67.
Burkle, Howard. "Jean-Paul Sartre: Social Freedom in Critique of Dialectical Reason." *The Review of Metaphysics* 19, no. 4 (June 1966): 742–57.
Catalano, Joseph. *A Commentary on Jean-Paul Sartre's Critique of Dialectical Reason*. Chicago: University of Chicago Press, 1986.
Clark, Dartunorro, and Garrett Haake. "Corker Calls GOP 'Cultish' and 'Fearful' under Trump." *NBC News*, January 13, 2018. https://www.nbcnews.com/politics/congress/republican-sen-bob-corker-calls-gop-cultish-fearful-under-trump-n882791.
Danto, Arthur. *Nietzsche as Philosopher*. New York: Macmillan, 1965.
Duffy, Michael, and Willard Mittelman. "Nietzsche's Attitude toward the Jews." *Journal of History of Ideas* 49, no. 2 (April–June 1998): 301–17.
Durkheim, Emile. *The Division of Labor in Society*. Translated by G. Simpson. New York: Macmillan, 1933.
Eire, Carlos. *Reformations: The Early Modern World, 1450–1650*. New Haven, CT: Yale University Press, 2016.
Evola, Julius. *The Elements of Racial Education*. https://evolaasheis.wordpress.com/author/evolaasheis/.
———. *Men among the Ruins: Postwar Reflections of a Radical Traditionalist*. Edited by Michael Moynihan. Translated by Guido Stucco. Rochester, VT: Inner Traditions, 2002.
———. *Metaphysics of War: Battle, Victory and Death in the World of Tradition*. Edited by John Morgan. London: Arktos, 2011.

———. *The Path of Cinnabar*. Edited by John Morgan. Translated by Sergio Knipe. London: Arktos, 2010.
———. "Preface to 'The Protocols of the Elders of Zion.'" https://evolaasheis.wordpress.com/2016/04/14/preface-to-the-protocols-of-the-elders-of-zion/.
———. *Revolt against the Modern World*. Translated by Guido Stucco. Rochester, VT: Inner Traditions, 1995.
———. *Ride the Tiger*. Translated by Joscelyn Godwin and Constance Fontana. Rochester, VT: Inner Directions, 2003.
Ferrer, J. N. "The Perennial Philosophy Revisited." *Journal of Transpersonal Psychology* 32, no. 1 (2000): 7–30.
Furlong, Paul. *Social and Political Thought of Julius Evola*. Milton Park: Routledge, 2011.
Goldstein, Joseph. "Alt-Right Gathering Exults in Trump Election with Nazi-Era Salute." *New York Times*, November 20, 2016. https://www.nytimes.com/2016/11/21/us/alt-right-salutes-donald-trump.html.
Gramsci, Antonio. *Selections from the Prison Notebooks*. Edited and translated by Quintin Hoare and Geoffrey Smith. New York: International Publishers, 2018.
Guénon, René. "Civilization and Progress." In *The Essential René Guénon: Metaphysics, Tradition, and the Crisis of Modernity*, edited by John Herlihy, 68–74. Bloomington, IN: World Wisdom, 2009.
———. *The Crisis of the Modern World*. Translated by Marco Pallis, Arthur Osborne, and Richard Nicholson. Hillsdale: Sophia Perennis, 2001.
———. *Introduction to the Study of Hindu Doctrines*. Translated by Marco Pallis. Hillsdale: Sophia Perennis, 2004.
———. *Le Roi du Monde*. Paris: Gallimard, 1927.
———. "Sanātana Dharma." In *The Essential René Guénon: Metaphysics, Tradition, and the Crisis of Modernity*, edited by John Herlihy, 108–16. Bloomington, IN: World Wisdom, 2009.
———. "Some Remarks on the Doctrine of Cosmic Cycles." In *The Essential René Guénon: Metaphysics, Tradition, and the Crisis of Modernity*, edited by John Herlihy, 117–23. Bloomington, IN: World Wisdom, 2009.
———. *The Reign of Quantity and the Signs of the Times*. Translated by Lord Northbourne. Hillsdale: Sophia Perennis, 2001.
Hansen, H. T. "A Short Introduction to Julius Evola." In *Revolt against the Modern World*. Translated by Guido Stucco. Rochester VT: Inner Traditions, 1995.
Hobbes, Thomas. *Behemoth*. Edited by Ferdinand Tönnies. Chicago: University of Chicago Press, 1990.
Huxley, Aldous. "Introduction." In *Bhagavad-Gita: The Song of God*. Translated by Swami Prabhavananda and Christopher Isherwood. New York: Mentor Books, 1951.
———. *The Perennial Philosophy*. New York: Perennial Modern Classics, 2009.
Isenberg, Nancy. *White Trash: The 400-Year Untold History of Class in America*. New York: Penguin Books, 2016.
Jacobs, Tom. "A Cult Expert Finds Familiar Pattern of Behavior in Trump's GOP." *Pacific Standard*, June 21, 2018. https://psmag.com/news/a-sociologist-explains-the-similarities-between-cults-and-trumps-gop.
Jones, Robert, Daniel Cox, Betsey Cooper, and Rachel Lienesch. "Anxiety, Nostalgia, and Mistrust: Findings from the 2015 American Values Survey." *PRRI*. Published November 17, 2015. https://www.prri.org/research/survey-anxiety-nostalgia-and-mistrust-findings-from-the-2015-american-values-survey/.
Judaken, Jonathan. *Jean-Paul Sartre and the Jewish Question*. Lincoln: University of Nebraska Press, 2006.
Kindy, Kimberly, and Kimbriell Kelly. "Thousands Dead, Few Prosecuted." *Washington Post*, April 1, 2015. https://www.washingtonpost.com/sf/investigative/2015/04/11/thousands-dead-few-prosecuted/?noredirect=on&utm_term=.0d098a97da93.
Kludt, Tom, and Brian Stelter. "White Anxiety Finds a Home at Fox News." *CNN*, August 9, 2018. https://www.cnn.com/2018/09/28/media/fox-news-laura-ingraham-tucker-carlson-white-nationalism/index.html.

Lee, Michelle Ye Hee. "Donald Trump's False Comments Connecting Mexican Immigrants and Crime." *Washington Post*, July 8, 2015. https://www.washingtonpost.com/news/fact-checker/wp/2015/07/08/donald-trumps-false-comments-connecting-mexican-immigrants-and-crime/?utm_term=.597dca090d92.

Levin, S., C. Frederico, J. Sidanius, and J. Rabinowitz. "Social Dominance Orientation and Intergroup Bias: The Legitimation of Favoritism for High-Status Groups." *Personality and Social Psychology Bulletin* 28, no. 2 (2002): 144–57.

Malraux, André. *Days of Hope*. Translated by Stuart Gilbert and Alastair MacDonald. London: George Routledge & Sons, 1938.

Massing, Michael. *Fatal Discord: Erasmus, Luther, and the Fight for the Western Mind*. New York: HarperCollins, 2018.

Mercier, Hugo, and Dan Sperber. *The Enigma of Reason*. Cambridge, MA: Harvard University Press, 2017.

Merton, Robert. "The Self-Fulfilling Prophecy." *The Antioch Review* 8, no. 2 (1948): 193–210.

Moscovici, Serge. "Notes toward a Description of Social Representations." *European Journal of Social Psychology* 18 (1988): 211–50.

Mutz, Diana. "Status Threat, Not Economic Hardship, Explains the 2016 Presidential Vote." *PNAS* 115, no. 19 (April 2018): 1–10.

Nietzsche, Friedrich. *Beyond Good and Evil*. Translated by Helen Zimmern. Amherst, NY: Prometheus Books, 1989.

———. *Daybreak: Thoughts on the Prejudices of Morality*. Edited by Maudmarie Clark and Brian Leiter. Translated by R. J. Hollingdale. Cambridge: Cambridge University Press, 1997.

———. *Ecce Homo*. Translated by Walter Kaufman. New York: Vintage Books, 1989.

———. *The Gay Science*. Translated by Walter Kaufman. New York: Vintage Books, 1974.

———. *Human, All Too Human*. Translated by R. J. Hollingdale. Cambridge: Cambridge University Press, 1986.

———. *On the Genealogy of Morals*. Translated by Walter Kaufman and R. J. Hollingdale. New York: Vintage Books, 1989.

———. *Thus Spoke Zarathustra*. Translated by Walter Kaufman. New York: Penguin Books, 1978.

———. *The Will to Power*. Translated by Walter Kaufman and R. J. Hollingdale. New York: Penguin Books, 1968.

Northbourne, Lord. "Looking Back on Progress." In *The Underlying Religion: An Introduction to Perennial Philosophy*, edited by Martin Lings and Clinton Minnaar, 18–32. Bloomington, IN: World Wisdom, 2007.

———. "Modernism: The Profane Point of View." In *The Underlying Religion: An Introduction to Perennial Philosophy*, edited by Martin Lings and Clinton Minnaar, 11–17. Bloomington, IN: World Wisdom, 2007.

———. "Religion and Tradition." In *The Underlying Religion: An Introduction to Perennial Philosophy*, edited by Martin Lings and Clinton Minnaar, 3–10. Bloomington, IN: World Wisdom, 2007.

Oldmeadow, Harry. *Traditionalism: Religion in the Light of the Perennial Philosophy*. San Rafael: Sophia Perennis, 2011.

O'Meara, Dominic. *Plotinus*. Oxford: Clarendon Press, 1993.

Pettigrew, Thomas. "Social Psychological Perspectives on Trump Supporters." *Journal of Social and Political Psychology* 5, no. 1 (2017): 107–16.

Pettigrew, Thomas, and L. Tropp. *When Groups Meet: The Dynamics of Intergroup Contact*. New York: Psychology Press, 2011.

Plato. *The Republic of Plato*. Translated by Allan Bloom. New York: Basic Books, 1991.

Plotinus. *Enneads IV*. Translated by Barrie Fleet. Las Vegas: Parmenides, 2016.

Putman, Robert. *The Comparative Study of Political Elites*. Englewood Cliffs, NJ: Prentice Hall, 1976.

Reginster, Bernard. "Nietzsche on *Ressentiment* and Valuation." *Philosophy and Phenomenological Research* 57, no. 2 (June 1997): 281–305.
Remley, William. "'Can You Justify Your Existence Then? Just a Little?': The Psychological Convergence of Sartre and Fanon." *Diogenes* 61, no. 1 (2016): 44–58.
The Rig Veda. Translated by Wendy O'Flaherty. Harmondsworth: Penguin Books, 1981.
Rivera, Lauren A. *Pedigree: How Elite Students Get Elite Jobs*. Princeton, NJ: Princeton University Press, 2015.
Santos, Barbara, and John Giodano. "René Guénon on the Realization of Traditional Knowledge." *Prajñā Vihara* 18, no. 1 (January–June 2017): 98–140.
Sartre Jean-Paul. *Anti-Semite and Jew*. Translated by George Becker. New York: Schoken Books, 1948.
——. *Being and Nothingness*. Translated by Hazel Barnes. New York: Washington Square Press, 1956.
——. *Critique of Dialectical Reason*. Vol. I. Translated by Alan Sheridan-Smith. Edited by Jonathan Rée. London: Verso, 2004.
——. *Critique of Dialectical Reason*. Vol. II. Translated by Quintin Hoare. Edited by Arlette Elkaïm-Sartre. London: Verso, 2006.
——. *Emotions: Outline of a Theory*. Translated by Bernard Frechtman. New York: The Wisdom Library, 1948.
——. *Notebooks for an Ethics*. Translated by David Pellauer. Chicago: University of Chicago Press, 1992.
——. *The Wall and Other Stories*. Translated by Lloyd Alexander. New York: New Directions Publishing Corporation, 1948.
Scheler, Max. "Ressentiment." In *Nietzsche: A Collection of Critical Essays*, edited by Robert Solomon, 242–57. Garden City, NY: Anchor Books, 1973.
Schuon, Frithjof. *Light on the Ancient Worlds*. Bloomington, IN: World Wisdom, 2006.
Scott, Jacqueline. "On the Use and Abuse of Race in Philosophy." In *Race and Racism in Continental Philosophy*, edited by Robert Bernasconi and Sybol Cook, 53–73. Bloomington: Indiana University Press, 2003.
Sedgwick, Mark. *Against the Modern World*. Oxford: Oxford University Press, 2004.
Sellin, Thorston. *Culture, Conflict, and Crime*. New York: Social Science Research Council, 1938.
Sherrard, Philip. "Modern Science and the Dehumanization of Man." In *The Underlying Religion: An Introduction to Perennial Philosophy*, edited by Martin Lings and Clinton Minnaar, 70–91. Bloomington, IN: World Wisdom, 2007.
Sidanius, Jim, and Felicia Pratto. *Social Dominance: An Integrated Theory of Social Hierarchy and Oppression*. Cambridge: Cambridge University Press, 2001.
Sidanius, Jim, Felicia Pratto, and Lawrence Bobo. "Racism, Conservatism, Affirmative Action, and Intellectual Sophistication: A Matter of Principled Conservatism or Group Dominance." *Journal of Personality and Social Psychology* 70, no. 3 (1996): 476–90.
Silver, Nate. "The Mythology of Trump's 'Working Class' Support." *FiveThirtyEight*, May 3, 2016. fivethirtyeight.com/features/the-mythology-of-trumps-working-class-support/
Sloman, Steven, and Philip Fernbach. *The Knowledge Illusion: Why We Never Think Alone*. New York: Riverhead Books, 2017.
Smith, Huston. "Is There a Perennial Philosophy?" *Journal of the American Academy of Religion* 55, no. 3 (1987): 553–66.
Solomon, Robert. "One Hundred Years of *Ressentiment*: Nietzsche's Genealogy of Morals." In *Nietzsche, Genealogy, Morality*, edited by Richard Schacht, 95–126. Berkeley: University of California Press, 1994.
Southern Poverty Law Center. *Extremist Files: Alliance Defending Freedom*. https://www.splcenter.org/fighting-hate/extremist-files/group/alliance-defending-freedom.

Stoddart, William. "Mysticism." In *The Underlying Religion: An Introduction to Perennial Philosophy*, edited by Martin Lings and Clinton Minnaar, 230–42. Bloomington, IN: World Wisdom, 2007.

Stone, Jon. "Far-Right European Governments Launch Plan to Take over EU with Anti-Immigration 'Axis.'" *Independent*, January 10, 2019. www.independent.co.uk/news/world/europe/far-right-europe-hungary-viktor-obran-italy-poland-immigration-axis-eu-a8720976.html.

Sumner, William. *Folkways: A Study of the Sociological Importance of Usages, Manners, Customs, and Morals*. Boston: Ginn and Co., 1906.

Taylor, Steve. "From Philosopher to Phenomenology: The Argument for a 'Soft' Perennialism." *International Journal of Transpersonal Studies* 35, no. 2 (2016): 17–41.

Trismegistus, Hermes. *The Emerald Tablet of Hermes*. Translated by Jabir ibin Hyyan. n.p.: Merchant Books, 2013.

———. *The Way of Hermes*. Translated by Clement Salaman, Dorine van Oyen, William Wharton, and Jean-Pierre Mahé. Rochester, VT: Inner Traditions, 2004.

Tversky, Amos, and Daniel Kahneman. "Judgment under Uncertainty: Heuristics and Biases." *Science, New Series* 185, no. 4157 (September 27, 1974): 1124–31.

Van den Berghe, Pierre. *Man in Society: A Biosocial View*. New York: Elsevie1978.

Versluis, Arthur. *Perennial Philosophy*. Minneapolis: New Culture Press, 2015.

Washington Post. "Deconstructing the Symbols and Slogans Spotted in Charlottesville." August 18, 2017. https://www.washingtonpost.com/graphics/2017/local/charlottesvillevideos/?noredirect=on&utm_term=.481daaca5353.

Watkins, Eli, and James Gary. "Let Them Call You Racist." *CNN*, March 10, 2018. https://www.cnn.com/2018/03/10/politics/steve-bannon-national-front/index.html.

Yockey, Francis Parker. *Imperium*. Newport Beach: Noontide Press, 1962.

Yovel, Yirmiyahu. *Dark Riddle: Hegel, Nietzsche, and the Jews*. Cambridge: Polity Press, 1998.

———. "Nietzsche, the Jews, and *Ressentiment*." In *Nietzsche, Genealogy, Morality*, edited by Richard Schact, 214–36. Berkeley: University of California Press, 1994.

Index

action, 60, 122, 136; aesthetes and, 74; contemplation and, 44–45, 74, 75; freedom and, 70; of group-in-fusion, 150; as interiorization, 151; reaction as, 168; Sartre on, 139; unreflective consciousness as, 170
active-passivity, 148
active resistance, task of, 64
ADF. *See* Alliance Defending Freedom
African Americans, 3, 101
age system, 10, 96, 97
aggregated individual discrimination, 99
aggregated institutional discrimination, 99
alchemy, 47
alienation, 14, 139
Alliance Defending Freedom (ADF), 100
alterity, 129, 144
alternative-right (alt-right), 1; *ressentiment* and, 161–176; traditionalism and, 16; Trump and, 2
anamnesis, 23–33
Ancien Régime, 106
Anti-Semite and Jew (Sartre), 163
anti-Semitism, 111, 164; discussion of, 16, 162–163; Nietzsche on, 168–169
Apocalypse, 128, 131, 155n11
arbitrary-set system, 10, 96; group-in-fusion and, 106; oppression and, 97
archives, 60
aristocracy, 51, 82, 85
Aristotle, 25
Aryans, 9, 65, 66; decline of, 76; discrimination and, 110; justification of, 111; social hierarchy and, 65; spirituality and, 80
asceticism, 73–74

astrology, 47
astronomy, 47
asylum seekers, 166
Atlantic Cycle, 78
atomization, 140
authoritarian governance, 151–152
authority, 42, 75, 83; foundation of, 67; sovereignty and, 149–154

Bachofen, Johann Jakob, 8, 60
bad conscience, 164, 168, 177n18
Bannon, Steve, 10, 64–65
Bäumler, Alfred, 163
behaviors, 111, 149; behavioral asymmetry, 101, 102; psychology and, 174
being, 120, 129; being-in-group and, 140
Being and Nothingness (Sartre), 123
beliefs, 1, 6, 109; contemplation and, 28; racism and, 104
Bhagavad Gita, 66
biology, 63
Black Skin White Masks (Fanon), 102
Blois, France, 37
blood, 70
bond, 143, 147; of sociality, 137–138
borders, 112
bourgeois, 65, 86
brahmin caste, 69
Buddhism, 30
burial, 80
Burkle, Howard, 156n13
Bush, George W., 171

capitalism, 86
caste system: doctrines and, 71–73; equality and, 72; function and, 49–50; principles and, 71. *See also specific castes*

Catalano, Joseph, 154n1
Catholicism, 38, 43, 56
Catholic Traditionalism, 2
certainty, 105
characteristics, 11, 132, 145; adoption of, 154; cults and, 152; nobility and, 168
Charlottesville, Virginia, 69
chemistry, 47
chivalry, 82
Christianity, 29, 80–81
chthonic theme, 79
civilizations, 43; of the Mother, 79–80; stories and, 77–80; types of, 80
civil rights movement, 19
class, 48, 49, 113
cleverness, 165
Clinton, Hillary, 84
collective, 81, 122; nationalism and, 87; seriality and, 119–120; series as, 120–125
confirmation bias, 125
conflict, 113, 141; avoidance of, 121; the pledged and, 144–146
consciousness, 45, 169; unreflective, 170
consecration, 69
consensuality, 104, 111; LM and, 112
conservatism, 110
conspiracy theories, 84
container (wall), 64; advantages of, 54–55; bond over, 143; enemies and, 152; protection of, 142; Trump and, 112
contemplation, 32; action and, 44–45, 74, 75; asceticism and, 74
contemplative ascent, 28–29, 30
Conway, Kellyanne, 153
Corker, Bob, 152
Corpus Hermeticum (hermeticism), 5
cosmos, 31
counterinitiation, 7
cremation, 80
The Crisis of the Modern World (Guénon), 6, 39–41
Critique of Dialectical Reason vols. I and II (Sartre), 3; topics in, 119–154
cult of personality, 14; leadership and, 15, 149–154

cults, 152

Dada movement, 59
Dark Age (*Kali Yuga*), 38, 39, 81, 90n52
Davis, Kim, 100
death, 134, 143
decadence, 40, 85; of the West, 87
deconsecration, 82
de Gobineau, Joseph Arthur, 117n26
degradation, 149
democracy, 51; equality and, 54; monarchy and, 85; traditionalism and, 48–51
demos, 68, 83
desacralization, 9
dharma, 72
dichotomy, 161
differences, 50
discrimination, 98, 99, 110; institutional discrimination, 101; institutional terror and, 100; legal system and, 114
disequilibrium, 45, 54
disorder, 50
disproportionate prosecution principle, 114
disunity, 49
Divine Essence, 24–25, 34n9
divine right, 69
doctrines, 27, 38; castes and, 71–73; of four ages, 77–80; perennialism and, 24–25; science and, 47
drive, 164, 173, 174
dualism, 28

the East, 46; encroachment upon, 55; the West *versus*, 43–44
economics, 53, 73, 86; elites and, 97; invention and, 53
egalitarianism, 81
Ehrlichman, John, 113
Eliot, T. S., 57
elites, 43, 44, 97; aristocracy and, 51; intellectual tradition and, 56; Plato and, 48
embeddedness, 104
The Emerald Tablet (Hermes), 30, 31
emotions, 169–170, 178n27

The Emotions: Outline of a Theory (Sartre), 169–170
empiricism, 52
Enneads (Plotinus), 29
equality, 50, 81, 103; caste system and, 72; democracy and, 54
esotericism, 6; exotericism and, 26–27; Nietzsche and, 32; perennialism and, 26
essentialness, 142
ethics, 23, 65
Etudes Traditionnelles journal, 38
Europe, 1, 64, 76; stratification and, 12, 107
evil, 166, 174
Evola, Julius, 3, 90n63; Guénon and, 9; traditionalism and, 59–88; translation by, 111; writings by, 8, 10, 62
exclusion, 143
existentialism, 170
exotericism, 6, 32; esotericism and, 26–27
experiences, 27, 67, 121
exteriority, 120

facts, 125
Fair Housing Act of 1968, 101
family, 75
Fanon, Frantz, 102, 116n15
fascism, 9; Evola and, 59–60, 61–62, 66; politics and, 62
fear, 16, 124, 175; of dispersal, 132; of dissolution, 142; freedom and, 143; structure and, 133–134; truth and, 171
fertility, 79
feudal system, 82
Ficino, Marsilio, 5
fides, 73, 85
Fifteenth Amendment to Constitution, US, 101
folk (*Volk*), 62, 89n9
formalism, 27
Formula of the Series, 121–122
fraternity, 135, 136
Fraternity-Terror, 136, 151
free common praxis, 135
free criticism, 42

freedom, 76; action and, 70; authority and, 83; human freedom as, 13, 119–154
Freemasonry, 60
French New Right, 2
French occultism, 37
French Revolution, 106, 124, 127
function, 48, 53, 157n32, 157n42; castes and, 49–50; conflict over, 145; essentialness of, 142; Evola on, 72–73; membership as, 96; sentiment and, 175; sovereignty and, 151; tasks and, 137
Futurist movement, 59

gender system, 10, 96; social control and, 97
A General Introduction to the Study of Hindu Doctrines (Guénon), 39
genocide, 97
Germany, Nazi era in, 69
goals, 18, 27; Evola and, 61; truth as, 32
God, 24–25, 29, 34n9; cult of personality and, 153; as telluric, 9, 61
Godhead, 24–25, 34n9
gold, 86
Golden Age, 77
government, 48; rejection of, 2; rise of, 86
The Great Fear of 1789, 124; public opinion and, 125
Great Replacement ideology, 8, 76–77
group-based dominance, 10, 12, 96; mechanisms for, 116; SDO and, 106–109
group-based social hierarchy, 98; behavioral asymmetry and, 101; consensus and, 106; LM, 104; oppression and, 102; processes for, 99
group formations, 13–15; *Critique of Dialectical Reason* and, 119–154
group-in-fusion, 14, 127–128; action of, 150; arbitrary-set system and, 106; Burkle on, 156n13; levels of, 137; mediated reciprocity and, 138; membership and, 138

groups, 14, 84, 125–126, 161;
  degradation of, 148; essentialness
  in, 142; *ressentiment* of, 4; seriality
  and, 128; structures and, 126;
  survival of, 131–132; transformation
  and, 130; unity and, 15, 131, 146. *See
  also specific types of groups*
Guénon, René, 3, 33n1, 57n5, 58n29;
  associates of, 6; Evola and, 9;
  initiation and, 6; traditionalist
  philosophy and, 37–57
Guizoit, François, 86

HA-legitimizing myths (HA-LM), 104
happiness, 54
Harper's Magazine, 113
hatred, 19, 169; predisposition to, 18, 170
hegemony, 110, 113, 117n23, 162
HE-legitimizing myths (HE-LM), 103–104
henosis, 29
Hermeticism, 5, 30
heroism, 63, 66, 74
hetaera, 80
heterogeneity, 137
hierarchical equilibrium, 105
hierarchy, 161. *See also* social hierarchy
hierarchy-attenuating (HA), 11;
  influence of, 98; position and, 102
hierarchy-enhancing (HE), 11;
  influence of, 98; position and, 102
hierarchy-terror principle, 115
Hinduism, 5, 77; castes and, 48–50,
  71–73; terminology and, 8–9;
  Vedanta and, 23, 30, 38, 58n29
homogeneity, 139
human ensemble, 122
human freedom, 13, 119–154
humanism, 38, 83; individualism and,
  84; secularism and, 40
humanitarianism, 53
humankind, 63, 65, 85
human relations, 67; cost of, 138;
  dangers of, 15; exteriority and, 120;
  identity and, 121; interiority and,
  129; to totality, 145. *See also*
  relationships
Hungary, 64

Huxley, Aldous, 24
Hyperborean, 10, 43, 78

ideals, 86
identity, 2, 172; human relations and,
  121; threat and, 145
ideologies, 102; amalgamation of, 1;
  change and, 13; discrimination and,
  109; fascism as, 62; Great
  Replacement as, 8, 76–77; inequality
  and, 109; social control and, 110–112
ignorance, 128–129
immigrants, 4
impact, 127
imperium, 80
impotence, 122; seriality of, 150;
  supremacy and, 167
inauthenticity, 164
individualism, 41–42; humanism and,
  84; revolt of, 84
industry, 46, 52–53
inequality, 12, 103; HE and, 98;
  ideologies and, 109
inertia, 139, 143; of institutionalization,
  147–149
inessentiality, 148
inferiority, 98, 167
information, 125
initiation, 61; Guénon and, 6;
  spirituality and, 83
institutionalism, 133
institutionalized group, 14, 15; Sartre
  on, 140–144
institutional terror, 99–100; legal
  system and, 113–116
Integral Christian Humanism, 38
intellectual intuition, 25
intellectuality, 8
intellectual tradition, 56
interchangeability, 121
interiority, 129, 137, 151, 154n1
invention, 53
inversion, 87
irrationalism, 172
Italy, 66

Jewish Law, 81
Jim Crow Laws, 101
justice, 72, 113

Kali Yuga (Dark Age), 38, 39, 81, 90n52
Kessler, Jason, 172
knowledge, 23, 45, 85; forms of, 41; Guénon and, 56; limitation of, 42; science and, 46
kshatriya (warrior caste), 8

Lalich, Janja, 152
language, 17, 145, 166
laws. *See specific laws*
leadership, 15, 149–154
legal system, 113–116
legitimacy, 25, 28, 51
legitimizing myths (LM), 13, 23; behavioral asymmetry and, 101; consensuality and, 112; policies and, 112; role of, 103–106; SDT and, 103
liberation movements, 83
LM. *See* legitimizing myths

magic, 4
Mahabharata, 66
Manafort, Paul, 153
Manichean terms, 17, 63, 166, 174
manifesto, 77
manvantara, 39
Marinetti, Filippo Tommaso, 59
Maritain, Jaques, 38
Marxian class conflict model, 113
mass/herd, 19, 123; mentalities of, 63, 172–173
material welfare, 54
mechanisms, 10, 111; characteristics and, 11; emotions as, 170; for group-based dominance, 116; law as, 133
mediated reciprocity, 130, 133; group-in-fusion and, 138
mediation, 128, 145; inertia and, 149; mediated reciprocity as, 130, 133, 138; mediational strength and, 105; praxis and, 130; sovereignty and, 151; victory through, 146
membership, 96, 136, 138, 150; group-in-fusion and, 138
men, 149; women and, 74–77
mentalities, 43, 55; of mass/herd, 63, 172–173; master and slave as, 16, 168. *See also specific mentalities*

metaphysics, 27, 37, 89n10; knowledge and, 23; legitimacy and, 25; science and, 47
methodology, 31
migration, 78
models: state and, 113–115. *See also specific models*
modern mentality, 43; unity and, 85
monarchy, 67, 69; democracy and, 85
morality, 163; master morality and, 164, 168; slave morality as, 165
Morgan, John, 61
Mother Earth, 79
multiplicity, 45, 120; unity and, 53, 121
Muslims, 170–171
Mutz, Diana, 176
mysticism, 5, 29, 63; role of, 27; ultimate reality and, 26

nation (*Volksgemeinschaft*), 62, 87
nationalism, 69; collective and, 87
National Policy Institute, 1
necessary culmination, 130
needs, 126
negation, 18, 169
negative social value, 95
neoreactionaries (NRx-ers), 1
Nietzsche, Friedrich, 8, 123; on -anti-Semitism, 168–169; on bad conscience, 168; on exotericism and esotericism, 32; on *ressentiment*, 4, 16–17, 163, 164–169; Sartre and, 174
nobility, 165; spirit of, 168
Northbourne, Lord, 24, 27
NRx-ers. *See* neoreactionaries
numen, 70

Obama, Barack, 161
objectives, 126
Olcott, Henry, 5
Oldmeadow, Harry, 24
the One, 31, 34n9
On the Genealogy of Morals (Solomon), 163
opportunity, 50
oppression, 10; arbitrary-set system and, 97; group-based social hierarchy and, 102; sociality and, 139

optimal intergroup contact, 112
Orbán, Viktor, 64
organized groups, 84; Sartre and, 136–139
ossification, 149
otherness, 123, 157n49, 173
outgroups, 19, 161
out of place principle, 114

paradoxical dependence, 173
passion, 18, 164; Sartre on, 169–170
passive-activity, 137, 148
passive defense, task of, 64
passiveness, 120
pater, 75
Peebles, Marc, 99
perennialism (*philosophia perennis*), 3, 34n13; anamnesis, 23–33; contemplative ascent and, 30; doctrines and, 24–25; esotericism and, 26; origins of, 5; science and, 31–33; traditionalism and, 7, 24
Perry, Whitall, 37
perspectives, 146, 162; nobility and, 168
philosophia perennis. *See* perennialism
physics (*physis*), 46
platforms, 96
Plato, 48, 72, 85
Platonism, 26, 30
the pledged: conflict and, 144–146; quasi-sovereignty and, 141; Sartre on, 14, 131–136, 156n22, 157n28; transcendence and, 134
Plotinus, 29
pluralist model, 113
plurality of unifications, 129
poets, 59
police brutality, 115
policies, 109; LM and, 112
politics, 61; alt-right and, 161; fascism and, 62; Guénon on, 48–51
Pompeo, Mike, 153
Pontifex, 67, 89n29
popularization, 50
populations, 76, 78
positive social value, 95
Posterior Analytics (Aristotle), 25
power, 10, 56, 98; danger and, 17; evil and, 166; legitimacy and, 51; *Pontifex* and, 67, 89n29; *ressentiment* and, 17; strength and, 168
power-man, 149
practical applications, 46
practical materialism, 52
practico-inert, 122–123; fear and, 124; sociality and, 155n4; structures as, 127
pragmatism, 44
praxis, 126, 135; collective and, 122; failure of, 150; forms of, 147; groups and, 126, 128; homogeneity and, 139; mediation and, 130; ossified praxis and, 149; sovereignty as, 129–130; unity and, 129, 132
principles, 16, 50, 60; absence of, 41; caste system and, 71; change and, 45; consciousness and, 45; of form, 83; form and, 73; relationships between, 79; religion and, 24; symbolism and, 75; understanding and, 44
professional athletes, 96
progressive materialization, 39, 53
progressive mentality, 24
property, 75
protest, 69, 130; freedom and, 131
Protestantism, 42
Protocols of the Elders of Zion manuscript, 111
PRRI. *See* Public Religion Research Institute
psyche, 164
psychology, 167; behavior and, 174; drive and, 173; terminology and, 163
public opinion, 124; The Great Fear and, 125
Public Religion Research Institute (PRRI), 110
the purge, 146–147
Putnam, Robert, 105

quantity, 85

race, 9; biology and, 63; dichotomy of, 161; racism and, 62–65; spirituality and, 62–63, 63; in United States, 12, 161

races of nature, 63
racism, 10, 117n26; Bannon and, 64–65; belief and, 104; disposition and, 18; hierarchy and, 65–66; magic and, 4; race and, 62–65; *ressentiment* and, 16; Sartre on, 18–19, 169–174; types of, 162
rationalism, 84, 85
reaction, 168
reason, 42
reciprocity, 126, 139, 156n15; dislocation of, 143; ignorance and, 128–129; mediated reciprocity and, 130, 133, 138; structures and, 129; worked reciprocity and, 138–139
redlining, 101
refusal, 151
Reginster, Bernard, 163
regression, 85, 87
relationships, 135–136, 156n15; principles and, 79
religion, 153, 171; change in, 37; esotericism and, 26; fall of, 42; mysticism and, 29; principles and, 24. *See also specific religions*
repressed vengeance, 17–18, 167
Republic (Plato), 48, 72, 85
research, 12, 19n2, 45
ressentiment, 54, 177n5; alt-right and, 161–176; groups and, 4; Nietzsche concept of, 4, 16–17, 163, 164–169; power and, 17; repressed vengeance and, 17–18, 167
revenge, 17, 166
Revolt against the Modern World (Evola), 60, 66–71, 88n2
right and duty, 133; tension of, 137
rites, 69, 70
royalty, 82
Rushing, Allison Jones, 100–101

sanctuary cities, 166
Sartre, Jean-Paul, 3; on action, 139; on anti-Semitism, 164; *Critique of Dialectical Reason* by, 3, 119–154; Fanon and, 116n15; group formations and, 13–15; Nietzsche and, 174; on organized groups, 136–139; passion, 169–170; on the pledged, 14, 131–136, 156n22, 157n28; on racism, 18–19, 169–174; SDT and, 95; on seriality, 131
satisfaction of wants, 54
science, 40, 85; of economics, 53; industry and, 46, 52–53; perennialism and, 31–33; research and, 45; sacredness/profaneness of, 45–47; the West and, 46, 52
SDO. *See* social dominance orientation
SDT. *See* social dominance theory
secularism, 40
self-domestication, 149
self-realization, 61
self-reflection, 19
sentiments: function and, 175; slogans and, 1
separation-secession, 143–144
seriality, 128; collective and, 119–120; danger of, 132; free common praxis and, 135; of impotence, 150; Sartre and, 131
series, 140, 155n2; collective as, 120–125; transformation from, 127
servitude, 123
Sessions, Jeff, 153
Sherrard, Philip, 31–32
skills, 96
slogans, 1, 13
social control, 97; ideologies and, 110–112
social dominance orientation (SDO), 11; acquisition of, 12; group-based dominance and, 106–109
social dominance theory (SDT), 3; assumptions about, 97–103; correlations and, 12; legal system and, 114; LM and, 103; oppression and, 102; outline of, 95–116; Putnam and, 105; social hierarchy and, 10
social hierarchy, 28, 48, 71; Aryans and, 65; *Critique of Dialectical Reason* and, 119–154; as individual-based, 96; institutional terror and, 114; negation of, 50; proximal process and, 11; racism and, 65–66; SDT and, 10; society as, 95
sociality, 123; bond of, 137–138; oppression and, 139; practico-inert

and, 155n4
social media, 101, 125
social organism, 49
social problems, 55–57
social role congruency principle, 115
society, 12, 67; crisis in bourgeois, 86; groups and, 161; as social hierarchy, 95; state and, 68; unity and, 71–73
Socrates, 72
solidification, 54
Solomon, Robert, 163
solutions, 55–57
sovereignty, 123; authority and, 149–154; limits of, 140–141; praxis as, 129–130; quasi-sovereignty and, 14–15, 141, 150; understanding of, 143
Spencer, Richard, 1, 172; on America, 2
Spicer, Sean, 153
spirituality, 39; Aryans and, 80; initiation and, 83; race and, 62–63, 63
standards of practice, 101
state: mechanisms, 133; models of law and, 113–115; society and, 68. *See also* legal system
state of mind, materialism as, 52
statute, 135
statutory group, 14, 131–136
stereotypes, 102
Stinson, Phillip, 115
Stoddart, William, 37
stories, 172; civilizations and, 77–80; purpose of, 103
stratifications, 12, 107; absence of, 97; status and, 13; systems of, 96
strength, 167, 168
structures, 120; Evola and, 63; fear and, 133–134; groups and, 126; of obedience, 151; as practico-inert, 127; reciprocity and, 129
subgroups, 144–146
submission, 151
subordinate groups, 110–112
superiority, 98
support, 162
supraformalism, 27
suprahuman order, 39, 41, 42, 56
supremacy, 10, 44; impotence and, 167

survival, 154; of groups, 131–132
symbolism, 75, 78, 79; as telluric, 79
syncretic outlook, 171
Synthesis of Racial Doctrine (Evola), 9

Tarrant, Brenton, 77
tasks: Evola on, 64; function and, 137. *See also specific tasks*
technology, 54
telluric, 8, 80; God as, 9, 61; symbolism as, 79
terminology, 17, 27, 74; atomization as, 140; distinctions in, 176; Fraternity-Terror as, 136, 151; Hinduism and, 8–9; humanism and, 40; intuition and, 25; language and, 166; psychology and, 163; technology and, 54; Western materialism as, 52
terror: as bond, 147; unity of, 135; violence and, 99–100, 134. *See also* institutional terror
Theosophical Society, 5
theosophy, 59, 88n1
theurgy, 28–29
The Third, 128–131
threat, 162; attitudes and, 175; identity and, 145; to status, 2, 4, 176
tolerance of abuse principle, 115
totality, 62, 124, 155n8
totalization, 130, 145
trade agreements, 175
traditionalism, 3; alt-right and, 16; beliefs and, 6; democracy and, 48–51; Evola and, 59–88; fascism and, 61; Guénon and, 39; humanity and, 63; interpretations by, 68; perennialism and, 7, 24; progress and, 77
traditionalist philosophy, 37–57
traditional mentality, 24
transcendence, 29–30, 73; dualism and, 28; the pledged and, 134
transformation, 26, 151; being-in-group and, 140; consequences and, 61; groups and, 130; from series, 127
Trismegistus, Hermes, 23, 30, 34n26; *The Emerald Tablet* by, 30, 31
Trump, Donald, 55, 57, 152; alt-right and, 2; cult of personality and,

153–154; Muslim ban attempt by, 170–171; wall and, 112
truth, 28; contemplation and, 30; fear and, 171; as goals, 32; universality of, 26; Western materialism and, 39
Tzara, Tristan, 59
Übermensche, 60

ultimate reality, 23, 34n9; mysticism and, 26
uniforms, 136
United States, 152; imprisonment in, 113; Muslims and, 170–171; race in, 12, 161; sanctuary cities in, 166
unity, 14, 49; of ensemble, 122; groups and, 15, 131, 146; modern mentality and, 85; multiplicity and, 53, 121; praxis and, 129, 132; society and, 71–73; subgroups and, 145; of terror, 135
Universal Declaration of Human Rights (1948), 104, 116n22
universality, 56, 81
unreflective consciousness, 170
unstructure, 127
uranic, 8; action and, 60; consecration as, 69

value consensus model, 113
value judgments, 163
Versluis, Arthur, 33n3
violence, 99–100, 134; fraternity of, 136
Volksgemeinschaft. *See* nation
vulnerability, 17, 166

war on drugs, 113–114
warrior caste (*kshatriya*), 8
weakness, 18, 167
wealth, 10, 86
Welch, Edgar, 84, 124
the West, 55; action and, 45; decadence of, 87; the East *versus*, 43–44; Evola on, 80–88; science and, 46, 52
Western decline, 7, 40; chivalry and, 82; individualism and, 41–42; solution for, 8
Western materialism, 7, 52–55; metaphysics and, 7; truth and, 39
whites. *See* Aryans
winter solstice, 79
women, 74–77
worked reciprocity, 138–139
World War II, 60
writings, 23, 162; by Evola, 8, 10, 62; Guénon and, 37, 38; Sartre and, 174; short story as, 172

About the Author

William Remley is lecturer in philosophy at Saint Peter's University, Jersey City, New Jersey.

www.ingramcontent.com/pod-product-compliance
Lightning Source LLC
Chambersburg PA
CBHW021850300426
44115CB00005B/91